CULINARY ECONOMICS

KV-312-619

293763

UCB

Cost Management is the Essence of This Book

CULINARY ECONOMICS

Chef Y.B. Mathur

Formerly
Senior Executive Chef
ITC Hotels

I.K. International Publishing House Pvt. Ltd.

NEW DELHI

UCB
293763

Published by
I.K. International Publishing House Pvt. Ltd.
S-25, Green Park Extension
Uphaar Cinema Market
New Delhi–110 016 (India)
E-mail: info@ikinternational.com
Website: www.ikbooks.com

ISBN 978-93-85909-19-1

© 2017 I.K. International Publishing House Pvt. Ltd.

All rights reserved. No part of this publication may be reproduced, stored in a retrieval system, or transmitted in any form or any means: electronic, mechanical, photocopying, recording, or otherwise, without the prior written permission from the publisher.

Published by Krishan Makhijani for I.K. International Publishing House Pvt. Ltd., S-25, Green Park Extension, Uphaar Cinema Market, New Delhi–110 016 and Printed by Rekha Printers Pvt. Ltd., Okhla Industrial Area, Phase II, New Delhi–110 020.

FOREWORD

 After reading 'Culinary Economics', I felt compelled to coin a new term to describe its admirable author, Chef Yaduvansh Mathur, namely "The Complete Chef". Truly, he has combined the sensibilities of the creative chef in him with the competencies of a corporate business leader to produce a comprehensive treatise that addresses the multi-dimensional challenge of running a profitable food service business.

His book is a labour of love, born out of his 'dharmic' conviction that he must leave behind a legacy for the next generation; and that legacy is not just the knowledge quotient contained in 'Culinary Economics', but also his strong message of perfectionism – a call to rise beyond excellence to create absolute benchmarks worthy of emulation. His devotion to his mission makes him a "Complete Man", a true karma yogi who looks upon his work as "tapasya" or "sadhana" undertaken in a totally ego-less spirit for the benefit of all.

Given its all-embracing content, 'Culinary Economics' is a classic textbook for students and practitioners alike. It will serve as a "go-to" compendium for chefs, restaurant owners, hospitality entrepreneurs, students, trainees and consultants in hotel management.

The book is panoramically sweeping in its content, integrating as it does the critical dimensions of F&B controls, procurement, inventory management and revenue strategy.

Leveraging his corporate experience, Mathur has impactfully highlighted the imperative of using audit and internal controls as effective instruments for not only plugging value leaks, but also as a means of enhancing quality and customer satisfaction.

The book has been imaginatively edited and formatted to set out the logical flow, from the macro to the micro, of the dynamics of the culinary business. Each module clearly provides the conceptual framework of the topic, including its context, criticality and significance, followed by detailed explanations and guidance. The exhibits are an invaluable supplement and ready reckoner, bringing focus to each part of the book's large canvas. The language and style seamlessly combine with the content and format to render the book an extremely reader-friendly experience.

In this painstakingly detailed work, Mathur has clearly demonstrated that the role of the chef has transformed in recent years from being a creative artist in the kitchen to that of a smart business manager who is expected to deliver a cost efficient and profitable food service business.

I am certain that for readers of '*Culinary Economics*' it will be an absorbing journey of discovery and mind expansion, from which they will emerge inspired and knowledgeable.

K. Vaidyanath

K. Vaidyanath is Non-Executive Director on the Board of ITC since 2011. Prior to this appointment, he was an Executive Director on the ITC Board for 10 years from January 2001, responsible for the Company's Finance, IT, Internal Audit and Corporate Communications functions, its investment subsidiary, its Paperboards, Paper, Packaging and Information Technology businesses.

Before his elevation to the Board as an Executive Director, he was the Company's Chief Financial Officer. An MBA from XLRI, Jamshedpur, in his 35-year tenure with ITC, Vaidyanath held various positions in the company's finance function. He has been a recipient of the 'Best CFO' Award from *Business Today* and the 'Best CFO in the FMCG category' Award from CNBC-TV18.

FOREWORD

 I am happy to introduce Chef Yaduvansh Mathur's book **Culinary Economics**. This is a unique, comprehensively researched book which has very useful insights on a variety of topics. The book will be of tremendous utility to chefs, F&B managers and others involved in running restaurant operations at both hotels and independent restaurants.

The book covers various areas including the culinary business, culinary ingredients, menu engineering, materials management and food production. The chapters have practical examples, case studies and other relevant material. There is a strong focus on F&B controls which is an essential component for a successful operation.

Leveraging his extensive industry experience, Chef Mathur has created a detailed yet practical to book for both professionals and students. The industry and fraternity should be grateful to him for creating this book.

I am sure the readers of Culinary Economics will gain immensely from the book and this will be used as reference material for many years.

Samir Kuckreja

Samir Kuckreja

Samir Kuckreja has 26 years of experience in the hospitality industry. He has worked in a variety of leading domestic and international brands and partnered with a PE fund. Samir is the Founder & CEO of Tasanaya Hospitality Pvt. Ltd. which specializes in consultancy work for the hospitality industry. Areas of work include advising start-up concepts, food technology companies, foreign companies on entry strategy, growth strategies and franchising, executive search and organization development, restaurant companies on fund raising and PE/VC funds on acquisitions.
Samir is a Trustee and was the President of National Restaurant Association of India from 2009 to 2014. He was CEO & MD of Nirula's from June 2006 till April 2012. He earlier worked with Yum Restaurants and Mars Hotel & Restaurants. Samir is a founding member of the Governing Council of the National Tourism and Hospitality Skill Council.
Samir has a BA in Economics Honours from St. Stephens College, Delhi and a BS in Hotel Administration from Cornell University, USA.

FOREWORD

 I am delighted to introduce Chef Yaduvansh Mathur's seminal work *Culinary Economics*, an original, well-researched and celebrated compendium of what his experience has to offer in its magnificent insights towards profitable food production operations. His vast experience as a stalwart in diligently chronicling and mapping our culinary processes to make business sense is indeed a revolutionary piece of work. He has spared no effort, having put in many years into the process of learning, documenting, experimenting and finally serving up this truly outstanding activity guide to make food production operations in business exciting and truly profitable in future years.

Outside of being extremely respectful of chef's knowledge as one of the leading lights amongst our most respected culinary art professionals, I have personally experienced his passion for detail when we hosted the World Skills Challenge Rounds at our institute last year. His professional demeanour, in protecting the integrity of food, the methodology and presentation often raised thoughts on the affordability of the initiative, but alongside his great artistry, he demonstrated great rationality and India hosted our Australian counterparts in the knowledge exchange process. Each food production exercise documented has been carefully chosen, treated with justice and transformed into a culinary entrepreneur's dream. Only a select few professionals may have been able to document their experience for the benefit of the chef community, by taking economics in kitchens so seriously.

As a hospitality professional and educator of nearly three decades, it gives me a great sense of fulfilment to see a great treasure trove of industry nuances that have been documented, to provide insights, otherwise lost in day-to-day cooking. Each chapter has been carefully modelled alongside illustrations and examples to make the reader's discovery of Culinary Economics, a wonderful learning experience.

Chef Mathur has evolved simple methods that could work in any geography, business landscape and is truly holistic in its approach to celebrating success as a professional business and chef manager, with an eye on profits alongside simply creating great food. The easy to follow instructions are like a refreshing shot of flavour in a learners evolving palate, enhancing what may have purely been a textbook compilation of facts, and potentially become a descriptive treatise.

Last but not the least, the purpose of this wonderful ready-reckoner on any aspect of number crunching in the kitchen, is to open incisive perspectives, by maintaining simple process consistencies to deliver on-going profitability oriented results, from any stressed food production operation. The robustness of chef's methods, their validity and simplicity are suggested from real experiences and must be adopted by all modern chefs. Simply because everything written here has been tested, ingested, digested and savoured — not only in the culinary sense, but also by happy business leaders, whose cash registers are ringing. The wealth of this book's foundation, the strength of its techniques and the simplicity of approaches suggested can be easily adapted by learners at any age and position in their career life cycle. The long-term benefits of practising culinary economics are purely documented for practical considerations. This is not simply a theoretical exercise but focuses on the real world of excitement as it exists in our kitchens today.

I wish every reader a wonderful voyage of discovery and experimentation, in the process of unearthing – Culinary Economics. Even as we adopt, modify and brand many international cuisines in our Indianization, here is a call for chefs to evolve into better business people first. At the end of the day, there is one outcome that makes sense for anyone connected with food, a smile on the face - when the culinary senses kick-in and cash in the till - to buy the next set of ingredients and verily start a new culinary journey. Except that after reading this book, it will definitely be a richer one!

Satish Jayaram

Satish Jayaram

Professor Satish Jayaram, PhD (Revenue Management) is serving as Principal, Institute of Hotel Management – Aurangabad, managed by the Taj Group. He is a fully engaged, creative and experimental 'true-blue' food and beverage enthusiast, focused on customer experience management, customer relationship management and real-time profitability in hospitality. His research in revenue management has evolved through the incorporation of stakeholders, customer co-option and mapping lifetime value into our business relationships.

FOREWORD

 Chef Y.B. Mathur is known for his dedication and creativity in the culinary arts. As author of 'Culinary Economics,' He portrays his depth of knowledge, skills enriched by experience, and his commitment to present his talent to future generations of chefs.

The book is a trend-setter, broaching a topic relevant to the present times wherein the subject of culinary economics is subject to the unpredictable market forces and finding good food value in terms of quality and price is an uphill task. The subject matter is of interest to all those in field of food production, ranging from managers of finance and F&B, executive chefs and their team, and students of catering institutes.

Chef Mathur helps impart training to prospective chefs and managers at the hospitality management institute run by ITC Hotels, the hotel from where he chose to retire as Senior Executive Chef. After putting in 43 years of service in various leading hotels, he took to educating chefs of the future, as he had once been trained at his alma mater, the Hotel Management, Nutrition & Catering Institute, Pusa, New Delhi.

After joining ITC Group in the hotels division in 1991, Mathur has worked in the group's properties in Bengaluru, Chennai, Jaipur and Hyderabad in different capacities. He also had a stint at ITC Welcomgroup Graduate School of Hotel Administration at Manipal between 2000 and 2002.

Chef Mathur has authored research books on French cuisine as well as culinary economics. He was also sent on an assignment to Texas, USA to prepare Indian cuisine for the most premier food importing organisation of America – The Tree of Life.

For many years, Chef Mathur was positioned as Regional Chef (South) - ITC Hotels. Chef Mathur has been responsible for total conceptualization and implementation of the Food & Beverages concepts of multiple hotel units. He is an expert in positioning and repositioning culinary business and creating benchmarks of commercial excellence and success. Chef Mathur was responsible for Culinary Product Development support for Foods Business Division of ITC, a premier organisation of the food processing industry.

This book is an encyclopedia for the current and future generations as it imparts practical knowledge about culinary economy ranging from subjects such as the business, engineering, ingredients, costs, pricing, materials management and related segments. The book looks at both sides of the coin by also elaborating on the economic disadvantages and limitations of the culinary business and the precautions to be taken to avoid these pitfalls.

Foreword

'Culinary Economics' should be mandatory reading for all those who want to gain insights from the prolific writings of a trained chef, experienced guide and motivated educationist. The style of instruction is simple, illustrated with examples, worksheets, flow charts and the step-by-step modular format makes the topics easy to read, understand and implement, when the occasion demands.

Recipient of many national and international awards, inclusion of this book in the course of catering institutes would be an additional feather in Chef Mathur's highly-decorated cap.

Anil Kumar Bhandari

Anil Kumar Bhandari is Chairman, AB Smart Concepts & AB Smart Placement. Earlier he has served as: Advisor ITC Ltd.– Travel, Tourism, Real Estate and Hotels; Chairman and Managing Director of India Tourism Development Corporation Limited; Managing Director of JHM Interstate Hotels, India; Managing Director of International Travel House Limited; and Managing Director, Hotel Corporation of India.

He has a Certificate in Hotel Administration from the Institute of American Hotel & Motel Association and is a former Fellow of the Institute of Hospitality, London.

PREFACE

The future of the Indian hospitality industry is surely upbeat. More than 40 international hotel brands, each with multiple sub-brands, have settled in India to do business. There is hardly a global hotel chain which is not eager to gain an entry into India. In a similar fashion, the restaurant industry is growing in geometric progressions each year. The market for food production and knowledgeable culinary professionals is burgeoning.

Thousands of culinary businesses close down within the very first year of operation. Most of these businesses have good concepts, involve large capital expenditure, and are started with the right intentions. The failure of the business, however, happens mostly due to operational inefficiencies and cost-overruns.

I strongly believe that world's best culinary businesses, and inherently their chefs, fail due to their poor knowledge and application of culinary economics.

This book would prove invaluable for hospitality professionals – students, trainers, chefs, food and beverage managers and consultants, entrepreneurs, operation and finance auditors, controllers and many more.

Chef Y.B. Mathur

INSPIRATION

We are all temporary custodians of the intellectual and emotional wealth of the Generation Next. The best use of this wealth is to share it with the younger generation.

In my confirmed opinion and way of life the Generation Next should stand on higher platforms of perfection and excellence, than we have ever achieved. That would be true salute to the country's interests. This has been the Scheme of Things for me - always.

We all have eaten the fruit from the trees that we did not plant. In the fullness of time, when it is our turn to give, it behooves us in turn to plant gardens that we may never eat the fruit of, which will largely benefit generations to come.

This is my sacred responsibility. And I have never failed in my responsibilities towards the next generation.

I dedicate "Culinary Economics" to the future of the country and to the Generation Next.

Rivers themselves do not drink of the water they carry.
Trees do not eat of the fruits they bear.
Clouds too do not eat of the rains they produce.
For the riches of the good are utilized for the welfare of others.

पिबन्ति नद्यः स्वयमेव नाम्भः

स्वयं न खादन्ति फलानि वृक्षाः ।

नादन्ति सस्यं स्वयमम्बुवाहाः

परोपकाराय सतां विभूतयः ॥

THE AUTHOR

Chef Y.B. Mathur is one of India's seniormost chefs. He retired from ITC Hotels as Senior Executive Chef. Chef Mathur's last posting while in service at ITC was at the ITC Hospitality Management Institute, an in-house training institute of the ITC Hotels. World class training is imparted to future chefs and managers in this institute, under various flagship courses.

Chef Mathur is passionate for the cause of the Generation Next. He continues to lecture and train management trainees of ITC Hotels at the ITC Hospitality Management Institute. Chef Mathur is the Cookery Skills Expert for World Skills International, a global organization encouraging development of skills, skill competitions as well as skills-led employment generation. In addition, he is actively involved in the national skills movement, a Government of India initiative to skill 500 million functionaries in hundreds of skills-related fields by 2022, through National Skills Development Corporation, which is spearheading the skilling process.

Chef Mathur is currently employed as Corporate Chef & Director Culinary Ventures with Zappfresh - A Fresh & Ready to cook Meat brand based out of NCR, The Brand has taken a oath to eradicate gaps in fresh meat category by working on Farm to Fork concept, The application of industry best practices covered in this book are being diligently applied in the food processing department of "Zappfresh" to effectively manage huge demand and supply challenge pertaining in the food industry.

Chef Mathur is an alumnus of the Institute of Hotel Management, Catering & Nutrition, at Pusa, New Delhi. He has led a dedicated career, spanning over 43 years, full of achievements. He has been recognised by the hospitality industry and bestowed with many prestigious national and international awards and accolades.

CONTENTS

This module deals with the understanding of the core characteristics, and business formats of culinary business. The module provides tips to the reader, especially an entrepreneur, to start and scale culinary business through concept-led benchmarks.

Contents

This module deals with the basic understanding of the building blocks of cuisine – the culinary ingredients. This module is a link between the first module and the rest of the modules of the book.

Contents

Contents

Contents

*This module presents cost-effectiveness through efficient stores management.
It explains why it is imperative to maintain low inventory and high turnover from
stores. The module further describes the process of issues from stores.*

Contents

This module examines the role of the Kitchen Steward and the stewarding department towards the success of the food & beverages outlet. Food production as well as food service must progress in a perfectionist manner. It is the role of the Kitchen Steward and his team to assist the food production and food service personnel. Food should be produced and served within the framework of the culinary concept, service guarantees, hygiene and HACCP control, statutory laws and the decided economic standards of the business.

13.   Objectivity and Subjectivity in Culinary Business   229

This module deals with key points and ideas to encourage higher objectivity in the operations of culinary business.

Product designing is largely led by objectivity in most types of business and manufacturing industries. Traditionally, culinary business has been a "touch and feel", creativity-led and subjective business in nature. Contemporary forms of culinary business – either as stand-alone entities or within a hotel are considered "revenue, profit and cost centres". Profits are the key prerequisites of culinary business. The enabler for higher profitability is enhanced objectivity in operations.

LIST OF EXHIBITS

The Indian Food & Beverage business

The future of the Indian hospitality industry is surely upbeat. Host of international hotel brands, each with multiple sub-brands; have settled in India to do business. There is hardly a global hotel chain which is not eager to gain entry into India.

In a similar fashion, the food & beverages industry is growing in geometric progression each year. New chains of food & beverages business are announced regularly. The industry is witnessing a number of mergers and acquisitions. The industry is already estimated to be worth $ 85 billion of yearly revenues and is growing at a rapid pace each year.

On the flip side

On the flip side thousands of food & beverages business close down within the very first year of their inception. Most of these business have good concepts, involve large capital expenditure, and are started with the right passion and intentions. These food & beverages business fail due to:

(i) changing customer choices;

(ii) fatigue in restaurant design;

(iii) cost overruns; and

(iv) most importantly due to insufficient knowledge of the economics of food production.

What does this book advocate?

The main theme of the book is cost-effectiveness of culinary operations. The book is packed with information and tips for chefs, operators and entrepreneurs to ensure profitability and success of the culinary business. The book identifies the economic pitfalls of the culinary business and details robust preventive as well as corrective measures.

1. **The importance of formulating a concept**

   To start with, "Culinary Economics" advocates a culinary business to formulate a strong concept as its foundation. Concept-led and concept-directed quality food pre-production and production processes must be the core activities of a culinary business.

2. **Structuring and maintaining benchmarks**

   The book advises operators and chefs to ensure the right benchmarks of tangible and intangible food and beverage products and services to a customer for a positive and memorable dining experience as well as repeat patronage. All benchmarks must be in line with the mandates of the concept.

3. **Backward integration of food production**

   Managements must create objectivity-centric backward integration of food production with robust standards for purchase and supplier management as well as those for the receipt of raw food products and ingredients, their storage and issuing. Food production must be planned and quantities of food production must be forecasted.

4. **Forward integration of food production**

   The food pre-production and production processes must be forward integrated with service guarantee-led food service benchmarks. Food production quality must be in line with the concept of the business and the marketing promises.

5. **Importance of culinary analytics and audits**

   Culinary analytics are important to study regularly to decide the immediate and future course of action, course correction wherever required, and the repositioning of the business itself, if required. Structured and regular reviews of benchmarks must be ingrained into the functioning of a culinary business. Audits and audit trails must be viewed as highly supportive of future actions.

6. **Controls and engineering**

   The book advises cost-efficiencies and non-negotiable controls at each of the functional and operational areas of a culinary business. The book refers to chefs and operators as "culinary engineers" and provides handy and step-by-step methodologies for positive engineering of food and beverage menu items.

7. **Objectivity in the business**

   Food production processes are thought of as highly subjective. The book identifies with the divide and balance between subjectivity and objectivity in a food-led business and directs operators and chefs to introduce as high objectivity into the system, as is possible. The book provides sequential information to achieve the same.

8. **The importance of service guarantees**

   The marketing functions of a business are often outsourced. The chefs and operators do not keep the marketing personnel adequately informed about the marketing promises of the business. The customer's dining expectations are mismatched with the actual. The book advocates declaration of service guarantees to offer the best dining experience to the customer at each moment of truth.

The roles of various functionaries are accurately and comprehensively delineated in the book. The text is **richly interspersed** with comprehensive "End of Module Notes" and **supported by exhibits**. The book presents the following types of exhibits.

(a) **Aids-to-memory exhibits,** for example, the Key to Classification of Menu Items as in Exhibit 6;

(b) Exhibits which would serve as a **case study,** for example, all the exhibits in Module 4;

(c) Exhibits detailing **aims & objectives,** for example, that of the Purchase Department as in Exhibit 13;

(d) Exhibits with **step-by-step process charts**, for example, a systematic development of Standard Purchase Specifications as in Exhibit 16;

(e) Exhibits which would serve as **ready-to-use templates** for entrepreneurs, for example, the Perishables Order Sheet and the Butchery Sheet, as in exhibits 17 and 18;

(f) Exhibits which are essentially **flowcharts,** for example as in exhibits 19 and 20;

(g) Exhibits which serve as **ready reference,** for example, like the one on Butcher Yield testing or the one on forecasting of food production quantities as in exhibit 30;

(h) Exhibits in the shape of **specimen formats** as in exhibits 31 to 33;

(i) Exhibits detailing zero-variables for example the Service Guarantees in exhibit 35;

(j) **Master exhibits** 13, 38 & 40:

- Exhibit 13 details efficient handling of food products and raw ingredients and integration of functional and operational areas.

- Exhibit 38 is the Control Chart and details the controls in the culinary business. It lists and details the eleven control points of the culinary business.

- Exhibit 40 details the cycle of strength of cost-effective culinary operations and is indeed a salute and tribute to Culinary Economics.

Culinary Economics would reflect the author's tireless striving towards perfection. The contents of the book are easy to understand and remember. The book is therefore a boon for students and entrepreneurs. No effort was considered too big and no detail was considered too small while writing this book.

This book would prove invaluable for hospitality professionals - students, trainers, chefs, food & beverage managers, corporates, venture capitalists, entrepreneurs, consultants, operations and finance auditors, food & beverages controllers and many more professionals related to the culinary business.

All the 40 exhibits provided in this book are also appended in the CD attached with this book. Exhibits 38 & 40 appear in elaborated form.

1

THE CULINARY BUSINESS

Essence of the Module

This module deals with the understanding of the core characteristics, and business formats of culinary business. The module provides tips to the reader, especially an entrepreneur, to start and scale culinary business through concept-led benchmarks.

Module Objectives and Competencies
1. To explain the challenging role of a chef in order to be successful.
2. To introduce the understanding of 'culinary business' to the reader.
3. To examine the types of culinary business:
(a) The existing formats of culinary business.
(b) The evolving formats of culinary business.
4. To present the requirement of knowledge management for the culinary business.
5. To identify the career opportunities in culinary business.
6. To introduce the core characteristics of culinary business.

1.1 INTRODUCTION TO THE CULINARY BUSINESS

Success of culinary business depends on the skills of its chefs and operators. The chefs and operators must develop their mental faculties, in addition to mastering culinary or operating skills. As has been scientifically proven, the left hemisphere of the brain seeks evidence, is goal-oriented and is always eager to reach conclusions. The left hemisphere is also responsible for logical-language based analytical and rational capacities and conclusions.

The right hemisphere of the brain is responsible for creativity and dreaming of options. The activities of the right hemisphere of the brain are more of inspirational nature. Exercising and continuous training of both the hemispheres of the brain is vital for developing the career goals of the chefs and the operators, as also to the success of the culinary business.

Chefs and operators must forever remain in a mode of self-actualization and continuously develop their own potential. Chefs must be concurrent and be careful of business disruptions. The turn of events can be most unpredictable. Fast unfolding events—socio-economic changes, changes in the country's laws—can disrupt plans in ways least expected. In case of a positive disruption in the marketplace or within the political or social ecosystem chefs should strive to gain maximum advantage for the culinary business. In case of negative disruptions chefs should cut losses for the business. Disruptions may be due to international and national awareness, fresh laws and notifications, demand and supply situations and weather conditions, for example:

- Change in dietary habits.
- Change in culinary trends.
- The slow-food movement.
- The locavore movement.
- The ethical-treatment-of-animals movement.

To be successful chefs must be:

- creative;
- skilled;
- experienced;
- goal oriented;
- eager to reach conclusions;
- decision makers;
- logical and sequential in their approach; and
- analytical and rational.

All the above-mentioned factors require the use of both the hemispheres of the brain.

1.2 FORMATS AND TYPES OF CULINARY BUSINESS

1. As part of culinary services of luxury and five-star hotels, and generally catering to business and upmarket travellers.

2. As part of culinary services of budget hotels catering to average and/or domestic business or leisure travellers.

3. As part of culinary services of heritage hotels. Heritage hotels represent palaces, havelis and forts converted into hotels. Very often wonderful and quality cuisine is created by established and fine culinary experts at these locations. Their expertise is difficult to replicate in other locations.

4. As part of culinary services of resorts and clubs. Premium or budget category of resorts and clubs are located in hill stations, at beach locations, at the central business districts in cities and other unique destinations.

5. As part of culinary services of flight catering units.

6. As part of inherent services of cruise ships.

7. As stand-alone culinary outlets of various dimensions, service benchmarks and culinary offers, for example:

   (a) **Fine dining:** A fine dining restaurant is a full service restaurant with a specific dedicated meal course. Décor, etiquette, restaurant infrastructure and table appointments feature high quality materials with an eye for the "atmosphere" desired by the restaurateur. The staff members are highly trained and wear formal attire. These restaurants often depend on the skills of the chef and of the bar manager for preparing culinary and beverages masterpieces, often at the site, and in view of the customers. The customers are expected to wear formal attire or smart casuals.

   (b) **Casual dining:** Casual dining restaurants serve moderately priced food in a casual atmosphere. These restaurants often have buffets for breakfast, lunch and dinner, and provision for beverages services. Sometimes they offer round-the-clock service.

(c) **Regional cuisine specific:**   These restaurants are cuisine-specific and serve typical cuisine from a geographical region like Karnataka, Kerala, Andhra or Tamil Nadu. Very often these restaurants also deal with cuisines of a region inside a state of India, e.g., Chettinad cuisine. In a similar manner regional cuisines of other countries can also be served in a region-cuisine-specific restaurant.

(d) **Multi-cuisine specific:**   Multi-cuisine restaurants are popular in India. In these restaurants multiple types of cuisines, for example, Indian, Chinese and European cuisines are served.

(e) **Food courts:**   Food courts are becoming popular in India, especially in shopping malls. Food courts also feature in airport, hospital and office complexes of large size.

(f) **Cafés:**   Cafés are format of food and beverages retailing. These comprise coffee/tea bars with selected food offerings. A few examples are Barista, Lavazza, Dunkin Donuts and Café Coffee Day. Student cafés are variations of food cafés which serve breakfast, coffee/tea, and selected food items. Some cafés offer open-air atmosphere, for example, the student café at Goethe-Institute, New Delhi.

(g) **Specialty restaurants:**   Examples of specialty restaurants are health food restaurants and restaurants with food influenced by Ayurveda. Certain specialty restaurants draw customers from beyond immediate neighbourhood due to celebrity chefs/cuisine and are often called destination restaurants.

(h) **Fast-food outlets:**   Examples of fast-food outlets are those that have been set up by international chains like McDonalds, Dominos, Pizza Hut, KFC, Papa John's Pizza, etc. These are also known as Quick Service Restaurants (QSRs). These are characterised by minimal table service and speed of service. The formats of "Take Away" and "Home Delivery" are essential parts of QSRs.

(i) **Restobars:**   Restobars offer services of a club, a bar and a restaurant together.

(j) **Cafeterias:**   Cafeterias serve food from series of hot and cold *bain-maries* which are part of a service counter. Cafeterias are often part of a business establishment's welfare activities, and the food is subsidized or free of charge. The price of menu items/composite meals is often controlled in cafeterias of hospitals and educational institutions.

(k) **Kiosks:**   Kiosks are relatively a new format. Examples of kiosks are stands that sell single or select items of Chinese, Italian, or Arabian cuisines or street food like kathi rolls, kababs, chaat, ice cream, etc.

(l) **Stand-alone banquets:**   In India, the tax structures as applicable to customers at banquet venues within hotels are higher as compared to tax structures applicable to them at stand-alone banqueting venues. This disparity has, over the years, encouraged large number of entrepreneurs to create quality stand-alone banqueting business as well as attract the MICE segment. The food and beverages offered in these stand-alone banquets match or exceed the quality offered by banquets within hotels, giving upscale hotels a run for their money. The trend is here to stay.

(m) **MICE business:**   Meetings, Incentives, Conferences and Exhibitions – known by the acronym **MICE** are a type of Food & Beverages business. Very often a central body of professionals arranges for a meeting, conference or exhibition to update or to review a particular industry's status and the way forward or to hold a seminar for academic purposes. MICE are usually profession, academic or trade linked. MICE get-togethers are usually planned well in advance, and are often contributory in nature.

Hotel Asia 2016, held at Singapore in April 2016 was a classic example of the MICE segment of business. Hotel Asia 2016 was an international exhibition of hotel, restaurant and food service equipment, supplies and services. The exhibition, together with other specialized events, for example, knowledge seminars was a structured and comprehensive trade show. The exhibition had convergence of thousands of global brands displaying products and services for view, sale and for partnership. The exhibition allowed for plenty of networking and business prospective opportunities for all visitors and exhibitors in the food and hospitality industry.

Quality of food and beverages at any MICE event often depends on the organizers. Multiple and disparate food outlets owned by different global restaurateurs offered different cuisines, quality of food and brands to support Hotel Asia 2016. In some MICE events the food and beverages services remain functional, supportive and economical. In other cases the food and beverages services can be of high quality and profile.

1.3 EMERGING CULINARY BUSINESS

Many national and international formats of culinary business are evolving. The business world would continue to present fresh challenges in doing business. Culinary business would evolve to cater to these challenges and to leisure activities. Few examples of such evolving formats of culinary business are given below.

1.3.1 Culinary Business at the Aerotropolis

The concept of aerotropolis has evolved due to globalization. The aerotropolis business model is that of a city spread out around the facilities of an airport. There is no need for travellers to enter the main city for any requirement whatsoever. Local people specific to the requirement of the aerotropolis reside around the complex.

The aerotropolis model allows for all business needs to be met. The business deals are done at a variety of dedicated business lounges in and around the airport, and at hotels situated within the airport. Dining and shopping facilities are available within the airport complex. This business model presents possibilities of a host of diverse culinary concepts, at different business scales and potential, within immediate vicinity of each other.

1.3.2 Culinary Business in Support of the Food Processing Industry

Culinary product development support is vital for the success of the food processing industry. In the future, many forms of culinary business would function solely to support the food processing industry. Different economic and food production benchmarks would govern such culinary business.

1.3.3 Culinary Business as Mother Kitchen

The mother kitchen is fast emerging as a format for operations of culinary business, especially those with multiple franchised or owned branded outlets. The mother kitchen model is like a food processing unit having guaranteed in-house customers (its own outlets), and which produces food exclusively for these outlets.

The mother kitchen produces food products in the format of:

(i)   ready-to-cook;

(ii) heat-and-serve;

(iii) scratch foods;

(iv) convenience foods; and

(v)   proprietary items like sauces, gravies, concentrates, marinades, flavour enhancers, spice blends – all specific to the needs of the business, including franchises.

The preparations from the mother kitchen are supplied to multiple outlets through a cold store chain under strict hygiene and HACCP conditions, mostly in and around the same geographical location. However, preservation processes like freezing, canning, bottling, vacuum packing, etc., allow the prepared items to be transferred to other national locations too. The mother kitchen treats each outlet as its customer.

The mother kitchen can be located at a property which is economical to operate in terms of lease values and access to suppliers. The mother kitchen **concept** ensures intrinsic quality, food safety and greater potential for economic efficiency. It has the following advantages:

(a) **At the mother kitchen level, it is feasible to:**
- produce large quantities of ready-to-use basic preparations and other proprietary menu items;
- centrally control quality of food production by competent and knowledgeable chefs and operators. This inherently allows for same product quality to be maintained at each of the outlets;
- maintain secrecy during food production and allow standard recipes to remain privy to a few senior personnel;
- carry out secret and in-house evaluation of existing and new products through a committee approach and through gourmet panels. New products can be developed through research and development. Quality of existing products can be improved through change of ingredients and recipe methodology;
- carry out laboratory check-ups of under-production items, and those picked up at random from the outlets;
- bring in greater efficiency in back-end logistics support in purchasing, receiving, storing and utilizing of food products and raw ingredients. Standard purchase specifications of food products and raw ingredients to be purchased can be maintained. Due to larger purchase volumes major suppliers, distributors and manufacturers would be interested in providing supplies;
- expect hundred per cent capacity utilization of the food production facilities. The mother kitchen can work round-the-clock and ensure economies of scale.
- introduce service design and service guarantees for items for internal efficiency; and
- maintain standard operating procedures.

(b) **At the outlets level, it is feasible to economise in:**
- training of junior staff especially for the finishing touches required for ready-to-use menu items and for the sales. This eliminates the need for higher paid and higher qualified production and service personnel;
- tremendous savings on labour costs. Highly skilled culinary professionals are not required at outlet level. Ready-to-use and ready-to-serve food products are received from the mother kitchen. Lesser number of food production and food service personnel are required at the outlet level;
- the requirement of equipment and food production facilities, keeping it to the minimum;
- the requirement of floor space for the outlet-kitchen. This allows leasing outlet space at premium locations. Very often, large outlet spaces are exorbitantly expensive at premium locations, and not available for culinary business;
- the maintenance of minimum inventories of purchased food products and raw ingredients; and
- replenishment of outlet requirements, for example, food embellishments, proprietary sauces and ingredients and those prepared by the mother kitchen on a daily or just-in-time basis.

There are further advantages at the outlets level, as follows:

- Enhanced efficiency through reduction in service and delivery time of customer orders;
- Elimination or reduction of wastage, pilferage and unauthorized consumption of prepared food items;
- Better supervision to control dishonesty among individual outlet operators;
- Faster and easier computerized controls of the mother kitchen as well as of individual outlets. Audits are easier and menu engineering formats could be implemented on a daily basis. Inventory management systems could be implemented for the entire product and production line.

1.3.4 Underwriting of Other Forms of Culinary Business

Large number of culinary business ventures fail because they are unable to garner the desired revenues and profits. In the future, many culinary ventures which are not doing well would invite external agencies to underwrite their business. The external agencies, run by professional chefs, would examine the existing working conditions; evaluate the current business scenario in terms of revenues, footfalls and activity schedules. They would then underwrite the business to guarantee specific revenues, footfalls and culinary activities.

The guarantees for business would be higher than the existing business potential. The external agencies would charge for their professional services and introduce menu engineering activities, food promotions and festivals, re-engineer banquet and à la carte menus, introduce business segments with a fresh creative approach suiting the geographical location, the weather conditions and other business opportunities. They would also examine higher utilization of the installed restaurant covers; floor areas as well as existing average customer spend per cover.

1.4 KNOWLEDGE MANAGEMENT FOR THE CULINARY BUSINESS

The culinary business is a "touch and feel" business. Culinary business requires skilled and knowledgeable professionals. In addition, chefs and chef trainers are required for culinary institutes, food processing industry, burgeoning food shows on television channels and for marketing campaigns.

The hotel and restaurant industry constantly upgrades its benchmarks. Hotel and restaurant companies of the world, settling into India have very high and contemporary benchmarks. Therefore, the demand of wannabe hospitality professionals is increasing day-by-day. Students from hotel management and culinary institutes must strive to upgrade their knowledge in line with the changing professional benchmarks. Once employed the students must continue to enhance their knowledge and skills through self-development and also through specific and structured developmental programmes.

1.5 CAREER OPPORTUNITIES IN THE CULINARY BUSINESS

The culinary business is vibrant with career opportunities. As a rule of thumb approximately 15% of total staff strength in hotels and 35% in restaurants are composed of culinary professionals. The Indian culinary industry requires about 9000 culinary professionals every year.

World over, there is growing need of skilled and trained culinary professionals in hotels, restaurants, cruise ships, and other catering establishments. Thousands of Indian culinary professionals take up assignments in the global hospitality industry.

There is no doubt that efficient, skilled and trained culinary professionals would continue to command great careers and greater emoluments towards enriching their lives. The author wishes to encourage students of hotel management and culinary institutes to take up the culinary profession as the aim and objective of their careers.

1.6 CORE CHARACTERISTICS OF CULINARY BUSINESS

1.6.1 Culinary Concept and Business Plan

The business must examine the aspirational values of the customer in relation to its culinary concept and culinary product delivery system. Culinary business typically relates to the specific needs of a geographical market and must fill the available niche. It can create the 'need' of its existence in the market through creating aspirational values linked to fresh product offers, identifying product quality, its convenience or cost-effectiveness or combination of all these.

Sufficient market research must be done to confirm that the market is ready for such a culinary offer. It must identify the value propositions for its customers and establish its benchmarks accordingly. In addition, a culinary concept must remain relevant to the customer, to the market and to the business enterprise. The culinary product and its delivery system must be designed and packaged carefully to work better than the competition.

An entrepreneurial inspiration must be developed into a decisively positioned culinary concept. Culinary concepts start with assumptions of the market conditions. These must synergize with the skill, knowledge and talent bank of the culinary business, its market position and its marketing promises. The developed culinary concept must be execution-friendly. The talent and skills of the chefs and other operators ensure that the business starts making profits and sufficient clientele comes into the business.

Chain operations introducing a fresh culinary offer into a new geographical market often place a copy of a tried and tested culinary concept. Chain operations observe their existing and successful culinary concept, identify the critical success factors, develop a template and duplicate it at another geographical location or introduce it with minor changes that are likely to work well in the new location.

In case of an altogether new culinary concept, chain operations must invest in an R&D kitchen or mother kitchen. Fresh culinary concepts must be eminently supported by stated and implied marketing promises and regular marketing, while maintaining strict service guarantees at the outlet.

The culinary business plan is an extension of the culinary concept. The process that should be ideally implemented is to identify an external specialist in case of a new venture. In case of chain operations, the in-house specialists support it. The next action is to work on the menu and identify the menu sections and menu items. Benchmarks of quality of food production are set in line with the value proposition that the culinary business intends to provide to the prospective customer.

Backward integration of the food production processes requires identifying the logistics of supplies required for food production. This includes firming-up of the process-framework for purchase, the identification of the right suppliers, the receiving and storage, as well as the pre-production.

Forward integration of the food production processes requires setting up benchmarks for quality of food service and other tangible products and intangible services. Example of tangible product is the quality of outlet infrastructure. Examples of intangible services are the quality of service delivery, training of service personnel, and warmth and hospitality desired by the customers in relation to the value proposition.

Making a business plan is an on-going exercise. An example of later additions to the original business plan is the setting up of all operational and back-of-the-house functional areas. Another example is dealing with many non-operational issues like taxation and statutory laws.

The culinary business plan inherently identifies the:

- culinary concept;
- aims and objectives of the culinary business;
- type of cuisine to be served;
- value proposition;

- investments;
- target market;
- marketing promises;
- marketing plan;
- menu/menu item sale price strategy;
- unique selling propositions—skills and intellectual advantage;
- profitability targets and the estimated returns on investments;
- logistics of supplies required for food production;
- chain of strength flowing through all operational areas, back-of-the-house functional areas and the administration; and
- assumptions.

The business plan also identifies whether the outlet would be limiting food services to a geographical area or be open for expansion. If multiple outlets are planned it is economical to institute processes for a mother kitchen and central purchases. The process may also include purchasing/leasing of cheaper space at a convenient location for purposes of the mother kitchen and central purchase.

In due course the culinary concept and business plan take shape as objective benchmarks. The business plan, as any other benchmark, must be reviewed periodically and value propositions for customers examined. Essentially, all forms of culinary business must reinvent themselves. Values of the culinary concept and the culinary business plan must be enhanced as business environments and technologies change and the concept repositioned. An important part of the success of any culinary business is the capability of the management to define guidelines for its continued commercial success. While developing as well as during any repositioning exercise chefs and operators must maintain focus on customer centricity.

This book is devoted to culinary economics. The author wishes to restrict the information contained in the book only to matters of economics of the culinary business.

1.6.2 Value Proposition

Customers come in to sample a culinary product based on recommendations of friends, family, colleagues, media and also because of claims of the culinary business placed as advertisements. The customer decides on a repeat visit based on his perception of values received during the first visit. In addition, on each of his visits the customer establishes and compares the values he receives in relation to his earlier visits.

The quality of food is not the only criteria for a customer to patronize or re-patronize a culinary offer in the market. Combinations of tangible and intangible services create the values of his experience.

A customer assesses a culinary product line for diverse values. The values depend on the:

- quality of the culinary product;
- quality of the tangible and intangible services; and
- ambience and features like: sitting arrangement, comfortable access.

The assessment of the culinary product and its delivery services are inseparable from each other. Values must be established and monitored based on the expectations of the target market. The customer's perception of value is very important in the evolving market competition scenario and is governed by the total dining experience. **Positive dining experience produces** high values.

The customer is becoming increasingly knowledgeable and selective on the matter of cuisine. He desires value for money. He is intelligently able to compare products and culinary offerings of different outlets, and reach his conclusions of value for his money. The needs of the customer are constantly changing. To stay in business and to remain profitable, culinary business should respond to the changing needs, desires and expectations of customers.

Business which constantly meets or exceeds guest expectations is a winner. The composite culinary product and the quality of service deliveries should evolve positively.

For any culinary business and in all geographical locations, the supply markets are becoming dearer. The additional cost burden cannot be borne by customers constantly. Evolving culinary product offers should create inherent efficiencies in service deliveries, be cost-effective and continue to remain in line with the culinary concept.

Operators of culinary business must maximize values to its customers in relation to the culinary concept, through the establishment of benchmarks at each stage of materials management. Operators must strive to introduce and maintain higher levels of objectivity in operations. (The process of introducing objectivity in quality of food production has been eminently explained in Module 13: "Objectivity and Subjectivity in Culinary Business", and specifically in the **Exhibit 39, p. 237**).

It is important for the business to review its culinary concept, product line, service guarantees, food production standards, materials management systems and the expected dining experience of the customer. Each of these needs benchmarks, and should be reviewed individually, collectively and periodically. Each benchmark depends on the performance of another benchmark. Each benchmark is also inseparable from another. Reviews and positive repositioning of deliverables support the transformation of a culinary product offer into a strong culinary brand.

The business would be able to evaluate the price points at which the products and services would sell and their relative costs through the initial and regular critical examination. The examination and calculations thereof would indicate the profitability. Examining the purchase systems would also reveal continuity in availability of raw food products and ingredients as well as continued viability of a particular menu item.

A price and quality relationship would be noticed due to these reviews. The relationship is described below.

The value received by a customer of a culinary business is a relationship between the quality of food and services and price paid within the parameters of the declared or implied marketing promise. The relationship can be expressed as follows:

$$\text{Value} = \frac{\text{Quality} \times \text{Service}}{\text{Price}}$$

Value varies directly with changes in the quality and/or service. Value decreases if price increases and there is no change in quality of food, service, delivery intangibles or ambience. If price remains constant, and quality of food, service, delivery intangibles or ambience improve, value increases. Therefore value has an inverse relationship with price. It is possible to retain value for a customer, even with price increase. (The possibilities are explained in Module 4: "Menu Engineering: Culinary Business Analytics".)

When a culinary business becomes the customer to a supplier, the connotations of value in relation to quality, service and price remain the same. (The reader would study these in Module 7: "Selecting the Right Supplier".)

1.6.3 External Specialist Resources

Stand-alone culinary business must engage external specialist resources. These specialist resources are in a position to take an "outside-in" view of the culinary business and play key roles to keep the business rejuvenated. For chain business the specialist resources can be their own corporate personnel of different specialties.

A consultant takes up a number of assignments. A consultant travels across geographical regions. He observes several forms of culinary business with different concepts. Each of these forms is governed by different management styles, strengths and weaknesses of the operators and of the cuisines. These characteristics serve as a window to the **fast-changing** business scenario in the hospitality/culinary environments.

Consultants spend time, energy and money in self-training of specific skill-sets. They also undertake specific and structured studies of the national and international data and industry trends for specific and purposeful support to a customer's needs.

The operators of stand-alone business are ensnared in their own business environments and day-to-day routine. With no exposure to business other than their own, the operators can get to be complacent with their own knowledge and skill-sets and tend to lose out against competition in the market. To remain competitive it is wise to adopt or **at least examine** evolving methodologies, technologies, fresh skills, better presentation styles, cost-effective styles and infrastructure layouts. To do so the advice of a consultant is crucial.

In addition, consultants often bring in specific culinary or management skills which are not available to investors of the culinary business. Consultants provide clarity and framework to the concept and associated managerial requirements to fulfil the "dream" of an investor. They therefore are very important for the right start-up of stand-alone culinary business.

Business which is not financially successful benefits from the advice of consultants. Consultants play decisive roles to bring in or maintain positive changes in the financial results of a culinary business. Repositioning of business and culinary concepts, described above are important for the positive financial regain.

1.6.4 Price Points

The menu is the most important tool of any form of culinary business. Menu items are like business verticals and each one of them should be accorded equal opportunity to succeed. Menu items can sell at higher price points if the product is exclusive and coveted. The menu items must be priced in line with:

(a) the culinary concept;

(b) production and service costs of each menu item;

(c) tangible and intangible values of the culinary product and the offer;

(d) aspirational values created by the stated and implied marketing promises; and

(e) the existing name of the culinary brand/hotel property in the market.

1.6.5 Cost, Revenue and Profit Centres

(a) **Cost centre:** All forms of culinary business are cost centres and must ensure that the expenses are within the budgets. Handling a predominantly perishable business requires drive and dedication. The culinary business has to handle the entire purchasing at lowest total cost, minimize financial investments in storage and supply line, and protect the cost structure of the business.

(b) **Revenue centre:** The existing and evolving formats of culinary business have been listed earlier in the current module. All forms of culinary business are revenue centres. Revenues are generated through sale of food, beverages and other necessary services.

Earlier, chefs were skilled but illiterate and were not expected to contribute to management of revenues. That is not the case now. The chefs are literate and are from hotel management and culinary institutes. In addition, chefs add to their initial training by undergoing structured knowledge and skill based programmes throughout their career.

The chefs have taken over the role of business managers. They take active part in interaction with customers, have mastered the art of fruitful negotiations, and take lead in sourcing additional business through exhibition of fresh talent. Chefs are able to create food promotions and food festivals and encourage higher customer footfalls. In this manner chefs are not only able to keep their business invigorated but maintain the same as a revenue centre. The culinary business faces the challenge of producing increasingly higher revenues each year.

(c) **Profit centre:** A well managed culinary business is a profit centre. If managed efficiently, culinary business can be a higher money spinner and can give higher and quicker returns on investments than any other business. It is imperative for chefs and other operators to support other departments to reduce administrative costs.

The chefs and other operators must control:

- costs related to pre-production of food;
- costs related to post-production of food; and
- operational expenses **(see pp. 42, 219)**.

(see pp. 42, 219)

1.6.6 Benchmarks

Setting up of benchmarks is an important exercise. Once benchmarks are fixed, future performances can be measured against these benchmarks. Variances observed during this exercise can be analyzed, and reasons established. Subsequent corrective action would ensure efficient operations.

The cycle of the benchmark exercise involves:

(a) setting up of benchmarks;

(b) examining the benchmarks at periodic intervals;

(c) analyzing the benchmarks; and

(d) upgrading or maintaining the benchmarks.

1.6.7 Audits

Benchmarks should be integrated with an efficient audit trail. **Audits are vital support functions for the operations.** Chefs and other operators must recognize this fact, follow all benchmarks and run the culinary business in an efficient and cost-effective manner. They must influence ways and means to increase revenues at comparatively lower costs than an earlier financial period.

Audits support examination of existing benchmarks and provide information and guidelines for improvements on performances in the matter of:

(a) costs;

(b) revenue-earning capacities;

(c) profits; and

(d) average customer-spend per cover.

It is essential to build an effective "report-back" format of each activity of operational/functional/administrative areas of the culinary business. Audits are critical for identifying problems and maintaining optimum performance. The benchmarks of the operational and functional areas should be periodically reviewed in relation to the audit report. The most important aim and objective of audit is to review financial transactions. Financial transactions assume larger meaning than actual cash transactions. These include:

(a) all steps of the materials management processes;

(b) acts of inherent cost-effectiveness; and

(c) efficiency of operations to prevent financial losses.

Shares of the business are often held by the public. In such cases audits are mandatory as per statutory laws. Audits become part of the performance schedules. The stocks-in-hand form the assets of the company. Efficient management of stocks encompassing purchase of entirety of stock keeping units (SKUs), their receipt into the business, their storage and their issue for usage and production is vital, and each step of the process is subject to audits.

Slackness or lack of management controls and systems may encourage employees to embezzle. Audits point out purposeful mistakes and thefts – often in the shape of pilferage committed by staff members. Such staff members should be kept under watch. If required their services should be terminated before they cause further financial losses to the business.

A chef or an operator may be performing his operational tasks to the best of his knowledge and skills. While in operations, it is often difficult for operators to keep a watch on other operators. Auditors are trained for the auditing functions. Auditors view and review operations as well as functional areas and area related documents with fresh "eyes". Interpretation from auditors often informs the operators as well as professionals of back-of-the-house functional areas what they miss observing in their daily routine. Auditors therefore provide a fresh perspective of the business, concept, target market, standard operating procedures and the marketing strategy.

Auditing is an objectivity-led process. Auditing functions have been greatly facilitated by computerization and property management systems. All listed benchmarks and their performance parameters are listed and formulated into checklists. Auditors work against ready-to-use checklists and keep evolving these in line with the evolving business. Auditors are external to operations, are unbiased, and are able to view operations with a fresh insight and point out deficiencies if any. In addition, in their audit report auditors suggest ways and means to add to the revenues, reduce costs, or both in an objective manner.

Culinary business faces three types of audits:

(a) **Internal audits:** Internal audits are part of the culinary business's financial performancte system. Internal auditors check day-to-day financial transactions, and caution the operators on an immediate basis. Many companies add audits of operations to the internal audit system. In addition audits of specific benchmarks of a company are audited by specific teams, for example 'environment and safety' audit and 'hygiene' audit.

(b) **External audits:** External audits are performed by external audit companies hired by the business. Their audit reports follow the statutory requirements. Their audit report is sent to the management first. The department heads and operators act on each audit point, as required.

(c) **Mystery audits:** Culinary business with chain operations hire external agencies to do secret audits of individual units of the chain. However, these audits are mostly to check the operations of the unit, and not to review the financial transactions. The auditors come into the units as customers and check the efficiency and value propositions of the unit. This is done without even the unit management's knowledge.

Audit Trail

External audits are conducted months after the actual operations. **An audit trail** is a series of chronologically listed records, documents, and reports that trace the flow of resources through any operation. The operation should maintain these records, documents and reports to enable future check-ups in so far as the accounting process is concerned for correctness of operations and against benchmarks.

Globally, statutory laws demand that shareholders of a business do not suffer financial losses due to pilferage thefts, unexplained shortage, spoilage and other acts of mismanagement. Stock-in-hand is considered an asset of a business for a particular period. All assets are subject to checking of their values by auditors.

The audit trail checks the accuracy and reliability of the financial statements of a culinary business. The audit trail is supported by evidence. The documents are maintained by a business to answer their own auditors as well as statutory auditors. The audit trail links the various departments of a business and their documentation in a systematic and analytical manner, and has a logical path. Transactions can be traced effectively if an audit trail is maintained correctly.

In relation to this book the audit trail exhibits the flow or processing of materials right from the stage of ordering and up to the payment made for them. For example, if the receipt of a quantity of commodities is accounted for in the production area, it is also accounted for in terms of payments to the supplier.

Audit trails are useful both for maintaining security and for noticing and recovering missing transactions. In addition to culinary materials management the audit trail traces all operational transactions.

1.6.8 High Customer Interface

Earlier, customers were not allowed in the food-production areas. Chefs were highly skilled in the culinary arts, but were semi-literate or illiterate. Hygiene of the kitchen, of the equipment and of the personnel did not have sufficient focus. Facility planning of the kitchen equipment layout and services was not up to the mark.

The situation has changed completely. Chefs are literate and from hospitality management/culinary management institutes. Most chefs have international exposure. Chefs, food production staff, other food handlers and kitchen stewarding personnel are increasingly aware of hygiene standards. They are well trained with soft skills and customer interface skills. Chefs take pride in interacting with customers and producing food as per customer's choice. Boundaries between the kitchen and the food service outlet are disappearing rapidly. Customers are encouraged to watch their food being cooked. Show kitchens have taken over.

The modern kitchens are well planned by trained facility planners with an eye for space planning. Equipment is scientifically, ergonomically and technologically superior. All pieces of equipment are positioned in their own places. The modern food production areas are a delight to work in and chefs take pride in allowing customers to walk in.

Culinary business must formulate strategies to sharpen its customer focus. The chefs and operators must utilize the opportunities of customer interface effectively and systematically. The business must leverage each of the customer contact points/occasions to advantage. The world of cuisine is evolving rapidly. Customer focus and innovation will generate a higher profitability and higher return on investments. If not utilized in a defined manner, customer contact is as perishable as the perishables the culinary business deals with.

1.6.9 Business to Customers (B2C) Orientation

Culinary business are typical formats of Business to Customers (B2C) orientation. A few examples of culinary business governed by the Business to Business (B2B) format are mother kitchens, food processing units, R&D kitchens, and flight-catering units.

1.6.10 Value of Customer Feedback

Great culinary brands are defined by the compelling emotional connection to their customers. Positive customer feedback acts as a great differentiator in the marketplace and enhances the strength of the culinary concept of established culinary business.

Encouraging customers to provide feedback on the cuisine and services is vital for the growth of culinary business. Chefs and other operators must devise an implementing force to ensure positive action on customer feedback. This would result in upgradation of benchmarks and overcoming deficiencies in quality of cuisine and services.

Listening to and acting on customer feedback, strict adherence to service guarantees, as well as ensuring quality intangible services improve customer experience and impacts them emotionally about the culinary brand. Future "moments-of-truth" ensure enriched and higher quality positive experiences for the customers.

The ideal conditions would be when the customer is happy to recommend the culinary outlet to a friend, colleague and family. When customers act as positive references they actually indicate that they have received good economic value from the outlet.

However, word-of-mouth publicity does not mean the same thing it did a few years back. Today's world is a world of megabits, megahertz, and megapixels. Today a customer can connect to the whole world through social media networks like Facebook, WhatsApp, Twitter, Instagram, YouTube and others in fractions of a minute. While positive feedback would give boost to the culinary business with rich rewards, the damage through bad feedback can be ruinous.

1.6.11 Menu Engineering: Culinary Business Analytics

Systems and databases are more reliable than human memory, observations and assumptions. Menu engineering is a process of culinary analytics. Information resulting from the systematic analysis of sales and financial data of the business supports repositioning exercises.

Culinary business responds well to the process of menu engineering. Sales figures of a certain period are examined and each menu item is assessed for its relative profitability and relative popularity. Menu engineering identifies menu items which the business should sell most and those that do not contribute as much as the other menu items.

Menu engineering manages all the menu items to make all of them individually profitable for the business and popular with the customers. Higher product value allows for higher customer satisfaction and higher popularity of the menu item. Menu engineering also creates focus on how to draw and increase the customer's attention to specific menu items. Menu engineering therefore works both as an audit as well as a **performance improving management exercise.**

1.6.12 Culinary Materials Management

In culinary business a large number of raw ingredients are purchased for production of the menu items listed on the menu. The raw ingredients are classified into perishables, highly perishable, and non-perishable, for internal management purposes. However, all food materials are perishable.

Raw food ingredients have prescribed shelf life and must display the dates of expiry. In addition, food ingredients are subject to statutory laws, which dictate their "usage-within" dates and other quality parameters. The present provisions of the Food Safety and Standards Act (2006) India are more robust, comprehensive and stricter than the earlier version – the Prevention of Food Adulteration Act, 1954. Globally also laws governing food safety are becoming stricter by the day. Extreme care is required for handling ingredients. Irresponsibility in handling food materials can result in food poisoning and damage to the reputation of the outlet.

Traditionally, in India the perishables and highly perishables are directly controlled by the chefs in the kitchens. The non-perishables are controlled by the stores department. The controls include the ordering of materials in time and in the right quantities and their storage under the right storage conditions. Ordering of perishables and non-perishables is controlled by systems and benchmarks.

Under-ordering of ingredients would result in their stocks to run out in the stores or in the kitchen. This would lead to menu items not being available. Hence, customer's dissatisfaction. Over-ordering would result in materials not consumed as regularly as desired. Over-ordering would also result in unauthorized consumption, pilferage, wastage, etc. Right ordering patterns have to be evolved by operators to ensure that the right quantities are ordered.

Right purchasing involves purchasing the right ingredients, of the right quality and in time. Benchmarks which are set up for right quality are called standard purchase specifications. Other systems and benchmarks govern the purchase processes.

Selecting the right supplier is the key objective of the purchasing systems. Right supplier supports the purchasing activities and is a key collaborator for the success of the business. The supplier's efficiencies relate up to the point of the customer receiving value for his dining experience.

Ingredients should be received and stored immediately. Benchmarks govern the receiving and storage processes. Ingredients, stored either in the kitchen or in main stores, must regularly move in the order of their purchase dates and be consumed in a profitable manner. This process of movement of ingredients is called first-in-first-out. Issues of ingredients from the stores or from the storage in the kitchen are controlled by certain benchmarks and systems.

Once the ingredients are issued for food production, the management of these materials involves:

(a) Achieving the right yields.

(b) Quality and quantity food production, in time, through the use of standard recipes and skills of the chefs.

(c) Holding ready-to-serve menu items under the right environment conditions and at the right temperature.

(d) The service of the prepared menu items using the benchmarks of service guarantees.

It is noticed that the management of materials is an on-going day-to-day process and is a cyclic activity. Materials must be managed to secure the best interests of the business, be cost-effective and timely. Benchmarks are set up for the movement of materials through the processes of ordering, purchasing, supplier selection, receiving, storing, issuing, food production and food service.

Depleting supplies must be reordered in time. Supplies are reordered under specific benchmarks. (The reader can see the details in Module 9: "Efficient Storing, Inventory Management and Right Issuing".)

The essence of materials management therefore is to obtain the right quantity of materials, of the right quality, from the right source, at the right time, for the right price and at the lowest administrative costs. Materials management encompasses effective inventory management, maintaining the cost structure of the business and handling of materials in the prescribed manner.

1.6.13 Creativity

Creativity is a business discipline. To succeed in culinary business one must adopt an affirmative approach to creativity. By using the left brain as well as the right brain one can cluster creative and emotional experiences with intellectual ones and arrive at definite business practices and solutions. Culinary business can easily maintain a competitive advantage in the marketplace and prosper through encouragement of creativity at the workplace.

It is imperative for culinary business and chefs to look at the culinary product line, culinary products, situations or problems **differently** to find a creative solution. It helps to step back and view any situation from a different angle.

Profits are the key prerequisite of culinary business. Creativity is linked to:

- profits and profitability/yields;
- capacity utilization;
- excitement in the marketplace;
- benchmarks/standard operating procedures;
- positioning and repositioning;
- pride in job performance; and
- creating opportunities and seizing opportunities.

To be more creative, chefs should discard preconceived, patented or long-standing ideas. Rigid approach is the worst enemy of creativity. Developing aesthetic benchmarks in line with the culinary concept and marketing promises is imperative for a creative journey. To be useful, an inspiration must be honed in by a trained chef's experience, sophistication and discipline.

Chefs must bring several senses into play simultaneously so that one sense enhances the other. They must stretch their abilities and talent. Brainstorming is a useful means towards higher creativity.

Quality culinary business decides presentation and plating designs of each menu item in advance and integrates the same with service design and service guarantees. Creative chefs re-plan the presentation style of the menu item in line with the essence of menu engineering, especially the menu items identified as "standards", and "puzzles".

Creativity could also mean examining and identifying opportunities of utilizing space and covers during non-business hours for generating revenues.

The marketplace presents regular disruptions. New policies are introduced by the political establishment of the day causing disruptions. Creativity also means overcoming negative disruptions of any kind and seizing advantage of an expected or actual positive disruption.

1.6.14 Food Promotions and Food Festivals

Culinary business must hold food promotions on a regular basis. Food promotions help in advertising the diverse talents of the chefs beyond the contents of à la carte menus, and the outlet's ability to create fresh culinary products. Culinary promotions and their excellence in execution lend a positive image in the minds of customers as a "happening place" and many visit outlets to experience something different from the à la carte menu. These special events also support the ever-widening culinary offers for banqueting business.

Food promotions are called as such when a special event/menu publicizes a special culinary preparation for a considerable period of time, for example, a week, or a menu item ready to be introduced into any menu or an ingredient, for example, promotion of olive oil, apples, prunes, etc.

The same food promotion is called a "food festival" if any festivities or social message or cultural programme is attached to it. The word "festivities" has a broader connotation and can include a romantic linkage, and /or a dance, or music.

1.6.15 Cuisine: An Art, a Science and Management

The primary duty of chefs is the preparation of food. However, chefs have redefined the preparation of food as specialized and often theme-oriented. By combining various raw ingredients, in specific measures and preparing them through specific step-by-step methods, chefs create **well-defined and specific** culinary preparations of:

- exciting flavours;
- lingering tastes;
- variety of textures;
- specific and wonderful natural colours; and
- delightful decorative appeal.

The chefs therefore use their knowledge, experience and skills to make food more enjoyable. Cooking raw ingredients makes them easily digestible, their flavour improves, and their textures become more appealing. Stimulating combination of flavours and tempting colour mix result due to culinary marriage of different ingredients. This part of the cooking process is therefore **an art in the preparation of food.**

In addition, chefs cater to the nutritional needs of the customers. Food must also be prepared hygienically and all HACCP requirements observed to safeguard the health of the customers. This part of the cooking process is **the science involved in the preparation of food.**

(This book takes the reader through systems and procedures, and detailing of benchmarks to ensure **cost-effectiveness** of the culinary business — the **core** theme of this book. The reader would read about the definite steps that are taken to manage costs through the process of materials management).

Understanding of food preparation in the backdrop of materials management is the **management** in the preparation of food. Quality food preparations must be served under pre-decided service guarantees. **Therefore, cuisine is an art, a science and management,** and all forms of culinary business must respond to all these three facets of cuisine to be successful.

1.6.16 Exclusive and Coveted Product Line

A culinary product/menu item which is exclusive and covetable is sure to generate:

- (a) higher number of footfalls into the business;
- (b) higher customer-spend per cover;
- (c) higher sales of "associated" products and services;
- (d) higher profitability;
- (e) higher revenues;
- (f) higher value-for-money for the customer; and
- (g) quality dining experience for the customer.

Examples of exclusive and coveted product lines are the Bukhara and Dum Pukht restaurants at the ITC Maurya Hotel, New Delhi.

1.6.17 Usage of Technology

Earlier, culinary business was driven by skills and creativity. Over the years culinary business has incorporated management processes. Cost-effectiveness, materials management and regular customer interface are the key improvements of this period.

Increasing technology quotient is driving the culinary industry. Contemporary technology is facilitating creativity. In addition, technology is fast changing:

- (a) ease of cooking;
- (b) business scenario;
- (c) ease of operation;

(d) quality of ready-to-serve culinary products; and

(e) revenue-earning potential.

Tedious and prolonged cooking processes associated with traditional cooking ranges has given way to enhanced usage of futuristic equipment, inbuilt with artificial intelligence. Examples of these technology led kitchen equipment are combi-ovens, turbojet ovens, turbojet cookers, sous vide cookers and blast freezers.

Culinary business has benefitted from technology towards reduction in wastage and longer shelf-life of perishable culinary products. Multi-purpose, multi-utility and futuristic kitchen equipment have reduced physical efforts. Technologically advanced equipment have facilitated seamless integration of different cooking methods.

Technology has also ensured that culinary business is also able to cut down on energy and labour costs and floor space. Market competition and corporate activities have forced culinary business to install environment-friendly equipment.

1.6.18 Property Management Systems and Digitalization

Digital technology is becoming pervasive in the materials management chain. Digital information from property management systems improves inventory turnover, rescues commitment of capital from non-utilization of financial resources and enables faster cycle times. The cost of using technology to collect and utilize information to advantage would keep dropping.

The roles of the chef and other culinary professionals are changing fast. The changing roles include shaping overall business strategy and ensuring cost-effectiveness. Chefs would be required to be responsible for culinary materials management. Property management systems and digital technology would guide chefs for the requirements.

1.6.19 Revenue Maximization

Almost all types of business respond to upselling. Marketers and salespersons are forever trying to persuade customers to buy expensive version of products. In the process the marketers are rewarded with higher sales and larger profits. However, customers respond to upselling of items of manufactured merchandise by purchasing either the lower-priced item or the higher-priced item. Customers do not respond to upselling by purchasing both items.

Marketers of culinary business — very often the chefs and food service personnel themselves — are able to upsell enhanced number of culinary/ beverages products than the customer would have otherwise purchased. These additional items can be beverages, side-dishes or non-listed items. These additional items can also be those that the customer would not notice and place orders for unless the same are suggested. Customers of culinary business respond to upselling at each moment-of-truth.

1.6.20 Economies of Scale

Culinary business typically responds to economies of scale. This is because it involves selling products which are highly perishable. If the quantities of portions produced match the portions sold, the business is a winner.

Customers can consume only a limited quantity of the culinary product at each occasion. If there are multiple cuisines on offer, the consumption of individual items would come down. Experience of chefs and operators, visual observations, and discussions with customers can help reduction in quantities of food produced. Yields get better and better on the volume route and costs reduce progressively. This is especially true for banqueting business. The cascading effect of the volumes of business support reductions in costs. A distinct link between costs, economies of scale (i.e., volume route), capacity utilization and food cost is noticed in culinary business.

1.6.21 Yields from Raw Products and Yield Tests

All foods are perishable and non-saleable portion of the product or ingredient is as perishable and as worthless as a room remaining unsold in the rooms division of the hotel business or a cover unsold in the restaurant business.

Therefore, the quality of as-purchased ingredients should be commensurate with the desired saleable value. The concept and class of culinary business decide the quality of as-purchased ingredients. Purchase of 'higher-than-required' quality of ingredients reduces profitability.

It is essential in business to understand the saleable value of a product or product line. In different types of business yield tests are done to identify different requirements. Yields in culinary business typically relate to the saleable value of a culinary product or ingredient. Yield tests are mostly done to calculate butcher raw weight yield tests.

Butcher raw weight yield tests are helpful for establishing cost per servable portion and cost factor of non-vegetarian items. (Yields and yield tests are elaborated in Module 10: "Economics of Food Production and Food Service".)

1.6.22 'A' Value Food Products and Raw Ingredients

Culinary business is typical and unparalleled to other manufacturing business sectors in the matter of using a few culinary products and raw ingredients which are:

(a) very expensive;

(b) highly perishable;

(c) consumed in larger quantities than other ingredients; or

(d) have subjective accountability.

These are called 'A' value food products and raw ingredients. 'A' value products and raw ingredients are a few in number, but carry high or very high costs. Few examples of very expensive food products and raw ingredients are *pâté de foie gras*, imported ready-to-cook portions of fishes, truffles, caviar and saffron. A few examples of highly perishable raw ingredients are lobsters and prawns. A few examples of raw ingredients consumed in larger quantities are onions, tomatoes and potatoes. Examples of food products that have subjective accountability are proprietary sauces, condiments, chocolates and other complimentary food items that are handed over to the food service personnel. Safe-keeping, strict care and just-sufficient usage of these 'A' value food products and raw ingredients would result in tremendous cost savings.

1.6.23 Highly Perishable

Culinary business involves dealing with highly perishable product line. All foods are perishable. Some are highly perishable, and deteriorate fast while others take time to deteriorate. Statutory laws stipulate usage of food products and raw ingredients within a certain time limit.

Food products and ingredients are expensive in addition to being perishable. Poor preparation styles, incorrect meat fabrication, overproduction, wastage and unauthorized consumption add to the costs of the business. Cost is incurred as soon as a food product is produced partially or completely. Semi-prepared food for à la carte business is an example of partially produced food. If the item is not ordered by customers the semi-prepared food is considered wastage.

Food production quantities cannot be flawlessly calculated. Incorrect estimation of number of footfalls into the business can result in overproduction of food. Food products, ingredients and ready-to-serve menu items which have deteriorated in quality become unfit for human consumption. (Methods of forecasting of quantities of food production have been detailed in Module 10: "Economics of Food Production and Food Service.)

Overstocking of food stores prevents efficient utilization of capital for other business requirements. Overstocking of food items results in spoilage and wastage.

The service outlet presents another area of perishability. The outlet is kept in readiness for customer service. Insufficient clientele for any dining period results in capacity not being utilized. If the restaurant covers are not sold for any of the possible meal period, the revenue which would have accrued otherwise is lost for ever. Unutilized capacities are highly perishable.

1.6.24 Budgets and Budgeting

Budgets are objectivity-led documents. Chefs and operators must have benchmarks of revenues, profits and expenditures to work against. Budgets are never made to allow the chefs and operators to increase their comfort level. "Logic-notes" are often provided by the investors/management to the chefs and operators at the time of the budgeting exercise. These logic-notes provide "outside-in" views and possibilities of enhanced revenues and profits for a period of operations ahead.

Budgets encourage the chefs and operators to think differently and above their operations and provide the right challenges to work harder, faster and smartly. Within the permissible range of the culinary concept and business plan, chefs and operators must seize all opportunities to add to revenues and profits.

Budgeting is an important exercise of setting benchmarks of financial and operational performance for a start-up as well as for a running culinary business. Budgeting of incomes and expenditures for a financial period involves parameters of viability and of marketing the new enterprise. Factors of demand and creativity of the product line change the parameters of budgeting.

While budgeting sales there is an opportunity for culinary business to price its product line higher. Higher selling prices of the culinary product line are possible in case of higher utilization of the creative talents of the chefs, and also if the product line is not available with the competition elsewhere in the same marketplace.

1.6.25 In a Buyer's Market

Earlier, there was a dearth of the right suppliers for culinary business. It was a seller's market and suppliers dictated the market and conditions of supply. Customers anxious for a steady supply of culinary products and ingredients had little room to negotiate purchase price.

While the situation may ring true today for some isolated proprietary products and ingredients and in a few isolated geographical locations, the scenario has changed completely. For most of the culinary business there is an overabundance of suppliers. Many new suppliers enter the supply market regularly.

Culinary business is placed in a buyer's market due to this trend. Under such conditions the costs of the purchasing activity can be brought down through:

(a) efficient study of the supply market;

(b) selection of the right suppliers;

(c) development of good relations with the supplier; and

(d) the right materials management.

In a similar manner there is overabundance of all forms of culinary business in the marketplace. The customer is spoilt for choice and is placed in a buyer's market. Fresh formats of culinary business are appearing on the market regularly. The ability of the culinary business to create value for its customers will differentiate it in the competition marketplace. Culinary business which creates value would reap the benefits through better sales price per portion of menu item sold, larger number of footfalls into the business, and higher revenue and contribution per available cover. The "better sales price" would be commensurate with the value customers perceive they are getting and the value which the business actually provides.

1.6.26 Research and Development

Culinary product adaptation for many forms culinary business has long been on the copy-cat and "me-too" platforms. Competition is increasing for culinary business. Stand-alone restaurants are successful in challenging the hitherto dominant position of upscale restaurants located in hotels.

Changing customer tastes and needs require fresher culinary products. The key to retain customers and increase footfalls is culinary research, development and documentation. Research and development, earlier associated with sectors like engineering is now required for culinary outlets also. Experienced, trained and skilled chefs must set aside structured time periods for research and development. Chefs can do culinary product development work.

Conscious and conscientious culinary business must invest in research and development within the business in a regular and structured manner. Research and development has the potential to introduce new:

(a) cuisine;

(b) culinary products;

(c) platforms of service; and

(d) cost-effective technology.

Culinary business must develop the culture and ecosystem of doing research. Culinary research and development can be done in the line of cuisine or in additional culinary products as extensions of existing culinary offer.

Research and development activities require effective, systematic, step-by-step and chronological documentation. Documentation allows continuity.

Research, development and documentation are imperative tools for expansion of culinary business beyond immediate geographical boundaries. "Thinking local" should be replaced by "thinking national" or "thinking global" for chain of culinary business. For a growing culinary business, there is merit and cost advantage in instituting its own R&D facility rather than sourcing data and product knowledge.

1.6.27 Speed of Delivery

Delivery of culinary products is strictly controlled by chronological guidelines. If it is not delivered within promised time frames, the best of culinary product would appear to be of poor value to a customer.

Quality and image conscious culinary business declares service guarantees as inherent marketing promises. Service guarantees are zero-defect, zero-variable and zero-tolerance benchmarks. An inherent part of a service guarantee is the service time once orders are placed. This part of the service guarantee is as sacrosanct as other parts in the service guarantee schedule of a particular menu item. Prepared menu items must be picked up from the pick-up point in the food preparation area in time. Culinary business succeeds greatly due to the effective training, coordination and speed of delivery.

1.7 END OF MODULE NOTES

1.7.1 Clearly Defining the Culinary Concept

Clearly defining the culinary concept is imperative to the success of culinary business. Defining the culinary concept is instrumental in cost-effectiveness of the business. The critical success factors in relation to culinary concepts are as follows:

1. Culinary concepts work like efficiently laid out business plans.

2. The chef/operator/investor must position/reposition the culinary concept **sharply** through careful designing.

3. The menu is the most important link between the culinary concept, the customer, the food production and food service processes.

4. The chef/operator/investor must ensure a price, quality and service relationship within the culinary concept and menu offers for the benefit of the customer.

5. The chef/operator/investor must match operational competencies with the product delivery.

6. The culinary business must position the standard purchase specifications in line with the values of the culinary concept—no more and no less.

7. The culinary business must reduce costs through continuous examination of the concept.

8. **Quality is not a fixed standard.** The chef/operator/investor must reposition the benchmarks of operational and functional areas if repositioning a concept.

9. Culinary business is typically a touch-and-feel business predominantly of the B2C type, is consumer facing, with intangible services often overriding tangible products and services.

10. The chef/operator/investor must ensure that the tangible products and services are value-led and cent-percent in line with the declared concept. The culinary business must ensure regular training of intangible services.

1.7.2 Corporate Social Responsibility (CSR)

Culinary business must adopt number of CSR activities. It is a format of corporate self-regulation built into its business model. CSR initiatives are individual to each organisation.

The most important aspect of CSR is active compliance with statutory laws, ethical standards and international norms. Companies endeavour to own responsibility for their actions and encourage a positive impact through its business activities.

A corporate's social responsibility initiatives encompass its employees, suppliers, customers, stakeholders and the environment. Purchasers often take written guarantees for tenets of corporate social responsibility from approved/wannabe suppliers.

1.7.3 Defining Food Products and Raw Ingredients

For the purpose of this book, food products are defined and identified as processed items. Examples are as follows:

(i) Ready-to-cook items.

(ii) Heat-and-serve items.

(iii) Scratch foods.

(iv) Convenience foods.

(v) Proprietary items like sauces, gravies, concentrates, marinades, flavour enhancers, spice blends – all specific to the needs of the business, including franchises.

Raw ingredients are defined and identified as natural and unblended items required for production.

2

CULINARY INGREDIENTS

Essence of the Module

This module deals with the basic understanding of the building blocks of cuisine – the culinary ingredients. This module is a link between the first module and the rest of the modules of the book.

Module Objectives and Competencies
The main themes of this book are cost effectiveness of culinary operations and economics of food production. This module introduces culinary ingredients to the reader. The objective of this module is not to detail ingredients as would be done in a cookery or cuisine-led book. The objectives of this module are: (a) to provide introductory knowledge about different aspects of culinary ingredients; and (b) to link this module to culinary business taken up in Module 1 and to the rest of the book. The sub-topics taken up in this module are: 1. Introduction to the world of ingredients. 2. Ingredients and formats of culinary business. 3. Globalization of culinary ingredients. 4. Ingredients and gastronomy. 5. Organic ingredients. 6. Locally farmed ingredients. 7. Indian culinary ingredients. 8. Ethnic ingredients and authentic recipes. Understanding taste imprinting. 9. Ingredients and responsibilities of chef.

2.1 INTRODUCTION TO THE WORLD OF INGREDIENTS

The true impression of the **quality** of ingredients is conveyed to a customer through the culinary preparation that he enjoys. Even before a customer tastes the food, the reminiscent aroma of the ingredients stimulates the appetite and heightens the anticipation of what is to come. A good experience with the ingredients and the menu items leads to a valuable dining experience.

Ingredients are all-pervasive in cuisines of the world. It is the skilful handling and marriage of ingredients which produce wonderful menu items which any culinary business wishes to sell.

Culinary ingredients and their right usage demand application of mind, skilled performance and businesslike approach. Research, development, and documentation coupled with creativity and adaptation ensure fresh values of culinary ingredients.

Chefs must respect the essential ingredients of a menu item and prepare them in a way that highlights their quality and flavour. All culinary ingredients display taste and flavour notes, affinity to colours and possible culinary marriages. Masking the flavours of the main ingredient with overpowering or rich gravies or sauces is strictly taboo. The main ingredient must retain its identity and not get "lost" while cutting, dissecting or preparing it for the table. Cooking should emphasize the flavour and quality of the ingredients instead of covering them up.

Seasonal ingredients are always better to use than non-seasonal ones. Introducing only such ingredients in menu items that do not become part of a seller's market is the right strategy to adopt to ensure cost-effectiveness of operations.

Ingredients can be variously described as being ornamental, colourful, fragrant, and nutritious as well as of medicinal and therapeutic properties. Many ingredients in Indian cuisines, for example, turmeric find veneration in addition to their culinary usage.

Ingredients would continue to be linked to economic, social and cultural trends and institutions. Global, organic and locally farmed ingredients would continue to influence culinary business in some measure. Indian chefs would increasingly take part in celebrating Indian culinary ingredients towards their establishment and tag as geographical indicators and get these registered in India's Geographical Indications Registry (GIR).

2.2 INGREDIENTS AND FORMATS OF CULINARY BUSINESS

Ideation of a culinary concept leads to formation of a menu which lists menu items. The purchasing process starts with the chefs identifying and listing all the ingredients that they would require for preparation of each of the menu item. This is true for both *table d'hôte* and a la carte menus.

Ingredients required for buffets are handled differently. The size and format of a buffet allows for numerous permutations and combinations of preparations from Indian and global cuisines. Market competition and specific demands from customers often drive the usage of variety of ingredients chosen for a day or an event. Food production planning for such buffets allows purchasing of culinary ingredients in time.

Culinary ingredients, cooking techniques and the traditional cooking vessels vary widely across the world, reflecting unique, historical, environmental, economic and cultural traditions and trends. Chefs, employed with a hotel that enjoys international clientele, are expected to have knowledge and experience of international cuisines and global ingredients. They have to fulfil the forever-challenging task of keeping the displays and menu items on in-house buffets attractive and trendy thereby enticing larger number of footfalls and higher spend per cover. Dynamic buffet set-ups including those for banquets respond to the creativity, knowledge, skills and experience of the chefs.

Artisanal products, cheeses, flavour-intense foods, heirloom vegetables, specialty seafood, wild foods, oils of the world, etc., and their usage in menu items, especially for in-house buffets would continue to attract customers who travel globally and sample such ingredients elsewhere.

Culinary business runs on many formats. It may be a quick service restaurant (QSR), a regional cuisine-specific restaurant or a fine dining restaurant. It may operate in any of the existing or evolving formats of culinary business (See for details Module 1: "The Culinary Business".) Quality ingredients – foods as well as beverages will always form the basis of a successful and profitable culinary concept.

Cooking with alcoholic beverages – wines, spirits, liqueurs, etc., has been a norm in Euro-American cuisine and alcoholic beverages have always been considered culinary ingredients. It would be worthwhile for the chefs and other operators of fine dining restaurants established under the tenets of French and other Euro-American cuisines to understand the culinary ingredients associated with the menu items. They must study the marriage of food-based culinary ingredients with wines as well as other alcoholic beverages. They must garner sound knowledge of wines, winemaking, wine analyses and viticulture. This, in turn, would increase their culinary repertoire and help establish the culinary business towards superior business platforms exhibiting wine and cuisine culture.

2.3 GLOBALIZATION OF CULINARY INGREDIENTS

Globalization of culinary ingredients is the norm of the day. The cuisines of the world, their related culture and related ingredients are becoming more entrenched around the globe. Interest in international cuisines has made chefs knowledgeable and familiar with the flavours and taste notes of global ingredients. We find description of these ingredients in almost all dictionaries of various languages. Culinary terms associated with each cuisine are being used for other cuisines, even without translation.

Globalization of culinary ingredients has definitely influenced delivery performances and quality of international cuisines and the evolution of professional cooking. Globalization of culinary ingredients has happened due to:

- improvement in transportation;
- improvement in infrastructure;
- improvement in communication systems;
- need to disseminate expertise and knowledge; and
- need to think global.

The process of international integration of culinary ingredients is on and would remain on.

2.4 INGREDIENTS AND GASTRONOMY

Gastronomy is the study of the relationship between **culinary ingredients** of a particular cuisine and its related culture. The term gastronomy is not limited exclusively to the art of cooking; otherwise a cook would also be known as a gourmet. Cooking is only a small part of the discipline of gastronomy.

Gastronomy explores various cultural components with culinary ingredients as the central axis. Study of gastronomy is therefore also related to the fine arts and social sciences, and even to the natural sciences in terms of the digestive system of the human body.

A gourmet's principal activities involve researching and discovering, tasting, experiencing, understanding and writing about culinary ingredients of a particular cuisine in addition to associated activities and exhibition of fine arts. Gastronomy is therefore an interdisciplinary activity.

All forms of culinary business almost always concentrate exclusively on the culinary ingredients of any particular cuisine. Such activity can be described only as business and not as gastronomic experience. On closer research and observation however, one can detect the culinary ingredients linked with the fine arts.

Dance, drama, dramatic skills, music, painting, sculpture, literature and other fine arts are integral parts of gastronomic studies in addition to the study and usage of culinary ingredients and specific food cultures. By conducting food festivals, culinary business can promote gastronomy through the exhibition of specific cuisines along with related fine arts.

Gastronomy is any cuisine supported by the:

- knowledge of effects of the ingredients used in the recipes of that cuisine;
- related culture;

- related history;
- sporting life of the geographical region supporting that cuisine;
- knowledge of nutrition of that cuisine; and
- lifestyle and natural science issues.

2.5 ORGANIC INGREDIENTS

Industrially farmed culinary ingredients are deluged with pesticides and are nutrient-deficient. These ingredients therefore do not deliver the nutrition which the human body needs.

Organic ingredients are produced using natural fertilizers and sustainable farming systems. In addition, these are not processed or refined. Meats from animals that have not been given any antibiotic or growth hormones are considered organic.

Organic ingredients are more advantageous to health than conventional ones. Organic fruits and vegetables contain more antioxidants than non-organic fruits and vegetables. Organic ingredients have good taste, natural flavour and higher nutrition values when compared to non-organic ingredients since they do not contain additives.

2.6 LOCALLY FARMED INGREDIENTS

The source of ingredients is most important to a conscientious chef. Time elapsed between the harvesting of ingredients and their usage should be as less as possible. It also means that such ingredients should be farmed when these are ready to be farmed and not earlier and have reached their full flavour potential and are received by the chef in better conditions.

Culinary ingredients, farmed in their natural environments and at a natural pace, are definitely superior to those ingredients that are artificially ripened. These possess greater depth of flavour than artificially ripened ingredients. In the same manner free-range birds and other livestock develop the right texture and are more flavourful.

Locally farmed ingredients, regional foods and sustainable food systems would continue to make their mark in the world of cuisine. Many culinary business ventures would adopt locavore ingredients as their USPs. The understanding of ingredients farmed in the immediate geography would create an altogether new identity for culinary business and their concepts in India, as it has already happened in the European culinary world.

2.7 INDIAN CULINARY INGREDIENTS

The need to understand the diversity of Indian culinary ingredients and Indian cuisines from an international business perspective is emerging. Indian food cultures are becoming ingrained with international food cultures. Synchronized with this trend are international efforts to conduct research on Indian cuisines.

India is the seventh largest country in the world. India is bounded to the southwest by the Arabian Sea, to the southeast by the Bay of Bengal and in the south by the Indian Ocean. Varieties of seafood produced by these three seas are essential culinary ingredients. Large number of rivers and lakes in the country add to the availability of variety of fishes as culinary ingredients.

Indian culinary ingredients have always been linked with:

- cultural traditions;
- local availability;

- festivals and festivities;
- history;
- sporting life of the region; and
- weather conditions.

The Indian culinary ingredients present multitudinous flavours and taste notes as well as textures. India has its own expensive and exotic culinary ingredients like 'zafran' and 'gucchi' which are used in cooking of regal and exotic cuisines like the Dum Pukht originating from Lucknow and the Nizami cuisine originating from Hyderabad.

As mentioned above, local ingredients are predominantly used for preparation of regional Indian cuisines. These cuisines change every 300 kilometres in some manner. Each geographical area presents different and distinct:

- schools of cuisines;
- cooking styles; and
- shelf life of ingredients.

Traditionally, herbs and spices were introduced into cuisine by herbalists to safeguard health. In addition, Indian culinary ingredients have taken strong influences of cuisines of the travellers, "invaders" and settlers.

2.8 ETHNIC INGREDIENTS AND AUTHENTIC RECIPES

The use of ethnic culinary ingredients in authentic recipes enhances the experience of tourists. Such ingredients play a role in the way tourists experience a destination. Many travellers visit and return to the same destination to savour the unique and authentic recipes and the ethnic culinary ingredients used in these recipes. Culinary business can evolve itself into a **culinary destination** via the route of using authentic recipes. When chefs take pride in cooking of authentic recipes with zeal for perfection and with care that comes from the heart, they in effect create "taste-imprinting" on the customers through their preparations.

Taste imprinting: Human beings consume homemade culinary preparations from infancy to adulthood in a repetitive manner over the years. The human physiology accepts the flavour and taste notes of these preparations as the best and concurrent with the perception of being well-fed and that of contentment. These flavour and taste notes, along with the strong memories of ingredients that constituted these preparations remain in their minds forever.

If due to pursuits of career or due to settling elsewhere does not allow possibilities of consumption of these preparations, the human brain and taste buds yearn for them. Even the best foods of the world prepared by master chefs are not good enough while matching with the culinary preparations with which one grew up. This phenomenon is known as "**taste imprinting**".

2.9 INGREDIENTS AND RESPONSIBILITIES OF A CHEF

Culinary business has the social and moral responsibility to take care of health and welfare of customers. Chefs must be sensitive to their sacred duty of safeguarding the health of their customers. Purchase of quality ingredients and their hygienic handling is of primary importance. The chefs should never compromise on matters of food safety even at the cost of paying higher purchase prices of the ingredients.

Chefs should never attempt to use spoilt and suspect ingredients and those which were inadvertently not used within their prescribed "best-before" period. Using such ingredients for the customers or even for staff invites trouble and displays poor professionalism. Through the food and beverages controller the chefs should ensure that warranties have been secured from suppliers for ingredients received.

2.10 END OF MODULE NOTES

This module on culinary ingredients is not proposed to guide the reader on the fine nuances of cuisine or detailing of cooking methods or recipes. Ingredients are the most fundamental requirement of culinary business. The intention here is to provide brief information on the topic of culinary ingredients and to be still in line with the main theme of the book, that is, economics of food production and cost-effectiveness of culinary business.

Managing ingredients in terms of the economics of their identification, purchase, receipt, storage, issue, pre-preparation, and preparation as specific menu items or creative culinary preparations has been taken up at length in different modules of this book. (This module therefore has **backward** linkages with the Module 1 and **forward** linkages to the rest of the modules of the book).

3 COSTS: CORE OF CULINARY ECONOMICS

Essence of the Module

This module deals with various types of costs and expenses of the operational and functional areas of culinary business. It explains how to reduce costs of different types and how to be cost-effective during adverse business scenario.

Module Objectives and Competencies
After going through this module the reader would be competent to understand the terminology related to costs and expenses of culinary business as well as the essentials of control of such costs and expenses. The module will take the reader through the following topics: 1. Defining, understanding and expressing costs.   2. Revenues — gross and net — and effects of reduction in net revenues.   3. Important and integral types of costs to food & beverages business.   4. Reducing labour costs and costs of water and energy resources.   5. Operational expenses, food costs and typicality of food costs.   6. Monthly food sales and calculations of monthly food costs.   7. Adjustments to monthly food costs.   8. Food costs in absolute terms and percentages.   9. Calculation of monthly food costs for the Euro-American format of storage.   10. The objectives of food cost control and the steps in the food cost control cycle.   11. An effective food & beverages control cycle.   12. Aids to food cost control.   13. Actions that a chef should take to control costs.   14. Yields and yield tests.   15. Outlet capacity, capacity utilization and calculation of outlet capacity utilization.   16. Cost recovery point, banquet matrix and economies of scale.   17. Profits and profitability. How to improve profitability?   18. Maximizing revenues.   19. Minimizing expenditures, creative efforts to minimize expenditures.   20. The SOS principle and concept of money.   21. The inquisitive and questioning management style.

3.1 DEFINITION OF "COSTS"

"Costs" can be simply defined as **resources invested** to achieve a specific objective. Costs are generally measured in monetary terms. Cost is the amount of actual or notional expenditure incurred on or attributable to a product or services.

Here we shall deal with more about a **food product** as well as a **menu item sold** or a **food service** rendered. However, the understanding can be applied to the entire hospitality industry.

3.2 UNDERSTANDING "COSTS"

In terms of food costs, a cost is incurred as soon as a menu item is produced partially or completely. Semi-prepared food for à la carte business is an example of partially produced food. The same prepared completely and ready for service to customers is an example of completely ready food. Many *pâtisserie* and *boulangerie* items are examples of completely ready foods.

A cost is incurred even if the product is spoilt due to non-usage or poor preparation style and finish and thrown away or if it is consumed illegally, i.e., pilfered. It is noticed that cost is incurred even when the prepared food is no longer available for sales, i.e., profitable use. This is due to the highly perishable nature of the culinary ingredients.

3.3 EXPRESSION OF COST: HOW IS COST EXPRESSED?

Cost of a product or a service can be expressed in many ways, as follows:

(a) **Cost can be expressed as value in units of weight.** Example: A portion of a Chicken Steak of 225 grams for Rs. 775.

(b) **Cost can be expressed as value in terms of units of volume.** Example: 250 ml of fruit juice for Rs. 15.

(c) **Cost can be expressed as value in terms of any other predetermined unit.** Examples:

- A plate for Rs. 750.
- A piece for Rs. 225.
- A casserole for Rs. 775.
- A bottle of soft drink for Rs. 15.
- A can of beer for Rs. 120.
- A large peg of whisky for Rs. 475.

The most important understanding of the entirety of this book is the following:

Profits are the key prerequisites of any business. Cuisine is always a profit centre. Cuisine is also always customer oriented. Therefore, it is important to be very careful of costs, and of maintaining cost-effectiveness in culinary business. When the business is good, it is easy to contain costs in terms of parameters of **cost percentages** or in **absolute terms**.

Food business is revenue led. When revenues of food are high, all fixed and semi-fixed costs are at lower percentages. Most costs in the business of food & beverages are based on net revenues.

Costs therefore look big when revenues start falling. The salaries, wages and benefits (SWB) is a fixed cost. As an example, SWB of a culinary business for the month of November 2015 was Rs. 10,47,000. The net revenues for the same month were Rs. 1,02,06,000. The net revenues for the month of December 2015 increased to Rs. 1,25,52,000.

The SWB for the month of November 2015 was:

$$= \text{Rs.} \ \frac{10,47,000 \times 100}{1,02,06,000} = 10.26\%$$

The SWB for the month of December 2015 was:

$$= \text{Rs.} \ \frac{10,47,000 \times 100}{1,25,52,000} = 8.34\%$$

The difference between the SWB percentages for the two months is 10.26% – 8.34% = 1.92%. SWB costs look less in December 2015 in comparison to November 2015 due to increase in business. In case of fall in revenues the reverse is true. Costs therefore look big when revenues start falling.

Cost is a **generic** term. When talking of cost or expressing it, additional information in terms of a prefix is provided. For example: **direct** costs. Cost is always a relative or referential term. Cost is ascertained with reference to some objects such as product or services. Each prefix to the generic word "cost" implies certain attributes, which explains its **nature** and also its **limitations**. To understand the prefixes faster a few examples relating to the food & beverages business are provided below.

3.4 TYPES OF COSTS

Different types of costs that are integral to culinary business are:

1. fixed costs;
2. variable costs/semi-variable costs;
3. budgeted costs;
4. standard costs;
5. direct costs;
6. indirect costs;
7. actual costs;
8. labour costs; and
9. costs of water and energy resources.

3.4.1 Fixed Costs

Fixed costs are those which remain constant irrespective of the quantum of product or service output. Fixed costs are generally related to the capacity that has been built up. Fixed costs are also called **'period'** costs, as they relate to a time period, for example, a month, a quarter (3 months period), or a year. Examples of fixed costs are: management and permanent worker's salaries, insurance of building and vehicles, etc.

Fixed costs can be of two types:

(a) Committed fixed costs.

(b) Discretionary fixed costs.

   (a) Committed fixed costs are costs like depreciation, property taxes, and salaries.

   (b) Discretionary fixed costs are costs like research & development costs, costs of sales promotions, and costs of external consultancy. Fixed amounts are set aside for these activities. However, in adverse business scenario, these activities can either be eliminated or reduced in scale of expenditure for a period. These are called discretionary fixed costs.

These are called discretionary as they are at the discretion of the management. These costs are therefore totally dependent on the human factor. These costs may or may not have any particular relationship to the product, its volume or level of activity. Discretionary costs may be totally or partially curtailed in a particular time period. Discretionary costs have indirect relevance to the following in small measures:

- Gross or net revenues.
- Quantum of profits.
- Other costs of the business.
- Productivity.

3.4.2 Variable Costs/Semi-Variable Costs

Variable costs are those costs that vary directly in proportion to the volume of output. These costs are also called **product costs** as these relate to a product. These costs increase or decrease in the **same proportion** as the output.

Some of the food & beverages costs are variable costs. Cost occurs only when preparing a food & beverages product or rendering a food & beverages service. An example of variable cost is number of à la carte portions of menu items kept in expectation of customer orders. Costs would increase in relation to the number of portions kept in semi-prepared state. Cordoning off a section of a restaurant during non-peak business hours is an example of controlling variable costs.

Semi-variable costs do vary, but not in direct proportion to the output. Up to a certain level costs remain fixed and increase or decrease with change in the output.

3.4.3 Budgeted Costs

Establishing budgeted costs is an exercise of setting benchmarks of financial performance. The task of setting up budgeted costs for a new business utilizes the existing food & beverages industry norms. These involve parameters of viability and of marketing the new enterprise. Budgeted costs in relation to budgeted net revenues for a new business enterprise are often allowed to be higher due to the requirement of lower entry price point of products, as a market penetration policy. Budgeted costs are also based on certain factors of demand, and creativity of the product line.

For an existing culinary business, previous year's (or years') achievements, the opportunities in the market, and its potential, and also the need to set new performance benchmarks decide the budgeted costs. These costs are calculated taking into consideration the average of working conditions and expected market scenario of the budgeted period. Budgeted cost is therefore the cost expected to be incurred in the budgeted period.

3.4.4 Standard Costs

Standard cost is a benchmarking device to measure **future performances**. It is therefore regulatory in nature. It refers to the technique which uses a standard for costs for the purpose of control through analysis of variances.

Standard cost is therefore a predetermined calculation of how much costs should be under specified working conditions. These averages of working conditions are often market related or period-of-time related. Examples are recipe costs in a period for which raw ingredient costs remain constant due to yearly tenders. These recipe costs are standard costs for the period and for the marketplace. Same recipe in another geographical area and with different purchase costs would not produce same recipe costs.

To build up and arrive at a standard cost, an assessment is made of the following during the period under review:

- The totality of cost elements.
- Correlated technical specifications (butcher yield tests, etc.).
- Qualification of materials. (mostly standard purchase specifications in the food & beverages business).
- Labour costs.
- Other operational costs.

Once a standard cost is fixed, actual of future performances is measured against these standards. Variances observed during this exercise are analyzed, and reasons established. Subsequent corrective action ensures efficient operations. The requirements are:

(i) to set standards;

(ii) to examine these standards at periodic intervals;

(iii) to analyze these standards;

(iv) to upgrade these standards; and

(v) to maintain these standards.

3.4.5 Direct Costs

Costs that can be directly and completely attributed to a product are called **direct costs**. Direct costs are identified with a product or a cost unit.

Direct costs are of the following types:

(a) Direct material costs.

(b) Direct labour costs.

(c) Direct expenses.

(a) Direct material costs: Those materials or raw ingredients which become an integral part of the finished product and have specific physical units are known as direct material, and the cost of such materials is called **direct material cost**. An example of direct material cost for a culinary business is the food cost.

(b) Direct labour costs: These have been detailed under the topic of "Labour Costs" below.

(c) Direct expenses: Those expenses which can be wholly and directly assigned to a specific culinary product or food & beverages service are known as **direct expenses**.

3.4.6 Indirect Costs

Those costs that cannot be identified with a particular product or service, but require to be accounted and allocated are called indirect costs. Indirect costs add value to a product or to a service and cannot be dispensed with.

Indirect costs are of the following types:

(a) Indirect material costs.

(b) Indirect labour costs.

(c) Indirect expenses.

(a) Indirect material costs: Those materials which are used for the purpose which cannot be conveniently assigned to a specific physical unit of a product or service are called indirect materials, e.g., cleaning supplies, printing & stationery, etc. The costs of these materials are called **indirect material costs**.

(b) Indirect labour costs: These have been detailed under the topic of "Labour Costs" below.

(c) Indirect expenses: Expenses which cannot be directly, conveniently and wholly allocated to a specific cost unit are called **indirect expenses**. Examples of indirect expenses are rent of the building, insurance charges, etc., in relation to the production of a menu item or rendering of a food & beverages service.

3.4.7   Actual Costs

Data from the previous financial years is taken to estimate the cost of services. The budgets of costs are set for the next financial year accordingly. Operators are often not conversant of the actual costs until these are incurred. During the course of the year the cost of a service may be more or less than the estimated costs. Negative disruptions in the particular geographical market where the culinary business is located can increase costs. The **actual** amount paid or incurred as against the estimated costs is known as **actual costs**. Actual costs, to pay for a specific service, are taken into account and are **reflected in the books of accounts.**

Analyses of actual costs of different financial years help the operators to identify increasing costs of services or production over the past financial years. Operators may identify the reasons for the increasing trend of costs and scout for cheaper alternatives or establish management practices to reduce such costs. An example of such a management practice forces longer intervals between silver plating services or printing of menu cards.

3.4.8   Labour Costs

Quality food production and food service require trained and skilled personnel. Culinary business has two types of labour costs, as follows:

(a)   Direct labour costs.

(b)   Indirect labour costs.

(a) Direct labour costs: Direct labour costs are also called direct manpower costs. These costs are defined as the costs of hiring and retaining personnel who take a direct and active part in the production of food or its service to the customer. These costs can be directly and suitably traced to the preparation of specific menu items or constituents of menu items and delivering specific food or beverages services for the benefit of the customer. All labour costs of maintaining the operational areas are examples of direct labour costs.

(b) Indirect labour costs: Indirect labour costs are also called indirect manpower costs. The costs of hiring and retaining personnel for the purpose of carrying out tasks which do not have any direct relation to goods produced or services rendered are known as **indirect labour costs**. Such labour does not alter the condition of menu items or its constituents or food & beverages service. In addition, such labour cannot be particularly traced to menu items or its constituents or food & beverages service.

All labour costs of maintaining the functional areas are examples of indirect labour costs. Personnel of the functional areas do not work exclusively for the food & beverages department. They work for other requirements of the culinary business also. Another example of indirect labour costs is the salary, wages and benefits of the sales manager. The sales manager does not sell the menu items only.

Note: The reader may like to refer to "Functional and Operational Areas" on **p. 208**

Reducing Labour Costs

Costs of labour and constant increases thereof are subject to:

- demand and supply relationship for the personnel of the same set of professional skills and knowledge;
- geographical conditions; and
- statutory laws.

Higher-than-normal or/and higher-than-budgeted labour costs point to personnel without sufficient work or poor productivity standards. Chefs and operators must strive to reduce labour costs as an on-going exercise. Offering lower salaries, wages and benefits is not the solution to reduce labour costs. The culinary business may not get the personnel with the right credentials due to generic or local competition. Removing higher paid professionals and substituting them with lesser paid ones is not the solution to reduce labour costs either. The lower paid professionals may not have the right professional skills and knowledge. These methods, to reduce labour costs, are signs of poor management.

The following are some actions to reduce labour costs:

(a) Managing staff schedules.

(b) Re-booting and boosting productivity through training.

(c) Encouraging higher internships.

(d) Using the mother kitchen format wherever possible.

(e) Ensuring use of artificial-intelligence aided equipment.

(f) Efficient designing of food production areas and outlets.

(a) Managing staff schedules

(i) Staff duty rosters must be thoughtfully planned and must not become standardized over the span of a business year. Earlier, for culinary business, the duty rosters used to "assemble" staff for "typical broken shifts", for example, like 1000 hours to 1500 hours, and 1900 hours to 2130 hours. These staff duty rosters **are passé.**

Culinary business must strive to be dynamic. As culinary business evolves, changes in customer profile, culinary preferences, and peak hours of business for each business day are noticed.

Professionally competent managements must utilize culinary analytics like menu engineering and introduce dynamic changes in scheduling of staff as well as specialist staff, in as much as the statutory laws allow. Most certainly, the labour costs can be reduced and kept at the right values in absolute terms and percentages in relation to net revenues, through **maximizing productivity**. Maximizing productivity is best achieved through the observation of work requirements in relation to:

- the season;
- the days of the week;
- the business on hand; and
- the business in the immediate future.

If the food production is planned, it has to necessarily align with availability of the right professionals at the right time, necessitating thoughtful planning of staff duty rosters. (Food production planning is an important subject within the boundaries of culinary economics, the essence of this book. The subject is dealt with in Module 10: "Economics of Food Production and Food Service".)

(ii) In addition to the above, specialist food production functions require staggering of duty rosters of specialists. A typical example is that of bakery specialists. To save on energy costs the daily bakery production schedule first produces bread products which require high temperatures of the baking oven, and which requires one set of specialists. Once such bread products are produced, products like *génoise* and sponges are baked. These items require lower temperatures of the oven and different specialists. Therefore, to save on labour costs the duty rosters for different specialists must be made in a staggering way.

(iii) In certain geographical locations, the culinary business may be placed in a seller's market. Under such circumstances the business may have to accept supplies — especially non-vegetarian raw items at lunch time or even later. The business may be required to purchase these items from the open market. In such cases, it is logical to roster meat fabrication staff for start of their day's duties closer to the time when the supplies are likely to be received.

(b) Re-booting and boosting productivity through training

Regular training is of vital importance. Generic and individualistic training originates from understanding of the concept of the business and the menu. The type of training to be provided is dynamic and evolves with the changing needs of the business and the needs of all individual employees.

Empowering workers with proper training ensures that the business executes customer's dining orders in a perfectionist manner. A few examples of regular training are:

- Daily briefing sessions.
- Analyzing case studies of earlier mistakes in delivery.
- Formal classroom training.

Every professional, junior, senior as well as a highly trained specialist, needs training to re-boot professional knowledge and skills. **There is no exception.** The business which recognizes this fact is a winner.

Professional and pleasant food service ensure savings on labour costs in relation to bungling and mishandling which would not only leave intangible scars on the customers but increase labour costs in "recovering" from the mistake. Service recoveries are always considered negative work schedules for any business.

The author has himself experienced working within the historic French style *"La Brigade de Cuisine"* - (the kitchen staff). *"La Brigade de Cuisine"* was an unbelievably large assemblage of highly specialized culinary professionals. These professionals used to hold job positions and physical sections of kitchens which dealt with food related to their professional skills. For example, a Roast cook was responsible for roasted food items only.

That system worked very well up to 1976 as the then lifestyle permitted good sales of individual culinary products produced by individual skilled professionals. Such large staff formations, with individual job positions linked to individual professional skills, are extinct even in France now.

It is imperative for the management of culinary business to define roles of individual employees. As part of the employee induction programme, managements must assign generic as well as specific job responsibilities of each employee.

Food production must be a planned activity. As each form of culinary business strives to be dynamic, food production schedules would change. This would allow different experience and performance challenges to employees and possibilities of fresh learnings for each culinary professional. Multi-skilling would provide avenues of career development as well as grasp of additional and alternative professional capabilities.

In a similar manner multi-skilling would benefit other functional and operational areas. Formal and on-the-job informal training of employees would ensure multi-skilling leading **to right-sizing of manpower, job-optimization** and **reduction** in labour costs.

(c) Encouraging higher internships

Professional chefs and operators often do not value the availability of in-house apprentices, seasonal trainees and interns who are about to complete their hotel/culinary management courses. The dire need is to recognize that such personnel are young, energetic, educated, and are knowledgeable about standards of hygiene, etc. They require the right mentoring and training to turn into good professionals themselves and be an asset to the hospitality/culinary industry.

Professional chefs and operators who are conscientious trainers acquire the loyalty of such trainees. This loyalty often translates into larger acceptability of the business as a responsible employer. It is imperative to use a blend of these youngsters and professionals while preparing duty rosters. Utilizing these youngsters helps in reducing labour costs.

(d) Using the mother kitchen format wherever possible

The concept of mother kitchen, especially for chain of restaurants positioned in the same geographical location works very well to save on labour costs. Highly skilled culinary professionals are not required at outlet level. Ready-to-use and ready-to-serve food products are received from the mother kitchen. Therefore, lesser number of food production and food service staff are required at the outlet level. (The reader may revisit the topic of **"Mother kitchens"** on p. 4).

(e) Ensuring use of artificial-intelligence aided equipment

Traditional kitchen equipment as well as kitchenette equipment are labour and time consuming. Those are fast becoming extinct. The traditional equipment are being replaced by technology and artificial-intelligence aided equipment and gadgets. These contemporary equipment and gadgets work harder, faster and smartly. The food is prepared in the desired manner and to a desired finished-product stage or better. There are huge savings in labour and time if such equipment and gadgets are used.

Usage of traditional equipment demanded labour at the end of each usage to clean and sanitize the equipment as well as the surrounding area. Time, labour and labour costs are saved by using contemporary equipment and technology. Examples of labour saving equipment and technology are:

1. combi-ovens;
2. blast freezers/chillers;
3. thermomix — heavy duty blender/emulsifier;
4. air fryers;
5. infrared cookers;
6. dehydraters;
7. sous vide equipment;
8. cook and chill systems;
9. turbo-jet technology; and
10. UV systems.

Labour and labour costs can be easily trimmed by using contemporary equipment, gadgets and technology.

(f) Efficient designing of food production areas and outlets

Kitchens and food & beverages outlets must be designed for various aesthetic and functional requirements. These must be "smart-designed" to ensure:

- ease in movement. Movement is related to labour;
- fast and efficient pick up of customer's food orders and their delivery; and
- enhanced staff productivity.

"Minimum-movement" kitchens are the norm of the day wherein culinary professionals have easy and immediate access to everything they need — raw ingredients, equipment, gadgets and service gear to prepare food and execute orders within the promised service guarantee.

"Smart" designed kitchens and outlets:

- save time;
- add convenience; and
- prevent bottlenecks in the work-flow.

Smart-designed kitchens ensure lowering of labour costs.

In conclusion, the best methods of reducing labour costs are individualistic and are available within the business itself. One (the management) can get what one demands (the answers to managing labour costs) by asking questions. An inquisitive and questioning management style is imperative. (The author wishes to draw the attention of the reader to **p. 14**). **Application of the mind ensures the right solutions.**

3.4.9 Costs of Water and Energy Resources

Water and energy resources — charcoal, electricity and gas—are used in operational areas of culinary business during pre-preparation, preparation, holding and service of food. Water and energy resources in some manner are also required at functional areas during receiving, storing and issuing functions. Chefs and operators must control the consumption of these precious and costly resources to ensure cost-effectiveness of operations.

Chefs exhibit competencies to identify ingredients required for the menu items and calculate their quantities for efficient food production. It is not difficult to process a menu for cost-effectiveness of water and energy resources in a similar manner.

An inquisitive and questioning management style can direct the control of consumption of water and energy resources to just what is necessary. Facility planners must synergize **designing of the kitchens** with the menu concept and the menu thereby focussing on energy savings. Minutely examining the menu can establish the real need of energy-consuming equipment. Over-equipping a food production facility can add to wastage of energy resources.

Energy resources are expensive and would continue to be so. Culinary business must opt for energy audits conducted by specialist agencies. To introduce an alternative into a running business is often expensive but worthwhile to reduce recurring costs.

Water: Water may not be as expensive as energy resources, but is a precious resource in any geographical area. Some ways to control wastage of water are:

- (a) by installing water restrictor on taps – depending upon the usage. Water restrictors control the pressure of water; and
- (b) by installing user-friendly taps in terms of their ease to close.

Hot water should be used only if required in relation to ambient temperature. It is necessary for cleaning of pots, pans and equipment and for the dishwasher. Use of hot water should be controlled by limiting the number of hot water taps.

Energy Resources: Culinary business uses three energy resources, namely:

(a) charcoal,

(b) electricity; and

(c) gas.

(a) Charcoal

Culinary business uses charcoal to light up and heat the tandoor, open-charcoal grills and specialist ovens. The following are some of the ways to reduce the consumption of charcoal:

1. By examining the menu carefully

- Installing a combination of larger and smaller sized tandoors can be just right instead of installing two large sized tandoors as is done traditionally.

- If only a few menu items require grilling, then it is wiser to install just two small open charcoal grills — one for vegetarian and the other for the non-vegetarian menu items. On the other hand a full-fledged grill outlet with extensive menu items to be grilled would require multiple grills at the same time.

2. By rescheduling the charging and refilling patterns

The tandoor and the charcoal grills require the right temperatures for preparation of different types of menu items and should be ready when food orders are received in the kitchen. It is a futile exercise to light up a tandoor or a charcoal grill many hours in advance, and keep refilling with fresh loads of charcoal closer to the time of actual usage. The loading of the tandoor or/and a charcoal grill with charcoal must be aligned to the business hours of the culinary business. Tandoori and grilled items are not required for almost 45 minutes of start of any lunch or dinner session.

Wastage can be avoided by deciding beforehand **and measuring** the decided quantities for charging and refilling. Twenty kilograms of charcoal is usually the right quantity to start up a tandoor and fifteen kilograms for its refill. Good quality of charcoal would take less than half an hour to light.

3. By specifying the quality of charcoal

The standard purchase specifications for purchase of charcoal should specify the right quality needed for the business. Small pieces of charcoal and charcoal dust serve no purpose. Charcoal is often stored in open by suppliers. During the receiving process, charcoal should be checked to ensure that it meets the standard purchase specifications and is not wet due to rains, etc.

4. At the time of completion of a cooking session

Even after the close of a cooking session the tandoors and charcoal grills retain heat which should be utilized to boil lentils, etc. Alternately placing a cover on the mouth of the tandoor or on the charcoal grill and closing the air vents to stop the charcoal from burning further helps to preserve the charcoal in whatever condition it is.

(b) Electricity

Electricity is the most expensive energy resource amongst the three energy resources – charcoal electricity and gas. Electrical energy costs extend to 70% to 75% of total energy costs of culinary business. The important facilities that consume electrical energy are detailed below. In continuation pointers on how to ensure savings in electrical energy related to each of the facilities are also detailed.

1. High electrical energy consuming equipment

High capacity electric elements are used in:

- ovens;
- salamanders;
- griddle plates;
- grillers;
- deep-fat fryers; and
- *réchauffé* lamps at the food pick-up counters.

During active food service timings chefs often allow the above-mentioned equipment to remain on to facilitate execution of food orders faster. However, this results in wastage of electrical energy.

Savings on Electrical Energy

(i) A few menu items require finishing touches like grilling, toasting or top-browning, etc., just before their pick-up and service. The chefs and operators must study menu engineering analytics. The study would identify the number of times such finishing touches are required and the peak periods of food orders requiring such finishing touches. The analysis would point to a solution to reduce consumption of electrical energy. Switching on the required equipment 'just-in-time' would be one such solution.

(ii) Analyzing menu items for their suitability to retain on the menu in relation to electricity that is consumed for their cooking may give options for future reduction of electrical energy. It is possible that there are just a few infrequently ordered menu items which require electrical equipment to be kept on. Such menu items can be removed from the menu.

(iii) The equipment in this category can be switched off or their usage reduced in case of a predominantly buffet-led outlet.

(iv) The equipment should be compatible to the requirement, for example, the food to be cooked in an oven should be sufficient for the deck space.

(v) The pick-up counters should have a user-friendly switch to save on the electrical energy used by the *réchauffé* lamps.

(vi) At the completion of a cooking session unplugging the electricity based equipment would be a good way to ensure that these equipment are not using any electrical energy at all.

2. Cold store, deep freezer and refrigeration equipment

The doors of the cold store and deep freezers must be closed immediately on entering the facility. Leaving doors open to kitchen temperatures allows cold air to escape and entry of warm air from the kitchen which is at higher temperature. To cool down the warmer air the machinery of the cold store and deep freezer has to work extra thereby increasing electricity consumption. Similarly, the doors of cabinet or chest type refrigeration equipment must be closed immediately after use. Right types of gaskets on the doors insulate the cold store, deep freezer and refrigeration equipment.

Savings on Electrical Energy

(i) By restricting frequent entry into the cold store and deep freezer. Right operational planning would ensure minimum entries into the cold store and deep freezer. Maintaining a logbook for entries into deep freezer may prove to be a deterrent.

(ii) By installing timer-based hooter indicating a door left open would act as a deterrent and warning to careless users.

(iii) By checking temperature of the cold store and deep freezer regularly and taking suitable action, if required.

(iv) By installing a curtain of thick plastic strips inside the cold store and deep freezer to reduce loss of cold air.

(v) By replacing worn-out or partially damaged gaskets of cold stores, deep freezers and other refrigeration equipment in the kitchen. This action would support reduction in quantum of electrical energy otherwise used.

(vi) By defrosting cold stores and deep freezers.

3. Ventilation

Understanding electricity consumption due to ventilation

Two blowers are involved in the process of ventilation. One blower is responsible for the exhaust function to remove stale air from the kitchen and outlet. The second blower is responsible for injecting fresh air into the kitchen and outlet. The capacity of the fresh air blower is normally 80% of the capacity of the exhaust blower. The capacity of the exhaust fan is determined by taking the size of the kitchen, size of the exhaust hood and type of cooking.

Savings on electrical energy: The capacity of the exhaust and fresh air blowers should be suitably designed for the purpose. It is possible to bring down the cost of electrical energy by using a variable frequency drive. A variable frequency drive would reduce the rpm (rounds per minute) of the exhaust and fresh air blowers and consume close to half the electrical energy otherwise used.

Ventilation system for multiple outlets in the same complex

The total spread of time of operation of an outlet and the size of each of the kitchen and outlet are often different. Therefore, the needs of ventilation (exhaust and fresh air injection) are different for each kitchen and outlet. Ideally, each kitchen and outlet should have its own set of exhaust and fresh air blowers which are compatible to their size and spread of time of operation.

However, to save on costs of installation of different sets of blowers, facility planners/owners of outlets often install only one pair of exhaust and fresh air blowers for all the kitchens and outlets in the same complex. The set of blowers have to work for the entire span of operations of all the outlets. While the installation costs are reduced, the recurring costs are huge and electrical energy is wasted during the operations of the kitchen and the outlet.

To save on electrical energy it is imperative to install a ventilation system which is compatible to the requirements.

4. Lighting of the kitchen and the outlet

Savings on electrical energy

(i) By installing or replacing incandescent bulbs with LED lights. LED bulbs consume 50% less electrical energy than incandescent ones. Quality LED bulbs last longer, and produce better quality of illumination.

(ii) By using motion sensors for lights. Motion sensors automatically turn lights on and off.

5. Bread toaster

Rotary toasters are placed on breakfast buffets for faster results and to enable a customer to toast selected type of bread.

Savings on electrical energy: To save on electricity consumption the peak timings of usage of a rotary toaster must be examined. During non-peak hours, instead of rotary toaster pop-up toaster may be used.

6. Dishwashing machine

Savings on electrical energy

Soft water should be used in the dishwasher. Hard water causes scaling which, in turn, causes continuous heating of water as the thermostat of the dishwater does not function properly.

(c) Gas

Pointers to save gas

1. Pilot burners are essential to add to the facility of igniting cooking gas. The pilot burners must be kept on only during the peak time of business and food-order execution. Gas is wasted during unproductive periods. Lighting up the pilot burners at the start of any cooking session is not correct. The pilot burners must be ideally installed at one point – normally the source point of gas inflow, and not along with each burner. **Ideally**, a user-friendly gas ignition system should be installed in place of pilot burners.

2. Blue flame emanating from gas burners indicates the right mix of cooking gas and atmospheric oxygen. On the other hand, yellow flame indicates higher proportion of oxygen, less thermal value of the combination of gas and oxygen, and wastage of gas. Hence, the burners should be properly maintained at blue flame.

3. Pressure regulators must be of the right size depending upon the usage or type of cooking. Pressure regulators must be individual to each of the gas fired cooking ranges, griddle plates and ovens. For effective monitoring of gas consumption pressure regulators must be backed up by pressure meters.

4. Gas burners must be cleaned regularly. In case of a spill the burners must be cleaned immediately.

General pointers to save energy costs

1. Good maintenance of equipment is imperative to bring down the cost of electricity or gas consumption.

2. Energy costs can be brought down by installing artificial-intelligence aided equipment and gadgets detailed in this module. Using such technologically advanced equipment results in high energy savings.

3.5   OPERATIONAL EXPENSES

Fixed costs cannot be minimized. Therefore, understanding of the different type of costs is utilized in keeping variable and semi-variable costs down. The important variable costs in food & beverages business are food costs and operational expenses.

Those expenses which are not costs of food as explained earlier **(p. 3)** and which can be directly traced to a final product or service are called **operational expenses**. These expenses alter the totality of the food & beverages dining experience and are always the **differentiators in relation to competition** in the market of the same nature. We must keep in mind that operational expenses are different from administrative expenses, for example, expenses incurred on insurance and training of personnel.

The following are the operational expenses of food & beverages operations:

1. Uniform.
2. Guest supplies.
3. House stationary.
4. Photocopying.

5. Menus – making charges for initial print and replacements.

6. Laundry costs.

7. Cleaning supplies.

8. Contract services.

9. Pest control services.

10. Garden supplies.

11. Replacement costs of chinaware.

12. Replacement costs of glassware.

13. Replacement costs of linen.

14. Replacement costs of silverware.

15. Replacement costs of cutlery.

16. Replacement costs of utensils.

17. Costs of silver plating.

18. Costs of special decorations for special events like Christmas, Diwali, Easter, etc.

19. Music and entertainment charges.

20. Local conveyance costs.

21. Spoilage costs.

22. Freight charges.

23. Costs of cooking gas.

24. Costs of buffet fuel.

25. Costs of charcoal.

26. Hire charges.

27. Basic excise duty and license fees.

28. Turnover tax – on volume of business.

The above listed operational expenses fall in the category of variable costs and can be controlled through discretionary methods, explained earlier.

3.6 FOOD COSTS

Costs which are directly attributable to preparation of a particular menu item, whether in terms of semi-prepared dishes, for example in à la carte operations, or completely ready-to-serve dishes; for example, in buffet operations, and costs of certain necessaries of our business are called food costs. Food costs include the following:

- Cost of decoration of a dish.

- Cost of accompaniments.

- Cost of food appointments or the service side-table (the cost of proprietary sauces, pickles, cruet sets) or on the table, for example, pre-positioned condiments.

- Cost of those items which enhance the value of the dining experience (mouth fresheners like saunf, supari, pan for Indian cuisine; *petit fours*/chocolates/mints for European cuisine).

3.6.1 Typicality of Food Costs

Ready-to-serve menu items are prepared in accordance to the standard recipes and with perfectionist zeal and love. Such food production is time consuming and labour intensive. In the absence of suitable controls employees are tempted to commit pilferage and unauthorized consumption of such foods.

Food products and ingredients perish with time and are expensive. Skill-trained food production personnel are required for the pre-preparation and preparation processes. If the right personnel are not available, loss of yield, wastage and spoilage result.

It is a physical impossibility to trace each item of food through the receiving, storage, issuing, production and service functions, and verifying its sale in relation to its purchase. Further it is an impossible task to relate **every** purchased ingredient to a saleable value in food business. Efforts should however be made to relate every non-vegetarian item to its saleable value. (This has been taken up in Module 10: "Economics of Food Production and Food Service" while discussing yields.)

Computers may help us come nearer to the above requirements. However, if the mental and physical efforts that would be required to analyze the same and benefit from the analysis are disproportionate to the benefits received, then the efforts are futile. This does not mean that detailed examinations are not required. As a rule the business must examine its 'A' value products, and yields of non-vegetarian items.

3.7 MONTHLY FOOD SALES

In addition to food, culinary business also sells related items, for example, beverages. The sales of all these non-food items must be removed from the totality of the customer's bills for calculation of actual food sales. It is easy to calculate actual food sales using the point-of-sale (PoS) system or property management system. The total of actual food sales of the **month** are required for calculating monthly food costs.

3.8 CALCULATION OF MONTHLY FOOD COSTS

The rule of thumb to calculate monthly food costs is to arrive at those costs which create the food sales. For example costs of employee meals do not create food sales. The cost of employee meals therefore is not included in the monthly food costs.

The monthly food costs are the total sum of two cost components, as follows:

1. The monthly cost of actual issues of non-perishable food items. These costs are calculated by costing the stores requisitions.

2. The monthly cost of the entirety of purchases of perishables and highly perishables. This is because in India it is the chefs who are responsible for management of perishables and highly perishables. These are not controlled by the stores management and therefore are not part of the stores requisition process.

3.8.1 The Adjustments to Monthly Food Costs

Depending on the framework of an individual culinary business certain adjustments are made to the monthly food costs, as arrived above. Examples of the adjustments are:

(i) costs of employees' meals;

(ii) cost of complimentary food;

(iii) cost of transfers of food items to the bar; and

(iv) cost of transfers of beverage items to the kitchen.

(i) Costs of employee meals

Treatment: The costs of employees' meals are deducted from the total monthly food costs.

> **Note:** The deduction is done only if the employees' meals are cooked in the same kitchen meant for customers. However, if the employees' meals are cooked in a separate cafeteria, the calculation of employee meal costs is handled differently. In such a case the perishables are ordered separately, and the non-perishables are requisitioned from the stores separately.

(ii) Cost of complimentary food

Treatment: The cost of the complimentary food for the month is deducted from the total monthly food costs.

(iii) Cost of transfers of food items to the bar

Treatment: The cost of food items transferred to the bar for the month is deducted from the total monthly food costs and debited to beverage costs.

(iv) Cost of transfers of beverage items to the kitchen

Treatment: The cost of transfers of beverage items to the kitchen is added to the monthly food costs and credited to the beverage costs.

3.9 FOOD COST IN ABSOLUTE FIGURES AND PERCENTAGES

Let us assume some figures and examine them:

	November 2015	December 2015
Food cost	Rs. 24,36,000	Rs. 31,52,870
Net revenue	Rs. 10,20,6,000	Rs. 12,55,2,000

From the absolute figures quoted above it is difficult to say whether cost is in order, it is on the lower side, or on the higher side in comparison, and in relation and proportion to net revenues. It is also difficult at a glance to relate to the two absolute figures of food costs and arrive at any conclusion. Comparison is easier if food cost percentages are calculated. The monthly food cost percentages are arrived at by dividing the monthly food costs by the monthly food sales and multiplying by 100.

$$\frac{\text{Monthly food costs} \times 100}{\text{Monthly food sales}}$$

From the above, food cost percentage is 23.87 % for November 2015, and 25.19% for December 2015. Instead of absolute terms if figures are converted into percentages, as is done, it is clear that in relation to net revenues, food cost is much higher in December 2015, even with higher net revenues, then in November 2015. This is the reason for emphasis on a percentage figure. It is easier to compare percentages, more so because right from school days everybody is tuned to understand percentages.

3.10 CALCULATION OF MONTHLY FOOD COSTS: EURO-AMERICAN FORMAT OF STORAGE

The Euro-American format of storing perishables and highly perishables has been explained on **p. 152**. If the business is operating under the Euro-American format the monthly stores inventory includes conducting inventories of non-perishables, perishables and highly perishables.

If the culinary business is operating under this format, the monthly food costs are calculated in five steps, as follows:

1st Step: Two costs are added. These costs are:

- The cost of monthly opening inventory. It is the same as the monthly closing inventory of the previous month.

- The cost of food purchases – non-perishables, perishables and highly perishables – for the month.

2nd Step: The cost of the month-end inventory is deducted from the costs received from the 1st Step.

3rd Step: As explained earlier, the adjustments are made.

The result from this step provides the usage of food – non-perishables, perishables and highly perishables, which is the food cost for the month. This figure is in absolute terms.

4th Step: Monthly food sales are calculated, as explained earlier.

5th Step: Food cost percentages are calculated as explained on **p. 45**.

3.11   THE OBJECTIVES OF FOOD COST CONTROL

The main objective of food cost control is not to be a report-back, but to actualize the desired actions at each point of the materials management chain with a view to optimize costs and reduce wastage. (see Module 11: "Controls".)

The steps in the food cost control cycle: The control cycle consists of:
- setting up of a potential food cost percentage, which is both desirable and attainable;
- establishing standard recipes and portion sizes;
- establishing yields of various 'A' value commodities, and relating these to the standard recipes; and
- calculating menu item costs.

This above is for the **food production control**. On the menu sales front the following are the steps in the control cycle:

- Determining the selling prices of the menu items.
- Periodically evaluating the actual results obtained.

An effective food & beverages control cycle consists of:
- (a)   setting benchmarks;
- (b)   examining the results achieved against the benchmarks; and
- (c)   evaluating the achievements against the benchmarks and setting higher benchmarks if the current ones are achieved. Using a committee approach with the food & beverages controls, the operators must compare the **actual** food cost percentage, **for a period,** with a **potential** food cost percentage. This evaluation is normally done during each review meeting, normally held each month.

    Or

    Examining why the benchmarks could not be achieved, and establish measures to counter the shortfalls.

The following are some **aids to food cost control:**

1. Through introducing and practising higher objectivity benchmarks within the functional and operational areas.

   - Through personal observations and an inquisitive and questioning management style.
   - Through the value of statistics and analytics.

2. Through actions on 'cost' and 'operating' reports.

3. Through actions on menu engineering reports.

4. Through practising usage of standard recipe cards.

5. Through costing of standard recipe cards.

6. Through establishment and implementation of standard portions.

7. Through usage of the right standard portion control tools.

8. Through establishment, practice and observation of variances of standard yields and course correction if/whenever required of the following:

   - Non-vegetarian ingredients.
   - Sub-recipes.
   - 'A' value food products and ingredients.

9. Through elimination of malpractices in the system.

10. Through well-defined food production schedules.

Actions that a chef should take to control costs

The chef must actively contribute to the project planning processes during the period immediately preceding the start of the culinary business. He must ensure that:

(a) The operational benchmarks are positioned correctly.

(b) There is a price, quality and service relationship within the culinary concept and the menu offer for the benefit of the customer. (This has been explained under the topic of **"Value Proposition" on p. 8**)

The above actions would ensure that the culinary business starts with a robust commitment to ensuring its financial success and costs are controlled in the right manner.

The chef must not:

Over-specify the quality benchmarks by means of standard purchase specifications. The quality benchmarks must be in line with the culinary concept.

The chef must:

(a) inculcate financial accountability amongst food production personnel;

(b) modify the menu items to eliminate or reduce purchases of food products and ingredients of a seller's market;

(c) use a tight-fisted approach to authorization of ingredient requisitioning from stores as well as purchasing of perishables and highly perishables;

(d) avoid emergency purchases;

(e) assist the receiving process through availability of knowledgeable and trained kitchen personnel to receive ordered food products and raw ingredients and check these against quality benchmarks;

(f) ensure that the perishables and highly perishables are stored and handled in the right manner immediately after the receipt;

(g) ensure that perishables and highly perishables move out of their storage areas into production while they are of optimum quality. This would ensure that there is no wastage due to partial spoilage;

(h) plan meat fabrication processes and order for purchase accordingly. The chef must control the meat fabrication process through:

- testing yields regularly for non-vegetarian ingredients using a sample size which is as large as is possible;
- assigning skilled personnel for the meat fabrication processes to achieve maximum possible yields;
- recording standard yields;
- analyzing future yields in relation to standard yields and acting upon negative variances; and
- ensuring profitable use of by-products, bones and wastage from the meat fabrication process.

(i) plan preparation of expensive sub-recipes, if any;

(j) study the daily sales reports and attempt forecasting the volume of sales of the day and the immediate future;

(k) plan food production and control the quantities of food production required for the day/ immediate future. Overproduction of menu items must be prevented;

(l) use standard recipes to ensure consistency in quality of food production. Wastage is controlled by adherence to standard recipes;

(m) ensure availability of tools to measure standard portion sizes;

(n) eliminate or conscientiously reduce unproductive costs: wastage, spoilage, pilferage, and unauthorized consumption during:

- meat fabrication and pre-preparation processes;
- food production;
- holding or storage of semi-prepared and ready-to-serve portions of menu items; and
- food service.

This can be achieved through planned food production, standardized cooking processes and control. Elimination or reduction of spoilage and unauthorized consumption is also achieved by synergies of the menu engineering reports with the food production process.

(o) ensure adherence to service guarantees during food service. Adherence to service guarantees results in high quality of dining experience for the customer. This, in turn, is responsible for customer satisfaction, repeat visits, higher revenues and higher profitability of the business. The effect is lowered costs;

(p) study the menu engineering reports regularly. Each are of the menu items must be profitable and popular. Changes should be made to enhance the profitability and/or popularity of each menu item. If required, each menu item should be repositioned in the menu with changes in:

- the sale price;
- the presentation;
- the composition; and
- the service guarantee.

> **Note:** Changes as above cannot be made on daily basis. Changes must be introduced during the half-yearly or yearly reviews or while repositioning the menu concept.

(q) reduce the operational expenses related to food production and keep these in line with budgets and current net revenues;

(r) introduce cost-effective ingredients if possible; and

(s) use or avoid using scratch foods, ready-to-cook foods and individually quick-frozen products depending on the culinary concept and volumes of business and profitability.

Yields and yield tests

(Introductory understanding of yields and yield tests has been taken up in Module 1: "The Culinary Business" and elaborated in Module 10: "Economics of Food Production and Food Service".)

3.12 UNDERSTANDING OF OUTLET CAPACITY UTILIZATION AND ITS CALCULATIONS

Capacity utilization and calculations thereof are the understanding of yields in the **outlet service business**. Outlet-wise capacity is calculated for a fixed period, for example: a day, a week, a month, or a year. Capacity utilization is calculated as per the outlet in question. The capacity utilization for a **lunch and dinner food & beverages outlet** is calculated as follows:

1. The number of services in the day.
2. The number of covers available.
3. The number of days of the study period.
4. The number of covers actually sold.

Calculation of capacity utilization:

$$\frac{\text{Number of covers actually sold in the period} \times 100}{\text{Number of covers available for sale in the period}}$$

Wherever the outlet design permits, section or sections of the outlet can be blocked off during lean hours and lighting and air conditioning switched off in the blocked section to save on energy costs. This practice is called "zoning" and is an important activity in the area of energy conservation. The same can also be applied in the banquet areas and unused section(s) can be partitioned off and lighting and air conditioning provided only to the section/s being used.

The capacity utilization of **banquets** is calculated differently. The parameters depend on 3 services per day, and 10 square feet of space required per customer. The following are the steps to calculate the monthly capacity utilization of banquets.

1. The total area of the banquet hall in terms of square feet is calculated.
2. This figure is divided by 10 and multiplied by 3 for three possible services (breakfast, lunch or dinner or lunch, snacks and dinner.)
3. The resultant figure is divided by 2. The rationale is that all three services cannot be sold every day. Only 1.5 services can be sold. Turnaround time is required for the setting up, and a fatigue factor would come in the business otherwise.
4. This resultant figure is multiplied by the days of the month.
5. The totality of the above provides the number of covers available per month.
6. The figure is measured against the actual covers sold in the month.

The following equation provides the monthly capacity utilization of banquets in percentages:

$$\frac{\text{Total number of banquet cover sold per month} \times 100}{\text{Total number of banquet covers available for the month}}$$

Multiple venues are available for banquets in a hotel property. In addition the capacities available in the outdoor banqueting services are enormous. The process of calculation of monthly capacity utilization of banquets for the totality of banquet outlets is processed in exactly the same way as above.

The capacity utilization of room service is calculated with linkages with the front of the house.

The number of room nights sold for the month multiplied by 4 gives the number of available covers for the month. The following equation provides the monthly capacity utilization of room service in percentage terms:

$$\frac{\text{Number of covers sold in the month} \times 100}{\text{Number of available covers}}$$

3.13   COST RECOVERY POINT

Cost recovery point is a financial situation, wherein the net revenues out of a particular number of covers, matches the cost of production of the entire food, of the same period. Cost recovery point can also be defined as a minimum sales volume required by a food service unit in order to avoid an operating loss and meet operational expenses. Cost recovery point is an immediate indication of fixing a target, and beyond. It is a benchmarking exercise. Any achievement less than the cost recovery point in terms of number of covers indicates losses to the operation for the day.

For buffets the menu product line is different from one day to another. The cost recovery point would be different each day. Through an inquisitive and questioning management style, operators can achieve the cost recovery point. Examining the sales summary sheets of each day of the week helps in the process.

3.14   BANQUET MATRIX

The study of a banquet menu offered to 100 persons, and the same to 500 persons, with reduced rates per person, revealed that even with a reduced **average per cover** (APC) the food cost had reduced.

Yields get better and better on the volume route and costs reduce progressively. This is the **cascading effect** of volumes of business vis-a-vis cost reduction. **Benefits of economies of scale** are normally passed on **to the customer.** A distinct link between costs, economies of scale, i.e., volume route, capacity utilization and food cost percentages are noticed.

3.15   PROFITS AND PROFITABILITY

Profits, revenues and expenditure are the three important factors of any business. Profits can be increased by:

1. maximizing revenues;
2. minimizing expenditure; or
3. a combination of the above two.

1. **Maximizing revenues:**   Maximizing revenues for a food & beverages outlet is normally achieved through the following conventional means:

- Suggestive selling.
- Instituting of regular food promotions and food festivals — creation of a "happening place".
- Upselling initiatives by each employee.
- Hoardings and advertisement campaigns.

Maximizing revenue is also achieved through a couple of unconventional means:

- Repositioning of food outlets, and cuisine. This removes the factor of fatigue, and introduces creativity.
- Handling of the needs of the customer – analyzing the reasons for his patronage to the outlet and identifying ways and means to ensure that he patronizes the outlet again.

A truly valuable dining experience for customers is when they leave with a feeling of having received full value for money spent, or better still, more than their own expectations. Such dining experiences are the result of a combination of quality cuisine, quality food service, **quality upselling**, and quality of intangible services. A valuable dining experience leads to re-patronage and recommendations to others. The process ensures maximization of revenues.

2. **Minimization of costs:** To achieve the goal of minimization of costs, it is important to identify:

- the nature and type of costs leading up to and including food service;
- operational expenses;
- unproductive costs related to food pre-preparation and food production. Examples of unproductive costs are wastage, overproduction and poor yields;
- excessive costs. Examples of excessive costs are higher purchase costs per stock keeping unit (SKU) as well as higher administrative costs, etc.;
- pilferage of food products and raw ingredients; and
- unauthorized consumption of ready-to-serve portions of menu items.

Actions to minimize costs would be related to:

- All control actions at all control points. (The 11 control points as well as control actions to be taken at each of the control points have been detailed in Module 11: "Controls".)
- Conscious and conscientious efforts to reduce operational expenses. A creative effort would be to list out all items of expenditure and work on them. Just 10% reduction of costs under each heading would help.

Profitability is yield in profits or returns on investments. Profitability is therefore a measure of operating efficiency. Profitability can be improved with the following means:

- Through examination of the geographical area of the business.
- Through examination of the competition.
- Through understanding the business.
- Through control of variable costs.
- Through control of 'A' value food products and raw ingredients.
- Through understanding of the needs of customers.
- Through the questioning mould.
- Through adopting of the SOS principle in times of distress.

3.16   THE SOS PRINCIPLE

The SOS principle does not mean "save our soul". However, the fundamental nature is the same. The SOS principle in its true essence is to **switch on** the mind. The principle is:

- Save On Something.
- Switch On Something.
- Switch Over (to) Something
- Switch Off Something.

3.17   CONCEPT OF MONEY

The understanding of the four kinds of money would help in keeping variable and semi-variable costs down. There are four kinds of monies:

1. one's own money to be spent on self;
2. one's own money to be spent on others;
3. other's money to be spent on yourself; and
4. other's money to be spent on self.

To achieve the situation of keeping the variable and semi-variable costs down, money has to be used efficiently, as money is related to costs. The types of monies to be controlled are those of other's to be spent on yourself and more importantly other's monies to be spent on others. During hard times, it is important to work **harder, faster and smartly.**

To control costs it is important to get into an inquisitive and questioning mould. One can get what one demands by asking questions like the following:

What?

How?

When?

Where?

Who?

The following is an example of an inquisitive and questioning management style:

EXHIBIT 1: Inquisitive and Questioning Management Style

Present Facts		Examine Reasons: Why?	
WHAT?	What is done now?	WHAT?	Why is it done?
HOW?	How is it done?	HOW?	Why in that way?
WHEN?	When is it done?	WHEN?	Why at that time?
WHERE?	Where is it done?	WHERE?	Why in that place?
WHO?	Who does it?	WHO?	Why that person?
Consider Alternatives		Evaluate Best Solution	
WHAT?	What else could be done?	WHAT?	What should be done?
HOW?	How else can it be done?	HOW?	How should it be done?
WHEN?	When else could it be done?	WHEN?	When should it be done?
WHERE?	Where else can it be done?	WHERE?	Where should it be done?
WHO?	Who else can do it?	WHO?	Who should do it?

3.18   END OF MODULE NOTES

3.18.1   Understanding 'Costs' of Culinary Business

The chef/operator/investor must understand the "costs" of the culinary business and ensure positive actions during operations to support healthy bottom-line management. The critical success factors for cost-management are outlined below. The chef/operator/investor/the culinary business must:

1. Obtain the maximum value of all unavoidable costs at the least expenditure point.
2. Improve yields through the volume route, if possible in line with the culinary concept.
3. Control variable costs. Operational expenses are variable and discretionary.
4. Control consumption of 'A' value ingredients and food products.
5. Eliminate unproductive costs: wastage, spoilage, pilferage, unauthorized consumption.
6. Achieve the cost recovery point at least during lean periods of business.
7. Introduce higher accountability amongst personnel.
8. Control money to be spent on the personnel and the money spent by the personnel on 'outsiders'.
9. Adopt the SOS principle in times of distress and adopt an inquisitive and questioning work-style.
10. Use statistical data for analysis of business.

4 MENU ENGINEERING: CULINARY BUSINESS ANALYTICS

Essence of the Module

Menu engineering is essentially a process of culinary analytics. This module deals with the most essential tool of culinary business – the menu. The module systematically explains the two vital pillars of the menu's success – the relative profitability and relative popularity of the menu items. In addition, the contents explain the processes to add values to the menu items. Menu engineering therefore works both as an audit as well as a performance improving management exercise.

Module Objectives and Competencies

After going through this module the reader would be competent to:

1. Understand the process of menu engineering.

2. Explain the meaning of the term "profitability" and "popularity" of menu items.

3. Show how menu engineering defines the profitability and popularity of menu items.

4. Explain the meaning of the term "contribution" of menu items.

5. Explain the tool called average contribution margin and calculation of its values. In addition, explain how the average contribution margin is used to appraise the profitability of a menu item in relation to another/other menu item's profitability.

6. Explain the tool called popularity index and calculations of its values. In addition explain how the popularity index is used to appraise the popularity of a menu item in relation to another/other menu item's popularity.

7. Identify the meaning of the terms **relative profitability** and **relative popularity** of menu items. In addition showcase a good menu item.

8. Showcase the worksheet method to figure out statistical data beneficial to the business. In the process understand:

   - Food Cost Worksheet.
   - Menu Engineering Worksheet.
   - Menu Item Analysis.
   - Menu Mix Analysis.
   - Menu Engineering Summary.
   - Four-Box Analysis.
   - Menu Engineering Graph/Pie Chart.

9. Explain the terms Menu Mix and Menu Mix percentages.

10. Define the classification of menu items and identify them as a Star, or a Standard, or a Puzzle or a Problem.

11. Delineate how the knowledge of menu engineering can help a chef.

12. Detail the methods to make:
    - Menu items classified as Standards into Star menu items.
    - Menu items classified as Puzzles into Star menu items.
    - Menu items classified as Problems into Star menu items.

13. Detail the methods to control menu items classified as Stars to maintain them as Stars.

14. List the advantages and identify the limitations of menu engineering.

15. Introduce the processes of computerized menu engineering.

16. List the similarities of manual and computerized menu management systems.

17. Understand weighted figures and averages.

18. Explain adjustment of food & beverages menu items.

19. Identify the different nomenclature in some countries in respect of menu engineering.

20. Understand the unexplored frontiers of menu engineering.

4.1 INTRODUCTION TO MENU ENGINEERING

The process of menu engineering is an indispensable tool in the hands of chefs, food & beverages managers/controllers and other operators. The process of menu engineering **evaluates**, and **enhances** the performances of individual menu items.

The **process** involves stages of deconstructing, reconstructing and repositioning of menu items. The viability of the culinary concept, the service guarantees and other business standards can be re-evaluated and repositioned after the study of the menu engineering process.

Menu engineering is essentially a process of **culinary analytics**, that of course is correction and value addition. Menu engineering makes repeated use of statistical data received from computerization of the menu items in terms of their cost and selling prices in absolute figures and in percentages; as well as their relative popularity over a larger chronological study.

Chefs often assume a particular menu item to be great. Menu engineering helps chefs to remove myths of the menu item, if any. Menu engineering helps to verify or disprove the strengths of each menu item on the menu and allows for its management towards higher popularity and/or higher profitability or recommendations for its removal from the menu. Menu engineering is therefore a process to de-mystify the success or failure of a menu and to arrive at the statistical-data driven decision. While studying and managing data emanating from the menu engineering process chefs can get wonderful and creative ideas for successful menu composition of the future.

Trends of consumption of menu items often set in culinary business through customer preferences. These popularity trends are often influenced by weather and market conditions, freshness and exclusivity of the culinary product line, and the price points of the menu item. These trends are identified by the menu engineering process. The process is therefore able to identify undiscovered patterns and establish hidden relationship between popularity and profitability. Continuity of the process over the entire financial year is imperative. The outcome of each study of statistical data must be applied to the previous result.

The food cost percentage of a menu item can be calculated. Similarly, the food cost percentage of a selection/section of the menu or that of the entire menu can be calculated. Food cost percentage of a menu item is calculated by dividing the food cost by the sale price, multiplied by 100. **Percentages** are figures which are understood at a quick pace. Right from school days the brain is conditioned to understand percentages for requirements of academics and sports. It is monies in absolute term which are bankable and which support understanding of the financial standing.

4.2   THE WORKSHEET

A worksheet can give vital facts to understand the business. If the figures of cost and the sales figure of the same menu item are available, profits made in selling a portion of that menu item can be calculated. The same is true for weighted figures.

4.3   CONTRIBUTION

The difference between the sale price and the cost price of per portion of a menu item is called the **contribution** for that particular menu item. A menu item is said to be providing positive contribution if it contributes profits to the bottom line. If the menu item is providing losses to the bottom line it is said to be providing negative contribution. Ideally, each of the menu items should produce positive contribution towards the bottom line. Business would do well only if it is **cost-effective and profitable. Profits are the key requisites of any business.**

The type of contributions being addressed here are the menu item contributions, or the contribution of a section of a menu, for example, soups, or the contribution of the menu in entirety. Contributions in absolute terms can be calculated easily from a worksheet.

> **Note:** The menu item contributions are very much different from departmental contributions, which are the figures arrived by duly working out the net revenues of a particular time period, and reducing these in relationship to the costs of SWB, the food costs, and operational expenses. (These terms has been taken up Module 3: "Costs – Core of Culinary Economics".)

4.4   THE MENU

The success or failure of a food and beverages operation is directly linked to the menu. Therefore, a menu is the **most important tool** of the business. How should menus be appraised and managed to determine and ensure that the most profitable menu items are being sold? In continuation, how should menus be appraised and managed to determine and ensure that each of the menu items is popular with the customers? The appraisal is done through the process of **menu engineering. Ideally,** every menu item should be profitable as well as popular, and the management of menus towards this goal has been taken up in this module.

4.5   AN EXCELLENT MENU ITEM

Any culinary business would require that each of its menu items generates profits towards the bottom line and is popular with the customers. The profitability and popularity of a menu item are therefore the two most important requirements. A profitable menu item generates a higher contribution margin, in relation to other menu items. If the menu items are frequently ordered by customers, they are called popular menu items. Menu items can be evaluated in terms of both their **profitability and popularity**.

The very essence of the **menu engineering system** centres on the following most important principles:

Menu items cannot be evaluated **individually**.

Each menu item's Contribution Margin (CM) and Menu Mix (MM) provides measures for the item's profitability and popularity **in relation to another/other menu item's profitability and popularity.**

The requirement is to evaluate how high or low the profitability and popularity of a menu item is in comparison with all other menu items. What constitutes a **high** level of profitability or popularity? **Unless compared** with contribution margins of other menu items in a relative manner, the menu item's contribution margin does not forecast any information about the relative profitability of the sale of the menu item. Similarly, the sales of a menu item do not represent sufficient knowledge about its popularity **unless compared** with the sales of other menu items in a relative manner.

Menu engineering analysis is therefore an examination of **relative** merits of each menu item in terms of **profitability** and **popularity.**

The relative merits of each menu item are evaluated through two tools:

1. Average Contribution Margin.
2. Popularity Index.

It is against these two tools that each menu item is evaluated to identify its **relative** profitability and popularity. It is important to understand the appraisal of each of the menu items for the purpose of establishing their menu item classification.

Menu engineering is an all-inclusive exercise:

(a) of periodically examining a menu through examination of the menu items;

(b) assessment of individual menu items for relative profitability and relative popularity; and

(c) adding values to the service guarantees of each menu item to ensure higher profitability and popularity of the composite menu.

The understanding of the menu engineering process continues in the current module. The understanding of how values can be added to individual menu items to improve relative profitability and/or relative popularity has also been dealt in this module. The service guarantees of an individual menu item changes once values are added. (The matter of service guarantees has been taken up in Module 10: "Economics of Food Production and Food Service".)

4.6 PROFITABILITY

To understand profitability in terms of menu engineering, the **Average Contribution Margin** should be understood first. The average contribution margin is calculated by dividing the total menu contribution margin by the total portions of menu items sold during the study period. The study period is the specified time period for which the data was collected. Alternately, the average contribution margin is calculated by dividing the total contribution margin of a selection/section of a menu under study by the total number of menu items sold during the study period. It can be calculated very easily.

$$\text{Average Contribution Margin} = \frac{\text{Total Contribution Margin}}{\text{Total portions of all menu items sold}}$$

The menu's **average contribution margin** provides a precise measure of each menu item's **profitability**. (For further understanding of the applications of the average contribution margin the reader is directed to study the Menu Engineering Worksheet, presented as **Exhibit 3, between pp. 60-61**).

A **high** contribution margin for an individual menu item would be one that is equal to or greater than the average contribution margin for all menu items. The figures of total food costs of **all the portions of all the menu items** sold in any time period of study can be calculated by summing up.

The total menu revenues (sales) can be determined by simply summing the figure of sales of each menu item. The total contribution margin for all menu items is calculated by subtracting total menu costs from total menu revenues. These figures are easily available from the computerized Point-of-Sale (PoS) data.

4.7 POPULARITY

The basis for measuring the degree of popularity of each menu item is called the **popularity index.** The popularity index is based on the assumption of **expected popularity.** Any culinary business can change this assumption.

For the purpose of analysis, each menu item is assumed to be equally popular. This means that each item is expected to contribute an equal share of total menu sales. Therefore, the popularity of each menu item is calculated by simply dividing 100% (i.e., total sales) by the number of items on the menu.

A case study has been taken up below. There are 15 menu items on the menu for analysis in the case study. If each menu item is assumed to be equally popular, the sales of each item would be equal to 6.67% of total sales (100 divided by 15 equals 6.67%). On the other hand, if there were ten items on any menu, each item on that particular menu would be expected to represent 10% of total sales (100% divided by 10 equals 10%).

The hospitality industry benchmark declares a menu item to be popular if its sales equals or exceeds 70% of what is expected. Thus, the popularity index for items on a given menu is defined as 70% of the possible popularity of each item on that menu.

However, it is a prerogative of each culinary business to declare its benchmarks as far as popularity index is concerned. The popularity index can be enhanced or reduced. The enhancement or reduction depends upon the individual management's benchmarks on selling popular and profitable items.

In continuation of our example a menu item on a 15-item menu would be considered popular if its sale is equal to or more than 4.67% of total sales (100% / 15 = 6.67% and 70% of 6.67% = 4.67%). The reader can understand more on this from the continuation of the case study.

On the other hand, a food item on a 10-item menu would be considered popular if it measured 7% or more of total sales (100% / 10 = 10% and 70% of 10 = 7%). The concept of popularity index makes it possible to measure the **relative** degree of popularity of each item on a given menu.

With the above understanding of menu engineering, each menu item can be appraised for **profitability** and **popularity**. The menu engineering method also allows menu items to be classified into Stars, Standards, Puzzles and Problems. (The methodology of classification has been explained under the heading Menu Engineering Process).

4.8 MENU ENGINEERING CASE STUDY

The menu engineering case study represents data of Riverside Grill, a premium European Grill cuisine restaurant belonging to Riverside Grill Enterprises Ltd. An extract of 15 menu items representing the non-vegetarian section of the lunch and dinner main courses of the Riverside Grill restaurant were taken up for a 14-days' study. The 15 menu items are listed below:

    (i)   Grilled Queen Lobster Tails. *Nantua sauce.*

    (ii)   Grilled Giant Bay Prawns. Whisky sauce.

    (iii)   Grilled Halibut *Filet.* Served with roasted *Portobello Mushrooms Sauce.*

    (iv)   Grilled Chilean Sea Bass. Served with Pineapple Salsa.

    (v)   Grilled Salmon Steak with pickled ginger and Lemongrass Butter Sauce.

    (vi)   Grilled Tuna steak with *fresh basil and tomato beurre blanc.*

    (vii)   Grilled Chicken *suprêmes.* Ginger cream sauce.

    (viii)   Grilled Chicken steak. *Four pepper jus.*

    (ix)   Slow grilled Duck breast. Whole grain mustard and fresh apricot sauce.

(x)   Grilled Quail. Light garlic sauce.

(xi)   Rack of New Zealand Lamb. Rosemary sauce.

(xii)   Grilled baby Lamb chops with *minted pesto rub*.

(xiii)   Grilled Sirloin Steak with *Béarnaise Sauce*.

(xiv)   Grilled veal rib chops with Plum Tomato salsa.

(xv)   Grilled *gremolata* stuffed centre cut Pork chops. *Charcutière sauce*.

Notes: The names of the menu items listed above have been shortened while detailing the process of menu engineering to facilitate the data entry into Microsoft Excel files.

4.9   THE PROCESS OF MENU ENGINEERING

The process of menu engineering is a continuous examination of various menu items through the following reports:

1.   The Food Cost worksheet – described below

2.   The Menu Engineering worksheet – described on p. 60.

3.   The Menu Item analysis – described on p. 63-64.

4.   The Menu Mix analysis – described on p. 65.

5.   The Menu Engineering summary – described on p. 67.

6.   The Four Box analysis – described on p. 68.

7.   The Menu Engineering graph/pie charts – described on p. 68

The reports are explained from this point onwards.

4.9.1   The Menu Engineering Process: The Food Cost Worksheet

The Food Cost Worksheet of the menu engineering case study has been presented as **Exhibit 2 between pp. 60-61**. Data regarding menu items was collected from various internal sources of the Riverside Grill restaurant and fed into the Food Cost Worksheet.

(a)   The figures of total number of portions sold each day were collected from the outlet's computerised point-of-sale (POS) data.

(b)   The sale price of individual menu items was copied from the outlet's menu.

(c)   The food cost per portion was received from the standard recipe cost calculations.

(d)   The portions sold for each menu item have been tabulated date-wise.

(e)   The total numbers of portions sold in the 14-day period have been entered in the column (A).

The figures in column A present an idea of the:

- customer's acceptability of different menu items during the period of study; and
- sales of each menu item in relation with the other menu item/items.

Column B records the portion sale price of each menu item. Column C records the total sales of the menu items individually. This is calculated by multiplying the number of portions of menu item sold listed in Column (A) with portion sale price listed in Column (B). The figures of food cost of each portion of each menu item are entered in Column (D). The total costs of each menu item are calculated by multiplying the number of portions of menu item sold with portion cost price. These are entered in

Column (E). Figures in Column (C) and Column (E) therefore represent weighted figures. The portion food cost percentages are entered in Column (F).

The relationship between per portion cost price and per portion sale price is clear at one glance from calculations done in the Food Cost Worksheet. At one glance the worksheet also presents the weighted sales and weighted costs for each menu item in relation to the number of portions sold over a particular period. It further provides the chef an understanding of the food cost percentage of each menu item. It is easier and faster to relate to percentage figures as against absolute figures.

4.9.2 The Menu Engineering Process: The Menu Engineering Worksheet

The statistics available from the Food Cost Worksheet were examined further and utilized to prepare the Menu Engineering Worksheet which is presented as **Exhibit 3 between pp. 60-61**.

The menu engineering worksheet presents a comprehensive study and data of the merits of each menu item and that of the entire group of menu items under study, as follows:

(a)   The compilation of the menu engineering worksheet started with all the 15 menu items being listed in Column (A).

(b)   The information about the collected sales of each menu item, over the 14-day study period was entered as total sold in Column (B). This column is also called the Menu Mix or MM column and the individual figures are called Menu Mix figures. Those menu items which customers order frequently are called **popular** items. These have **relatively** high **menu mix**.

(c)   The number of portions sold as depicted in Column (B) is summed up. A total number of 1520 portions, representing the 15 menu items were sold during the study period. This total has been entered in Box (R).

(d)   The **menu mix percentage** (MM%) of individual menu items is a percentage relationship of the total number of portions sold of that menu item and the total portions sold of all the menu items. Menu mix of each menu item in terms of percentages is listed in Column (C).

44 portions of Grilled Queen Lobster Tails served with *Nantua Sauce* were sold out of the total menu sales of 1520 portions. Therefore the menu mix percentage of the menu item Grilled Queen Lobster Tails served with *Nantua Sauce* would be:

$$= \frac{44 \times 100}{1520} = 2.90\%$$

In a similar manner MM% of each of the menu items was calculated and listed in Column (C).

(e)   Each of the menu item's per portion sale price is recorded in Column (D).

(f)   Each of the menu items per portion food cost is recorded in Column (E).

(g)   Each of the menu items per portion Contribution Margin (CM) is recorded in Column (F). For example, to calculate the Contribution Margin for the Grilled Queen Lobster Tails served with *Nantua Sauce*, its cost (Rs. 480) listed in Column (E) is subtracted from its selling price (Rs. 1400), listed in Column (D); arriving at a contribution margin of Rs. 920. In a similar manner CM of each of the menu item was calculated.

(h)   The combined figures of sale prices of all the portions of each menu item for the study period are listed in Column (G). These are weighted figures. These are calculated by multiplying the number of each item sold, listed in Column (B) by its selling price listed in Column (D). For example, the menu revenue for 44 portions of the Grilled Queen Lobster Tails served with *Nantua Sauce* would be 44 × Rs. 1400 = Rs. 61,600. In a similar manner menu item sale of each of the menu items was calculated.

(i)   The combined figures of cost price of all the portions of each menu item for the study period are listed in Column (H). These are weighted figures. These are calculated by multiplying the number of each item sold, listed in Column (B) by the item food cost listed in Column (E). For example, the menu cost for 44 portions of the Grilled Queen Lobster Tails served with *Nantua Sauce* was 44 × 480 = Rs. 21,120. In similar manner menu item costs of each of the menu item was calculated.

(j)   The total Contribution Margin (CM) for all the portions of each menu item sold during the study period is listed in Column (I). These are weighted figures. CM figures are calculated by subtracting the combined figures of menu item costs listed in Column (H) from the combined figures of menu item sales listed in Column (G). In continuation, the menu item contribution for 44 portions of the Grilled Queen Lobster Tails served with *Nantua Sauce* would be Rs. 61,600 – Rs. 21,120 = Rs. 40,480. In a similar manner the contribution margin in respect of each of the menu item was calculated.

(k)   The total menu sales are the combined sales of all the portions of all the menu items. These have been listed in Box (M). These are weighted figures. In the case study, the total menu sales of all 1520 portions sold are calculated by summing up the individual sale for each menu item. These are equal to Rs. 10,53,350.

(l)   The total menu costs are the combined costs of all the portions of all the menu items. These have been listed in Box (N). These are weighted figures. In the example, the total menu costs of all 1520 portions are calculated by summing up the menu costs for individual menu items. These are equal to Rs. 3,19,630.

(m)   The total menu contributions are the combined contributions received from the sale of all the portions of all the menu items for the 14-day study period. These are weighted figures and are listed in Box (O). These are calculated by summing up the menu item Contribution Margin of each menu item listed in Column (I). These are equal to Rs. 7,33,720. The total menu contribution margin can also be calculated by subtracting the figures of total menu item costs listed in Box (N) from total menu items sales listed in (Box M).

Note: It is now possible to determine the **Average Contribution Margin**, and the **Popularity Index.**

(n)   **The Average Contribution Margin** is calculated in Box (S) and listed in Box (P). The average contribution margin is calculated by dividing the total menu CM listed in Box (O) by the total number of portions sold during the study period listed in Box (R).

A total of 1520 portions were sold (Box R) and the total menu contributions margin was Rs. 7,33,720. Therefore, the average contribution margin would be Rs. 7,33,720/1520 = Rs. 482.71. The average contribution margin is **the tool** against which individual menu item's contribution listed in Column (F) would be appraised.

The result would be the individual menu item's CM category and listed in Column (J). The individual menu item's CM category would be listed as High if its contribution is equal to or higher than the average contribution margin. In continuation, the individual menu item's CM category would be listed as Low if its contribution is lower than the average contribution margin.

(o)   Menu food cost percentage (food cost percentage of the entire group of menu items under study) is calculated by dividing total menu costs listed in Box (N) by total menu sales listed in Box (M), and multiplying by 100.

(p)   The concept of **relative popularity** has been explained earlier. Since there are 15 menu items in the case study, each menu item has an expected popularity of 100%/ 15 = 6.67%. Assuming that the sales of a popular item should equal 70% of what is expected for it, the popularity index is 70% × 6.67 = 4.67%. The calculations for arriving at the popularity index have been done in Box (U). The popularity index is listed in Box (Q).

The popularity index is **the tool** against which individual menu item's popularity (MM %) listed in Column (C) would be appraised. The MM% category of individual menu item is listed in Column (K). The individual menu item's MM% category would be listed as High if its menu mix is equal to or higher than the popularity index. In continuation, the individual menu item's MM% category would be listed as Low if its menu mix is lower than the popularity index.

In the case study the relatively popular menu items are those whose sales are equal to or more than the **Popularity Index of 4.67%.**

(q) Menu item classification in terms of whether the menu item is a Star, or a Standard, or a Puzzle or a Problem – was listed in Column (L).

In continuation, those items of the menu that are profitable (i.e., those with a high contribution margin) are those whose contribution margin is equal to or greater than the average contribution margin for all menu items — Rs. 482.71. In the case study, the following six menu items of the Riverside Grill restaurant turn out to represent high contribution margin:

(i) Grilled Queen Lobster Tails served with *Nantua Sauce*.

(ii) Grilled Giant Bay Prawns topped with Whisky Sauce.

(iii) Grilled Halibut *Filet* served with roasted *Portobello Mushrooms Sauce*.

(iv) Grilled Chilean Sea Bass served with Pineapple *Salsa*.

(v) Grilled Salmon Steak *served with pickled ginger and Lemongrass Butter Sauce*.

(vi) Grilled Sirloin Steak *served with Béarnaise Sauce*.

All the other 9 menu items have lower Contribution Margin than the average contribution margin, i.e., Rs. 482.71. Once the contribution of all the menu items is worked out, it is easy to identify which menu items are giving more contribution and which are giving less contribution to the bottom lines. One **yardstick of evaluation** of a menu is the **profitability** of its menu items.

Column (K) of the Menu Engineering Worksheet, in the case study indicates the assessment of each item's popularity. The figures are for Menu Mix (MM) percentage category. By comparing each item's menu mix percentage, available Column (C) with the popularity index, conclusions can be made.

The menu mix percentage, in Column (C) for Grilled Queen Lobster Tails served with *Nantua Sauce* is 2.90%. When compared against the popularity index – 4.67%, it is low. Therefore, the MM% category is entered as Low.

The menu mix percentage, in Column (C) for Grilled Halibut *Filet* served with roasted *Portobello Mushrooms Sauce* is 7.24%. When compared against the popularity index – 4.67%, it is high. Therefore, the MM% category is entered as High.

In a similar manner, MM% categories for all menu items are entered in Column K. It is noticed that there were certain items which were **frequently ordered** by customers. This indicated that these were popular menu items. **The second yardstick of evaluation** of a menu is the **popularity** of its menu items. Therefore, menu items can be evaluated in terms of **both their popularity and profitability.**

On further study it is noticed that menu item Grilled Queen Lobster Tails served with *Nantua Sauce* is high on CM category and low on MM% category. This means that it has a high contribution margin in relation to the average contribution margin, but does not sell enough number of portions. Such menu items are called **Puzzles** in the language of menu engineering. Therefore, the subject menu item is classified as a **Puzzle**.

The menu item - Grilled Halibut Filet served with roasted *Portobello* Mushrooms Sauce is high on CM category and high on MM% category. Therefore, the subject menu item is classified as a **Star**.

The classification of all menu items is similarly done and the result entered in Column (L).

The following data emerged from the study of the Menu Engineering Worksheet:

- Some menu items are popular (high sales). This means that they have relatively **high menu mix percentages**. In addition, these menu items are profitable also, indicating high contribution margin. These menu items are called **Stars.**

- Some menu items are popular (high sales). This means that they have relatively **high menu mix percentages**. However, these menu items are not profitable, indicating low contribution margin. These menu items are called **Standards.**

- Some menu items are not popular (low sales). This means that they have relatively low **menu mix percentages**. However, these menu items are profitable, indicating high contribution margin. These menus items are called **Puzzles.**

- Some menu items are neither popular (low sales-low menu mix percentages) nor profitable (low contribution margin). These menu items are called **Problems.**

Menu engineering classifies all menu items in the above manner. Therefore, each menu item is either of the following:

- A Star.
- A Standard.
- A Puzzle.
- A Problem.

This classification would indicate the **relative profitability** and **relative popularity** of each menu item. A key to classification of menu items is presented above.

Appraisal of menu items

Menu items can be appraised and classified for the purpose of menu engineering. It is important to understand the appraisal of menu items for the purposes of establishing their menu item classification.

As explained earlier, **menu engineering process** is also a continuous examination of various aspects of menu items. A menu item's profitability is *not* the level of **its food cost**, but **its contribution margin**. A menu item with a lower food cost percentage is not necessarily the more profitable item on the menu. The goal of effective menu planning and evaluation should be to increase the contribution margin of each menu item – not decrease its food cost percentage.

4.9.3 The Menu Engineering Process: The Menu Item Analysis

Menu item analysis is a portion analysis of each menu item of the menu. The analysis presents the following data:

(a) Total portions sold of each menu item during the study period.
(b) Sale price of each portion of each menu item.
(c) Cost price of each portion of each menu item.
(d) Contribution margin of each portion of each menu item.

The primary purpose of this report is to provide the user with analysis of each menu item under study. This is especially helpful if the data is entered manually into the data sheet. (The **Menu Item Analysis** for the main course items of Riverside Grill restaurant is presented as **Exhibit 4, p. 64.**)

EXHIBIT 4: Menu Item Analysis

RG Riverside Grill				
		In January 2016		
(A)	**(B)**	**(C)**	**(D)**	**(F)**
Menu Items	**Total Portions Sold (MM) Nos.**	**Portion Sale Price Rs.**	**Portion Food Cost Rs.**	**Portion CM (C) – (D) Rs.**
Grilled queen Lobster tails. *Nantua* sauce	44	1400	480	920
Grilled giant bay Prawns. Whisky sauce	65	1200	350	850
Grilled Halibut *filet*. *Portobello* sauce	110	900	280	620
Grilled Chilean Seabass. Pineapple salsa	108	900	275	625
Grilled Salmon steak. Lemongrass butter sauce	134	750	210	540
Grilled Tuna steak. Basil & Tomato *beurre blanc*	81	625	175	450
Grilled Chicken *suprêmes*. Ginger cream sauce	95	525	150	375
Grilled Chicken steak. Four pepper *jus*	130	500	130	370
Grilled Duck breast. Apricot & Mustard sauce	87	525	175	350
Grilled Quail. Light garlic sauce	78	500	125	375
Grilled rack of New Zealand Lamb. Rosemary sauce	170	750	280	470
Grilled baby Lamb chops. Minted *pesto rub*	133	625	190	435
Grilled Sirloin steak. *Béarnaise* sauce	90	675	180	495
Grilled Veal rib chops. Plum Tomato salsa	140	525	155	370
Grilled *Gremolata* stuffed Pork chops. *Charcutière* sauce	55	400	110	290

4.9.4   The Menu Engineering Process: Menu Mix Analysis

Menu Mix Analysis has two parts, as follows:

(a)   the popularity analysis, and

(b)   the profitability analysis.

Based on the above, the menu item classification is listed for each menu item.

(a)   The **popularity analysis** lists the following:

- The number of portions of each menu item sold in the study period.

- The MM% share of each menu item in relation to the total number of portions of all the menu items sold.

- The popularity ranking of each menu item in relation to the popularity index.

(b)   The **profitability analysis** lists the following:

- The contribution margin of each portion of each menu item.

- The menu contribution margin—the total contribution due to sale of all the portions of the menu items taken up for study during the study period.

- The profitability ranking of each menu item in relation to the average contribution margin.

Menu Mix Analysis is a comprehensive study of all menu items of a menu under study during a study period, in relation to each other. The analysis evaluates each menu item's participation in the overall menu's performance. It provides at-a-glance figures and also the menu item classification. (The **Menu Mix Analysis** for the main course items of Riverside Grill restaurant is presented as **Exhibit 5 between pp. 64-65.**)

4.9.5   The Menu Engineering Process: Menu Engineering Summary

The menu engineering summary lists all summarized values of a menu and menu items under study in a comprehensive manner, as follows:

(a)   Price section lists:

- Total menu revenues.

- A portion's average selling price.

- Lowest selling price per portion.

- Highest selling price per portion.

- Name of the menu item with the lowest selling price per portion.

- Name of the menu item with the highest selling price per portion.

(b)   Food cost section lists:

- Total menu costs (weighted figures)

- Average food cost per portion.

- Lowest food cost per portion.

- Highest food cost per portion.

- Name of the menu item with the lowest food cost per portion.

- Name of the menu item with the highest food cost per portion.

EXHIBIT 6: Key to Classification of Menu Items

	Popularity	Profitability	Key result	Menu items classified as
Case I **Best case**	High sales (Relatively higher menu mix percentage than the Popularity Index)	High contribution margin (Relatively higher contribution than the Average Contribution Margin)	Popular and profitable	Stars
Case II	High sales (Relatively higher Menu Mix percentage than the Popularity Index)	Low contribution margin (Relatively lower contribution than the Average Contribution Margin)	Popular but not profitable	Standards
Case III	Low sales (Relatively lower Menu Mix percentage than the Popularity Index)	High contribution margin (Relatively higher contribu-tion than the Average Contribution Margin)	Not popular but profitable	Puzzles
Case IV **Worst case**	Low sales (Relatively lower Menu Mix percentage than the Popularity Index)	Low contribution Margin (Relatively lower contribution than the Average Contribution Margin)	Not popular and not profitable	Problems

(c) Contribution margin section lists:

- Total menu contribution margin (weighted figures)
- Average contribution margin per portion.
- Lowest contribution margin per portion.
- Highest contribution margin per portion.
- Name of the menu item with the lowest contribution margin per portion.
- Name of the menu item with the highest contribution margin per portion.

(d) Popularity factor section lists:

- Total number of portions sold.
- Average number of portions sold per day.
- Lowest number of portions sold in a day.
- Highest number of portions sold in a day.
- Date when lowest number of portions were sold for the day. Some variations of the menu engineering summary list the day of the week in addition to identify it with business scenario of that particular day.
- Date when highest number of portions were sold for the day. Some variations of the menu engineering summary list the day of the week in addition to identify it with business scenario of that particular day.

(e) Food cost percentage (weighted figure)

(f) Number of menu items.

Information sourced from the menu engineering summary is used elsewhere in the menu management system. For example, the **lowest** and **highest** selling prices on the menu can be used to identify target market.

This helps marketing campaigns, as the marketer is clear about the variances of price points and the variances of a menu in terms of lowest cost menu item and the highest cost menu item. The menu engineering summary helps the chefs and operators to identify the 'high' and 'low' points of their business of the period under study. (The menu engineering summary for the main course items of Riverside Grill restaurant under study is presented as **Exhibit 7 below.**)

EXHIBIT 7: Menu Engineering Summary: Riverside Grill (In January 2016)

℞ Riverside Grill					
1.	Price	Total menu revenues	Average portion selling price	Lowest selling price per portion	Highest selling price per portion
		Rs. 1053350	Rs. 693	Rs. 400	Rs. 1400
				Gremolata stuffed Pork chops. *Charcutière* sauce	Queen Lobster tails. *Nantua sauce*
2.	Food cost	Total menu costs (weighted figures)	Average food cost per portion	Lowest food cost per portion	Highest food cost per portion
		Rs. 319630	Rs. 210.28	Rs. 110	Rs. 480
				Gremolata stuffed Pork chops. *Charcutière* sauce	Queen Lobster tails. *Nantua sauce*
3.	Contribution margin	Total menu contribution margin (weighted figures)	Average contribution margin per portion	Lowest contribution margin per portion	Highest contribution margin per portion
		Rs. 733720	Rs. 482.71	Rs. 290	Rs. 920
				Gremolata stuffed Pork chops. *Charcutière* sauce	Queen Lobster tails. *Nantua sauce*
4.	Popularity Factor	Total no. of portions sold	Average no. of portions sold per day	Lowest no. of portions sold in a day	Highest no. of portions sold in a day
		1520 Nos.	108.57 Nos.	75 Nos.	126 Nos.
				On 14.01.2016	On 04.01.2016
5.	Food cost percentage	(Weighted figure)			
		30.34%			
6.	No. of menu items	15 Nos.			

4.9.6   The Menu Engineering Process: Four-Box Analysis

Four-box analysis is an important tool for the day-to-day knowledge of a chef. It indexes the menu classifications developed in the menu mix analysis report. It lists the Stars, Standards, Puzzles and Problems of a menu for a study period at a glance in individual boxes.

The case study has presented the following data:

- There are 4 menu items which have found classification as Stars.
- There are 8 menu items which have found classification as Standards.
- There are 2 menu items which have found classification as Puzzles.
- There is 1 menu item which has found classification as a Problem.

The four-box analysis places a chef into a questioning mould, for example:

(a)   Are 4 Star menu items out of 15 menu items too little for profitable business?

(b)   Are 4 Star menu items out of 15 menu items justified for the start-up of the business?

(c)   Are 4 Star menu items out of 15 menu items justified for the geographical location of the business?

The four-box analysis gives immediate focus on menu items which need support to convert them into **Star** menu items, which is the most important requirement of culinary business. Many other queries are thrown up, for example:

- Can the menu item classified as problem be eliminated? Or restructured to become a Star menu item?
- How to convert the 8 menu items classified as Standards into Star menu items?
- How to convert the 2 menu items classified as Puzzles into Star menu items.

This type of evaluation process begins with the four-box matrix and continues through with the menu engineering graph/menu engineering pie chart. The four-box analysis places a chef in an advantageous position to manage the day-to-day production activity of à la carte menu items in a cost effective way, i.e., controlling number of portions of each menu item to be cooked during the day, or in readiness for customer order.

The four-box analysis encourages a chef to analyze methods to control wastage, spoilage, and unauthorized consumption of individual menu items. (**Four-Box Analysis** for the main course items of Riverside Grill restaurant under study is presented as **Exhibit 8, p. 69.**)

4.9.7   The Menu Engineering Process: Menu Engineering Graph/Menu Engineering Pie Chart

The menu engineering graph or the menu engineering pie chart is useful to evolve decision strategies. It positions each menu item in the case study in relation to other menu items of the case study.

The most important requirement of a culinary business is to compare each menu item's **relative** values in terms of popularity and popularity. Popularity is identified through Menu Mix (MM) and profitability is identified through Contribution Margin (CM). The menu engineering graph or the menu engineering pie chart presents this opportunity. Both have same functions and advantages and present the MM and CM of all the menu items under study. (The values of MM and CM are plotted in the graph. The graph has been presented as **Exhibit 9, p. 71.**)

This technique, therefore, points out that a different menu engineering strategy may be appropriate for menu items even though they are similarly segmented. Main course items of the Riverside Grill, for example, shall present a very different profile than the study of the restaurant's soups, or salads, or desserts. (Two menu engineering pie charts have been presented on **pp. 72-73**. The pie chart presented

EXHIBIT 8: Four-Box Analysis

RG Riverside Grill

Profitability ───→ Low

Popularity (Low / High)

Stars

1. Popularity characteristic: Relatively high menu mix percentage than the Popularity Index.
2. Profitability characteristic: Relatively high contribution than the Average Contribution Margin.

Menu items classified as "Stars" are popular and profitable.

Four "Star" menu items identified in the case study:

1. Grilled Halibut *filet. Portobello* sauce
2. Grilled Chilean *Seabass.* Pineapple *salsa*
3. Grilled Salmon steak. Lemongrass butter sauce
4. Grilled Sirloin steak. *Béarnaise* sauce

Standards

1. Popularity characteristic: Relatively high menu mix percentage than the Popularity Index.
2. Profitability characteristic: Relatively low contribution than the Average Contribution Margin.

Menu items classified as "Standards" are popular but not profitable.

Eight "Standard" menu items identified in the case study:

1. Grilled Tuna steak. Basil & Tomato *beurre blanc*
2. Grilled Chicken *suprêmes.* Ginger cream sauce
3. Grilled Chicken steak. *Four Pepper jus*
4. Grilled Duck breast. Apricot & Mustard sauce
5. Grilled Quail. Light Garlic sauce
6. Grilled rack of New Zealand Lamb. *Rosemary* sauce
7. Grilled baby Lamb chops. Minted *pesto rub*
8. Grilled Veal rib chops. Plum Tomato *salsa*

Puzzles

1. Popularity characteristic: Relatively low menu mix percentage than the Popularity Index.
2. Profitability characteristic: Relatively high contribution than the Average Contribution Margin.

Menu items classsified as "Puzzles" are not popular but are profitable.

Two "Puzzle" menu items identified in the case study:

1. Grilled queen Lobster tails. *Nantua* sauce
2. Grilled giant bay Prawns. Whisky sauce

Problems

1. Popularity characteristic: Relatively low menu mix percentage than the Popularity Index.
2. Profitability characteristic: Relatively low contribution than the Average Contribution Margin.

Menu items classified as "Problems" are neither popular nor profitable.

One "Problem" menu item identified in the case study:

1. Grilled *Gremolata* Stuffed Pork chops. Charcutière sauce

as **Exhibit 10, p. 72** illustrates the relative popularity of all the menu items. The pie chart presented as **Exhibit 11, p. 73** illustrates the relative profitability of all the menu items.)

4.10   MENU ENGINEERING SUPPORT TO A CHEF

Information received from the menu engineering analyses should be used to improve the menu. Once menu items are evaluated into Stars, Standards, Puzzles and Problems, dedicated efforts are required by the chef to manage transformation of each of these classified menu items into Stars, and maintaining Star menu items as Stars.

4.10.1   Transforming Standards into Stars

Standards are those menu items that are low in contribution margin, but high in popularity. Customers like these items, but unfortunately, **Standards** do not contribute their fair share of contribution margin. The menu items have relatively high Menu Mix percentages. The requirement is to enhance the profitability of these menu items, and increase its contribution to equal or exceed the average contribution margin, so that these menu items become **Star** menu items.

As a result of Menu Engineering Analysis, the case study has thrown up the following menu items as Standards:

(i)   Grilled Tuna steak with *fresh basil and tomato beurre blanc.*

(ii)   Rack of New Zealand Lamb. Rosemary sauce.

(iii)   Slow grilled duck breast. Whole grain mustard and fresh apricot sauce.

(iv)   Grilled Chicken steak. *Four pepper jus.*

(v)   Grilled Chicken *suprêmes.* Ginger cream sauce.

(vi)   Grilled Quail. Light garlic sauce.

(vii)   Grilled baby Lamb chops with *minted pesto rub.*

(viii)   Grilled veal rib chops with Plum Tomato salsa.

The dilemma of culinary business is that a wide variety of menu item offerings are required to attract a customer.

What can be done to the above Standards to make them into Star menu items? The obvious strategies would revolve around reducing the standard recipe cost of the menu item or increasing its sales price. The following are some ways to convert a **Standard** into a **Star**:

(a)   The menu item may be popular because its sale price per portion is low. The menu item presents a good value for money to customers. The menu sale price should be increased carefully. If prices are increased, the menu item may continue to be good value for money. The menu item may continue to be as popular as earlier. However, the menu item would start generating a higher contribution margin.

The decision to increase menu item's sale price is most appropriate when the menu items or the menu itself are exclusive to the culinary business and cannot be obtained elsewhere in the same geographical area. Such menu items are coveted by the customers and are often part of the menu of a speciality restaurant or are signature culinary creations of the chefs.

(b)   If customers accept the price increase for the menu item, and it still remains a popular menu item, it is desirable to repackage and reposition it. Repackaging may be to offer **additional** low-cost accompaniments and garnishes to improve the acceptability of the menu item and increasing its contribution margin through the price increase. Prices should be increased in

EXHIBIT 9: Menu Engineering Graph

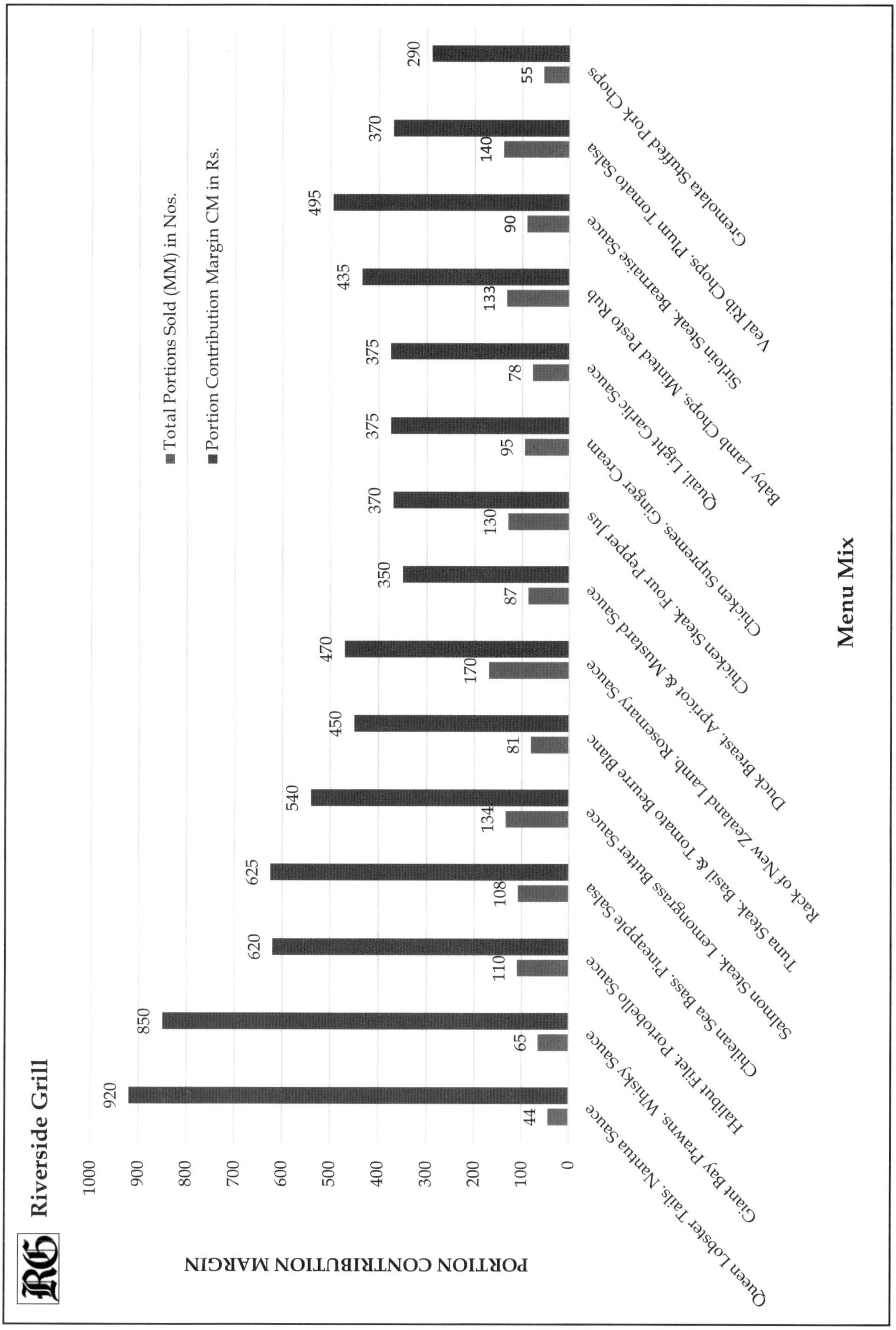

Riverside Grill

Menu Mix

■ Total Portions Sold (MM) in Nos.
■ Portion Contribution Margin CM in Rs.

PORTION CONTRIBUTION MARGIN

Data by item (Total Portions Sold / Portion CM):
- Queen Lobster Tails, Nantua Sauce: 920 / 44
- Giant Bay Prawns, Whisky Sauce: 850 / 65
- Halibut Filet, Portobello Sauce: 620 / 110
- Chilean Sea Bass, Pineapple Salsa: 625 / 108
- Salmon Steak, Lemongrass Butter Sauce: 540 / 134
- Tuna Steak, Basil & Tomato Beurre Blanc: 450 / 81
- Rack of New Zealand Lamb, Rosemary Sauce: 470 / 170
- Duck Breast, Apricot & Mustard Sauce: 350 / 87
- Chicken Steak, Four Pepper Jus: 370 / 130
- Chicken Supremes, Ginger Cream: 375 / 95
- Quail, Light Garlic Sauce: 375 / 78
- Baby Lamb Chops, Minted Pesto Rub: 435 / 133
- Sirloin Steak, Bearnaise Sauce: 495 / 90
- Veal Rib Chops, Plum Tomato Salsa: 370 / 140
- Gremolata Stuffed Pork Chops: 290 / 55

EXHIBIT 10: Popularity Analysis: Menu Mix Percentage

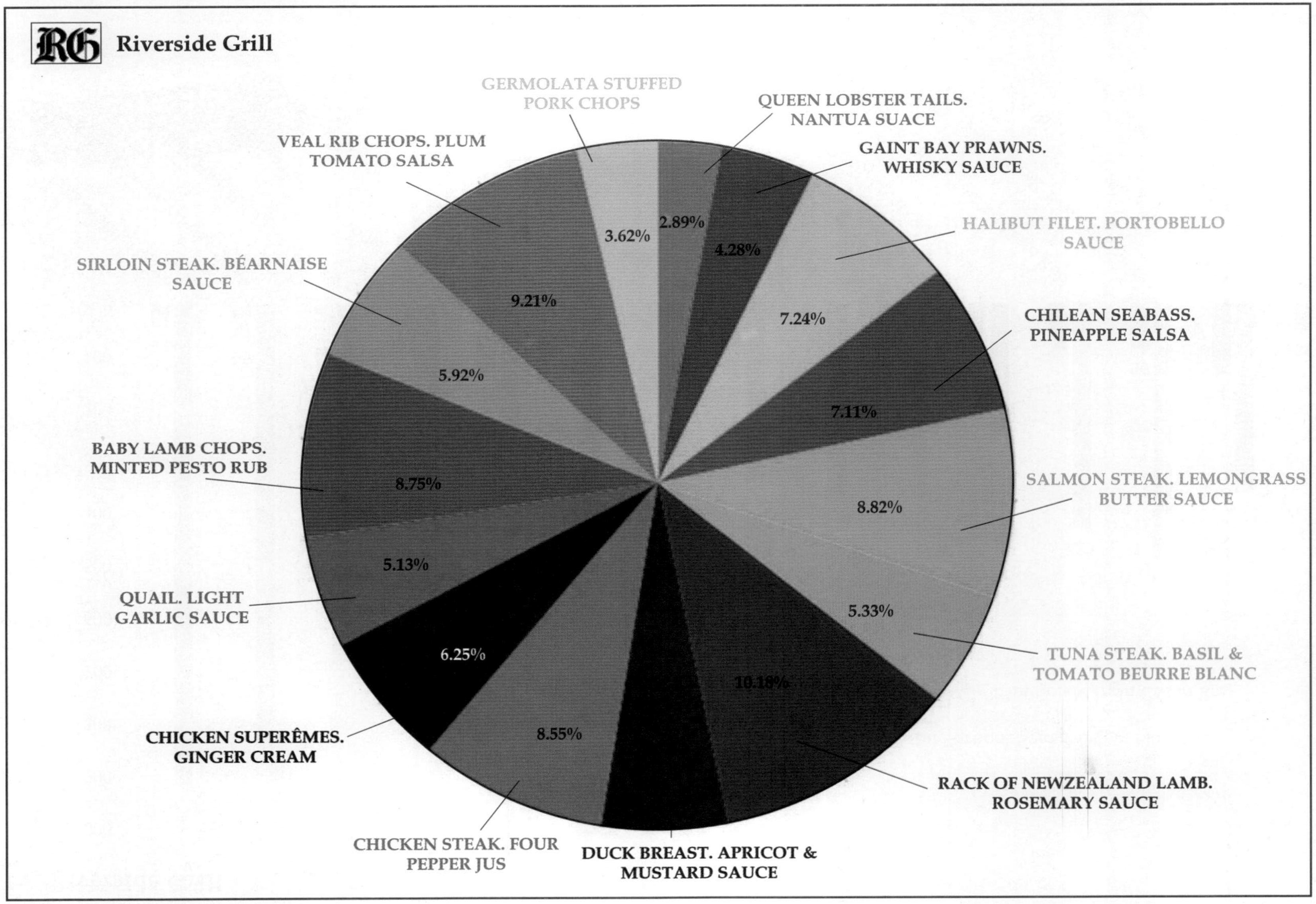

RG Riverside Grill

CHILEAN SEABASS. PINEAPPLE SALSA

HALIBUT FILET. PORTOBELLO SAUCE

SALMON STEAK. LEMONGRASS BUTTER SAUCE

GAINT BAY PRAWNS. WHISKY SAUCE

TUNA STEAK. BASIL & TOMATO BEURRE BLANC

QUEEN LOBSTER TAILS. NANTUA SUACE

RACK OF NEWZEALAND LAMB. ROSEMARY SAUCE

GERMOLATA STUFFED PORK CHOPS

DUCK BREAST. APRICOT & MUSTARD SAUCE

VEAL RIB CHOPS. PLUM TOMATO SALSA

CHICKEN STEAK. FOUR PEPPER JUS

SIRLOIN STEAK. BÉARNAISE SAUCE

CHICKEN SUPERÊMES. GINGER CREAM

BABY LAMB CHOPS. MINTED PESTO RUB

QUAIL. LIGHT GARLIC SAUCE

8.82%

5.33%

7.11%

7.24%

4.28%

2.89%

3.62%

10.18%

9.21%

5.92%

8.75%

5.13%

6.25%

8.55%

EXHIBIT 11: Profitability Analysis: Percentage Contribution Margin

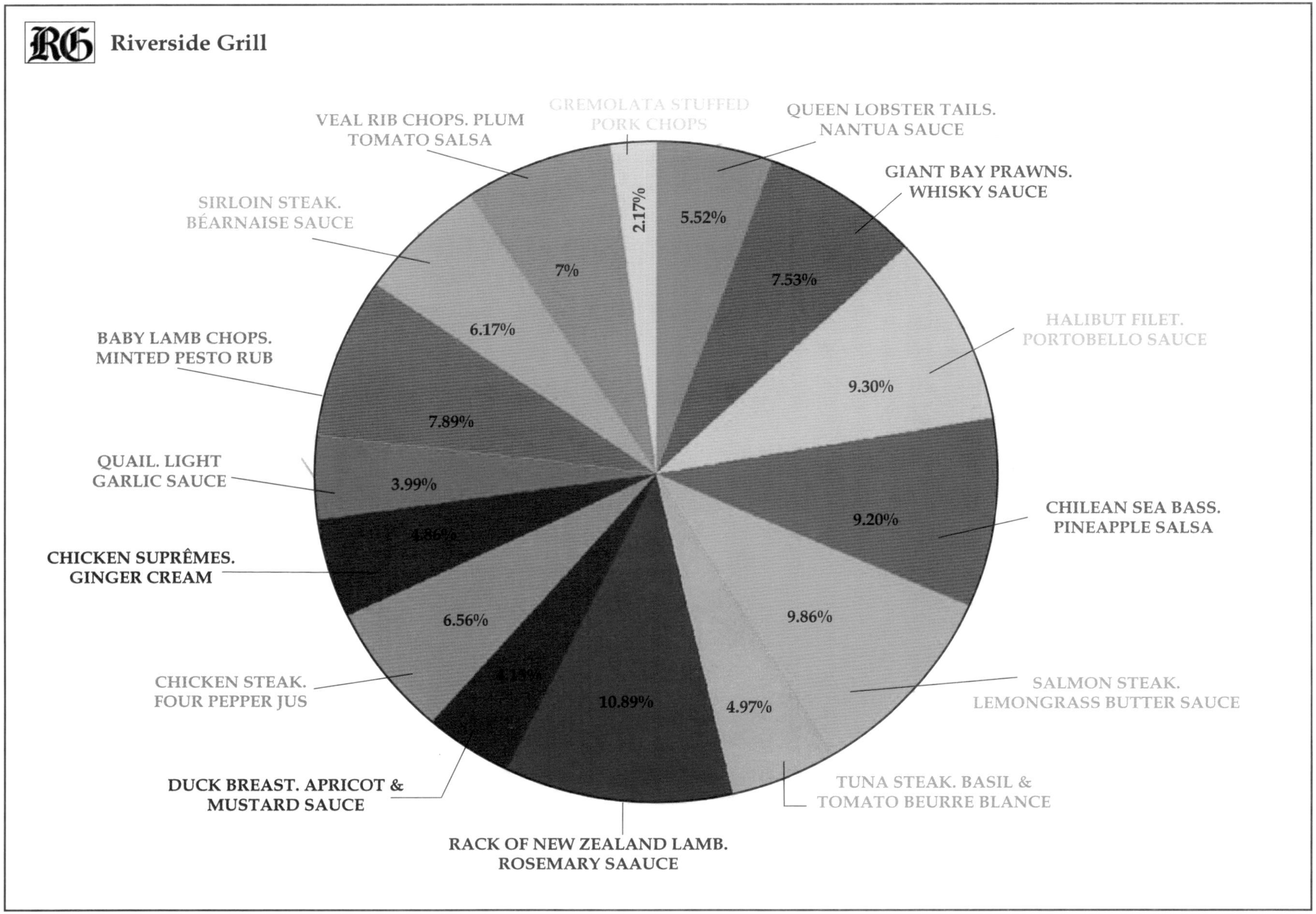

Riverside Grill

HALIBUT FILET. PORTOBELLO SAUCE

CHILEAN SEA BASS. PINEAPPLE SALSA

SALMON STEAK. LEMONGRASS BUTTER SAUCE

GIANT BAY PRAWNS. WHISKY SAUCE

QUEEN LOBSTER TAILS. NANTUA SAUCE

TUNA STEAK. BASIL & TOMATO BEURRE BLANCE

GREMOLATA STUFFED PORK CHOPS

VEAL RIB CHOPS. PLUM TOMATO SALSA

SIRLOIN STEAK. BÉARNAISE SAUCE

RACK OF NEW ZEALAND LAMB. ROSEMARY SAAUCE

BABY LAMB CHOPS. MINTED PESTO RUB

QUAIL. LIGHT GARLIC SAUCE

CHICKEN SUPRÊMES. GINGER CREAM

CHICKEN STEAK. FOUR PEPPER JUS

DUCK BREAST. APRICOT & MUSTARD SAUCE

9.30%
9.20%
9.86%
7.53%
4.97%
5.52%
2.17%
7%
6.17%
7.89%
3.99%
6.86%
6.56%
4.13%
10.89%

small measures. Quality of food preparation and delivery benchmarks should be upgraded or retained within the service guarantees.

(c) If possible, the menu item should be relocated to a lower profile on the menu. Additionally, the pitch of personal recommendations should be lowered for it. Depending on the menu layout, certain areas of the menu represent a better location than others. A **Standard** can be relocated to a less desirable area of the menu. Since the item is popular, some customers will search it out. Other customers will be drawn to higher profile areas of the menu that list more profitable items the outlet would like to sell. Relocation of menu items is not possible in structured à *la carte* menu formats. It is possible only in case of informally structured menus like those of a student cafeteria.

(d) The values of service guarantee fixed for the menu items identified as Standards should be re-evaluated. Accompaniments to the main dish should be combined with lower cost products. The contribution margin of a Standard can be increased if lower cost meal accompaniments are offered with the entrée. This becomes a case of reworking and re-costing of the Standard Recipe for the menu item, and also re-stating the service guarantee for that particular item.

For example, higher priced vegetables, potatoes, accompanying salads, and sauces can be replaced with other, less expensive items, without reducing the item's popularity. If this works, the lesser costing would mean additional contribution for the item, and would increase the level to equal or more than the average contribution margin. This would make the menu item into a Star.

On many occasions main course menu items, declared as Standards through the menu engineering process are combined with soups, salads and desserts and presented as a combo. Reworking the menu to present these menu items – soups, salads and desserts in an enhanced cost effective way can also reduce food costs and increase the menu item's contribution. The portion size of menu items in combo offers need not be as big as the portion size of the components, if sold separately. A customer may not be in a position to consume everything.

(e) The portion size of the menu items declared as Standards should be examined. The portion size may be too large for consumption by one person. It is possible that the menu item is being shared by more than one customer. This could be the reason for the menu item's popularity.

Consider reduction in size of the portion. If the portion size is reduced, the recipe cost will be decreased and the contribution margin will increase. However, this method of transforming a Standard into a Star is rarely used. A regular customer's perception of value may decrease if portion size is reduced. It is best to critically examine portion size before the launch of the culinary business and the menu.

4.10.2 Transforming Puzzles into Stars

Puzzles are menu items that are high in contribution margin but low in popularity. The chef desires to sell these menu items since their contribution margin is relatively high. Unfortunately the menu item does not find large acceptability amongst customers. In relation to the other menu items the Puzzles have a low menu mix percentage. The challenge is to find ways to increase the number of customers ordering these items.

As a result of analysis of menu items for the case study, the Menu Engineering Worksheet has thrown up the following two menu items as Puzzles:

(i) Grilled Queen Lobster tails. *Nantua sauce.*

(ii) Grilled Giant Bay Prawns. Whisky sauce.

To offer expensive ingredients and seafood on the menu is important for the overall acceptability of the concept of the menu in this case.

The purchase price of the ingredients required for these menu items is very high, and the standard recipe cost is very high in relation to other menu items. The sale price of each of these menu items is also very high. This may be the reason why customers do not order these menu items frequently. What can be done to the above Puzzles to make them into Star menu items? The following are some ways to convert a **Puzzle** into a **Star**:

(a) The subject menu item should be repositioned to more visible areas of the menu, or renamed. Personal recommendations for the menu item should be used, marketing campaigns should be developed, table tent cards should be used, and the menu item on the menu boards at the entrance to the food & beverages outlet should be highlighted. These strategies to focus demand to these menu items would improve the popularity of the menu item.

(b) The menu items should be repackaged with free offers normally given by ingredient or liquor companies. This effort may increase the acceptability of the menu item, and more portions of the same would sell.

(c) These menu items should be repackaged with additional offers in terms of beverages, free soups, or salads or desserts. Even with the additional costs of the additional offers, the menu item would continue to produce sufficient contribution above the average contribution margin. Repackaging would enhance its popularity.

(d) The prices of the menu item should be decreased. The menu item may be low in popularity because it does not represent a value to customers. If this is the case, the selling price might be reduced with the contribution margin still remaining higher than the average. This could lead to increased popularity, since a reduced selling price would represent a greater value to the customer. More customers would order the menu item. If the reduced prices are announced through personal recommendations, the menu item would increase its popularity.

(e) Subtle initiatives to make customers partner in the cooking process would be helpful in increasing the acceptability of the menu item.

For example, the challenge of preparing the lobster tails in the style demanded by the customers would add to the menu item's popularity.

(f) Values should be added to the menu item. Offering a larger portion size, adding more expensive meal accompaniments, sauces or garnishes, and using higher quality ingredients are among the ways that value can be increased. These techniques may lead to increased popularity and to a contribution margin that is lower than the earlier contribution margin, but still higher than the average contribution margin generated by the section of the menu under study.

4.10.3 Transforming Problems into Stars

Problems are those menu items that are low in contribution margin and low in popularity. These menu items do not contribute their fair share of contribution margin and they are not popular. As a result of Menu Engineering Analysis, the case study has thrown up the following menu item as Puzzle:

Grilled *gremolata* stuffed centre cut Pork chops. *Charcutière sauce.*

These menu items should be removed from the menu. However, an honest attempt should be made to convert these Problem menu items into Stars. Some suggested ways to make Problem menu items into Star menu items:

(a) The recipe should be examined. *Gremolata* is a great garnish, stuffing and flavour. Pork chops have been constant favourites. The marination of pineapple, touch of molasses, herbs and seasonings improve the quality of the pork meat and introduces great flavours and taste notes. The *Charcutière sauce* marries well with the pork with its tanginess.

(b) Other cheaper pork cuts like the fillet or steaks can be substituted for pork chops. The garnish and preparation styles can remain the same. The acceptability may improve, and customers may order more of the menu item. Obviously, the menu item would require renaming accordingly.

(c) The selling price of the menu item can be increased. A higher contribution margin would be the result.

(d) Subsequently, the same tactics to increase its popularity as those used for converting Puzzles into Stars, mentioned earlier can be applied.

4.10.4 Maintaining Stars as Stars

Stars are menu items that are high in contribution margin and high in popularity. These are those menu items which the chef wishes to sell the most. The following four menu items from the case study have emerged as Star menu items:

(i) Grilled Halibut *Filet*. Served with roasted *Portobello Mushrooms Sauce*.

(ii) Grilled Chilean Sea Bass. Served with Pineapple Salsa.

(iii) Grilled Salmon Steak with pickled ginger and Lemongrass Butter Sauce.

(iv) Grilled Sirloin Steak with *Béarnaise Sauce*.

Some of the suggested ways to maintain Stars as Stars are:

(a) Through ensuring that all service guarantees are adhered to. Rigid quality and delivery benchmarks must be maintained. All service guarantees must be examined at regular intervals and upgraded if necessary. There should be no attempt to alter the quality of the menu item being served. There should not be any change in the service styles. Accompaniments, garnishes, and other values should remain sacrosanct or upgraded.

(b) The menu item should be positioned to a highly visible location. Customers should be aware of the menu item's availability. Relocation is not always possible in structured à *la carte* menus.

(c) Efforts should be made to examine if the Star is popular because it is a significant value to the customers. It is possible that the Star is not available in its existing form elsewhere in the same marketplace. The menu item may also be a signature creation of the chef. The selling price of such a coveted menu item can be increased without a decrease in popularity.

(d) Suggestive selling techniques should be used. Some of the techniques for focusing demand mentioned earlier might be useful.

(e) Recipe production should be highly controlled. Standard recipes should not vary from one production schedule to another. If required, specific staff should handle production of Star menu items. The author successfully used this strategy while in service. Specific staff prepared sections of menu, thereby highly perfecting and tuning the production benchmarks.

Note: An operator may adopt any strategy to convert any/all menu items into Stars. The service guarantees should be changed accordingly. In addition, a careful observation of consequence of the changes must be made.

4.11 OTHER ADVANTAGES OF MENU ENGINEERING

1. The process and tools of menu engineering can be used to appraise **the entire menu**.

2. The process and tools of menu engineering can be used to appraise **menu revisions**.

3. The *à la carte* portions can be adequately controlled. By examining the menu engineering summary each day, a chef can easily spot the portions sold the previous day, and can stipulate production for the day or the next day or demand justification of losses in portions. This places the staff on guard, and expensive portions prepared especially for the customers are not lost to pilferage and unauthorized consumption.

Menu engineering is therefore the most important methodology in the hands of a chef or a food & beverages manager to understand the culinary business in terms of profitability. With the tools of menu engineering, the worth of a revised menu can be objectively assessed.

The following two examples illustrate how a revised or repackaged menu item can become a Star menu item.

Example One: The menu sale price of the menu item: Grilled Tuna Steak with *fresh basil and tomato beurre blanc* was increased. As a result of this measure, the contribution margin became higher than the earlier average contribution margin. The menu item continued being popular and customers asked for it specially. The menu item continued to represent a great value to the customers.

Example Two: The menu item: Grilled baby lamb chops with *minted pesto rub* were repackaged with low cost accompaniments and garnishes than the earlier ones. Expensive English vegetables like celery, leeks, and sweet pimentos were prepared individually and presented as vegetable accompaniments to the preparation earlier. These were replaced with lesser expensive vegetables like carrots, turnips, beans, etc. Almond potatoes were replaced with chateau potatoes. Salad prepared with expensive ingredients and served as an accompaniment to the main course was substituted with a mixed green salad.

The result of these changes enhanced the contribution margins of the menu item to more than the earlier average contribution margin. The lamb chops continued to be a favourite to regular customers with a result in good menu mix for the menu item.

The above are examples of the popularity of individual menu items remaining stable, while their contribution margin increased. The revised service guarantees of the menu items allowed changes in their standard recipes to provide for lower cost ingredients. Lower cost ingredients meant reduced cost of the standard recipes and higher Contribution Margin (CM) as the sale price of the menu items remained the same. Higher CM allowed the menu items identified earlier as a Standard become a Star menu item. The revised configuration of the menu item, most importantly its service guarantees turned out to be well positioned.

In a similar fashion all the menu items classified as Standards, or Puzzles or Problems can be repositioned.

Increasing the popularity of menu items classified as Puzzles and Problems, and increasing the profitability of menu items classified as Standards and Problems in different ways ensures that the culinary outlet emerges with more of menu items which would be classified as Star menu items, which is essentially the requirement of the business.

Further, while doing the above exercises it is clear that with the tools of menu engineering, the worth of an existing or revised menu item can be objectively assessed.

4.12 LIMITATIONS OF MENU ENGINEERING

There are a few limitations of menu engineering. These are:

1. Fast and efficient delivery of ordered menu items against individual service guarantees is facilitated by semi-preparation of a pre-planned number of portions of all à la carte menu items. Menu engineering does not respond to items ready for sales, or those that are partially cooked, but not sold.

2. The calculations of menu item cost price are limited to the costs mentioned in the Standard Recipe Card. The inputs are sometimes inaccurate and approximate.

3. The menu engineering process, by itself, does not accurately point to portions of food items lost due to spoilage or unauthorized consumption.

Notes:

(i) Production of à la carte menu items should be recorded in food production registers regularly. The record can be maintained digitally.

(ii) The synchronized study of such a food production record and the menu engineering reports of the day would definitely help in the identification of the number of portions that have not been accounted for inherently indicating their unauthorized consumption. Future discrepancies can be prevented through suitable management actions.

(iii) The synchronized study of the records and reports would ensure high accountability from food production personnel. These records and reports are as follows:

- The forecast of the food production quantities.
- The records of the actual food production quantities.
- The menu engineering reports.

The menu engineering process is advantageous to culinary business in many ways, and the limitations are just a few. Through a combination of sheer experience, and study of menu engineering reports of each day, a chef or a food & beverages manager can keep the menu and menu revisions profitable to the business.

(For the methods of forecasting quantities of food production see Module 10: "Economics of Food Production and Food Service".)

4.13 COMPUTERIZED MENU MANAGEMENT

Culinary concepts start with assumptions of the market conditions. The talent and skills of the chefs ensure that the business starts making profits and sufficient clientele comes into the business.

Essentially, culinary business must reinvent itself. A very important part of the success of any culinary business is the capability of the management to define guidelines for its continued commercial success.

The most important tool of culinary business is the menu. Menus must evolve in terms of the profitability and popularity of the menu items. The right approach to achieve that would be menu engineering led. Menu engineering is the approach the hospitality industry has used to identify the requirements and reposition menus for enhanced profitability and enhanced popularity of the menu items. Therefore, menu management is essentially menu engineering and vice versa.

The Menu engineering process can be handled manually as explained already, or through the use of computers. Computerized menu engineering systems depend upon software created to exhibit the entire menu engineering process. The computerized menu engineering **output** is composed of the following reports:

1. The Food Cost Worksheet.
2. The Menu Engineering Worksheet.
3. The Menu Item Analysis.
4. The Menu Mix Analysis.

5. The Menu Engineering Summary.

6. The Four-Box Analysis.

7. The Menu Engineering Graph/Pie Chart.

These reports are essentially establishing relationships between various menu items in terms of profitability and popularity at-a-glance. The computerized menu engineering systems are therefore a logical extension of understanding of the menu engineering process done manually or through Microsoft Excel sheet calculations.

The computer software allows faster and instant calculations and presentation of required data. Just as manual calculations reveal various cost, value and efficiency data, computer software ensures faster and accurate data presentation of the same. The computerized menu engineering software application supports evaluation of decisions regarding current and future menu pricing, design, and contents. To identify weaknesses of menu items in terms of their profitability and popularity the computerized system is easier, faster and accurate.

With the computerized system it is easier to evaluate new menu items in relation to existing or earlier menu items. The computerization process identifies the quantum by which a new menu item is better than the earlier one, either in terms of profitability or popularity. Computerized menu engineering systems further support the possibilities of repackaging and representing menu items, as is done for handling menu items classified as Standards and converting them into menu items known as Stars.

In a similar fashion as the manual menu engineering process, the computerized version allows for instant understanding of how to increase value to the customer. It helps to identify the price points and menu mixes with which a culinary business can maximize its profitability. This directly ensures balancing the **menu pricing structure** to arrive at the most profitable price to assign to a menu item.

The computerized menu engineering system identifies each menu item and examines its potential to be retained, replaced, re-priced or repositioned on the menu. In terms of à *la carte* business, computerized menu engineering system identifies positives or errors of production levels. This activity supports possibilities of cost reductions.

All the above points relate to a computerized menu engineering system's capabilities to evaluate the success of a menu change and to further understand the relative success of the culinary outlet and menu product line in relation to the price points of the outlet and similar offers in the market place.

An important guideline for all statistical work is to use as large a sample size as is possible. Manual calculations or those done through Microsoft Excel sheets limit the sample size. Menu engineering software allows as large a sample size as is available. As the days of a business year or a business month progress, the sample size can be made larger and still larger. The menu engineering reports are much more accurate. In addition, computerized menu engineering allows for record and storage of data for many years. The data can be placed on "cloud" and used later. It can also be accessed from another geographical location.

The computerized menu engineering applications are dependent on entering all the information about the menu items which supports the calculations into the software program's database, for example:

- The figures of total number of portions sold each day during the entire study period in respect of each menu item.

- The sale price of the menu item from the outlet menu.

- The food cost per portion from the standard recipe cost calculations.

Menu interface with other computerized systems, for example, the POS (the point-of-sale system) supports exchange of the above data to the menu engineering software. The above minimal inputs are sufficient to generate the entire lot of computerized reports listed above. Following the entering of this data into the software program the software's output represents each menu item in light of its Menu Mix (MM), which can be attributed to the marketing success of the menu; and Contribution Margin (CM), which can be attributed to the pricing success of the menu.

The computerized menu engineering process continues with decisive examination of each menu item through the generation of the reports listed earlier.

4.14   END OF MODULE NOTES

4.14.1   Cost-effectiveness Through Menu Engineering

The menu of a culinary outlet is its most important business tool. The menu should be designed well. The culinary product offer listing the menu items must relate to the culinary concept. The success or failure of a culinary operation is directly linked to the menu. Periodic examination and 'engineering' of the menu ensures commercial success of the culinary business. The understanding, **key areas** and **success factors** in relation to menu engineering are:

1. The menu represents the culinary concept, the culinary product offer and indicates the price points of each of the menu items.

2. It is important to **regularly** examine the menu items in relation to the concept and the marketing promises.

3. It is imperative to sell **all** the menu items and sell them profitably.

4. Operators must regularly study the menu engineering reports.

5. Large sample size of the sales study is vital.

6. Menu items cannot be evaluated individually.

7. The relative profitability and relative popularity of each of the menu items should be increased through value additions and strategic actions.

8. If required changes should be made in

    (a) the composition and/or presentation of menu/menu item, and/or

    (b) the price points.

9. Foot-falls into the business should be increased through focus on marketing and repositioning.

10. Service guarantees should be strictly adhered to.

4.14.2   The Successful Culinary "Engineer"

1. **Re**-examines the quality and delivery benchmarks of each menu item.

2. **Re**-prices selected menu items if the market presents the opportunity.

3. **Re**-designs the composition of service guarantees of the menu items as and when required.

4. **Re**-locates the menu item on the menu if possible.

5. **Re**-positions the menu item with fresh inputs like menu item description to attract customer's attention.

6. **Re**-markets the menu items through intrinsic marketing promises.

7. **Re**-trains food service personnel on the finer nuances and inherent positives of the menu items for the purpose of up selling initiatives.

4.14.3 Weighted Average

Weighted average is an average in which each quantity to be averaged is assigned a weight. These weights determine the relative importance of each quantity on the average.

4.14.4 Adjustments of Food & Beverages Menu Items

The information received from the data of various menu engineering worksheets and reports present enormous support to the requirements of re-pricing menu items and also to the quality and economic connotations of food production.

The requirement of converting all menu items of a menu into Star menu items throws **challenges** and **also opportunities** to chefs for the following:

1. To introduce objective financial and culinary accountability in the kitchens.
2. To prevent the losses arising out of overproduction.
3. To prevent revenue leakages in terms of unauthorized consumption.
4. To ensure prevention of malpractices at the outlet level in connection with raising of customer's check.
5. To implement the changes required in the service guarantee parameters.
6. To upgrade the standard purchase specifications.
7. To retain supremacy of the menu concept in the market, in terms of quality, profitability, and popularity.

4.14.5 Nomenclature

Menu engineering and its applications are used globally. However, in a few countries **Standards** are known as **Plowhorses** or **Workhorses**; and **Problems** are known as **Dogs**. The other two names, i.e., **Stars** and **Puzzles** remain the same.

4.14.6 Unexplored Frontiers of Menu Engineering: Understanding and Applications

Menu is a generic word. All types of business whether in the manufacturing sector or in the FMCG sector have menus. The generic meaning of 'menu' relates to the product or product line offer. Sale price of individual items on such menus are listed. In continuation, the number of units of each item sold can be established. The business must find a way to accurately calculate the cost price of individual items.

The essential elements of menu engineering are:
1. Cost price of individual item.
2. Sale price of individual item.
3. The number of units sold.

The menu engineering applications can be used for all such business where the three elements are known or can be calculated. Utilizing the elements of profitability and popularity, the applications of menu engineering can be used for any business.

5

CULINARY MATERIALS MANAGEMENT: THE CONCEPT

Essence of the Module

This module deals with the understanding of the concept of culinary materials management. The mainstay of any culinary business is the cost-effectiveness of operations. The module identifies the structural pillars of materials handling.

Module Objectives and Competencies
After going through this module the reader would be competent to: 1. Explain the concept of materials management. 2. Detail the aims and objectives of culinary materials management. 3. Discuss the benefits and financial gains of efficient culinary materials management.

5.1 INTRODUCTION TO THE MATERIALS MANAGEMENT CONCEPT

The important **aspects** of the materials management system are 'materials', 'time', and 'space'. The operation of the materials management system aims to overcome the problems of 'supply', 'distance' and 'time', in order to obtain product for the minimum cost under the constraint of established benchmarks of food production and food service.

5.2 DEFINING MATERIALS MANAGEMENT

Materials management is to obtain the right quantity of materials, of the right quality, from the right source, at the right time, for the right price.

Materials management can further be qualified as the organization, planning, implementation, and control of the procurement and movement process of all materials activities needed to ensure the production of the finished culinary product, and its sales under prescribed service guarantees of the business. This means that materials management is directly involved with the activities of many **functional areas** including purchasing, receiving, storing, issuing; as well as those of **operational areas** like food production planning, food pre-production, food production and of food service. Efficient materials management requires selection of the 'right' suppliers of culinary ingredients.

Functional areas must be kept integrated for value addition as well as cost-effectiveness. Each functional area has forward and backward linkages and integration with another functional area. Culinary materials management is a cycle of operations. Cost-effectiveness of each of the functional and operational area is important for the overall cost-effectiveness of the culinary business. (The reader may like to read the process chart **(Exhibit 40)** entitled "Cycle of Strength: Cost-effective Culinary Operations" on **p. 240.**)

Controls of one functional area often overlap that of another. The purchase system is broader and often includes functions of the receiving and supplier-coordination. The perishable nature of supplies introduces possibilities of manipulation and malpractices within the purchasing and receiving functions and must be controlled. Overlapping of controls is true recognition of the cycle of strength.

5.3   AIMS & OBJECTIVES OF CULINARY MATERIALS MANAGEMENT

- Provisioning of materials in specified quantity in a cost-effective manner.
- Ensuring materials quality required by the food production department.
- Maintenance of supplies in line with the production requirements and in time.
- Minimizing investments in storage and supply-line.
- Maintaining high inventory turnover.
- Maintaining low inventories.

5.4   CHARACTERISTICS OF CULINARY MATERIALS MANAGEMENT

The chef/operator/investor must understand the characteristics of culinary materials management. Materials management for any culinary business is unlike materials management of other industries. The distinction is due to the following reasons.

5.4.1   Perishable Nature of the Business

(a) **Popularity and perishability of the *à la carte* menu items:**   Each business has products to sell. For culinary business the products to sell are the menu items. The number of portions of menu items ordered by customers indicates their popularity. (The reader may like to revisit the understanding of popularity in Module 4: "Menu Engineering: Culinary Business Analytics".)

It is impossible to accurately estimate the number of portions of menu items that would be sold in a business day. A chef's forecast can only come nearer to the actual. The popularity of each menu item is subject to a customer's forever-changing needs and preferences. (Methodologies to forecast the approximate number of à la carte portions that would be required for a day's business have been detailed in Module 10: "Economics of Food Production and Food Service".)

The sales of menu items are designed with marketing promises in the nature of service guarantees. These service guarantees are highly objective in their design. An important service guarantee is the obligation to serve the menu item within a guaranteed time frame. This obligation requires semi-preparedness of the menu items in numbers which would be more than the possible number of portions that would be ordered. If unsold within the day or within the reasonable shelf life, the semi-prepared menu items are considered "over-produced" and unfit for sales. Costs have been incurred for the preparations. This is the understanding of the perishability of the à la carte menu items.

(b) **Popularity and perishability of the banquet menu items:**   Quality food production is not only the result of the usage of right ingredients and standard recipes but is also the result of the skills of the culinary masters. Right quality of food production always involves "cooking from the heart" – with love, care and with due diligence to the nuances involved in any food production. The right quality of culinary preparations therefore requires time and effective production planning.

Chefs and operators regularly 'inform' the immediate geographical scene as well as existing and potential customers of their knowledge, skills and quality benchmarks through regular and well-pitched food promotions and food festivals. In chain operations, the directions and inputs of the corporate management supports these special events and freshness of culinary offers.

The banquet customer is increasingly aware of the same and places fresh demands on the chefs and operators in terms of menu items from these special events. The agreed-to menu for any banquet therefore does not necessarily conform to formatted banquet menus. Ordering items from multiple cuisines for a banquet is very often the custom.

In addition and typically for banquet functions in India, the customer invariably provides lesser numbers of guests expected as minimum guarantee figures. The uncertainty of the total number of guests and not knowing what items would be consumed more the chefs tend to produce more of each of the menu items than would possibly be consumed. Certain quantities of each of the menu items prepared for banquets are always left over. This is the understanding of the perishability of the banquet menu items.

(c) **Perishability of the ingredients:** Culinary business involves dealing with highly perishable product line. All foods are perishable. Some are highly perishable, and deteriorate fast while others take time to deteriorate. Statutory laws stipulate usage of food products and raw ingredients within a certain time limit.

Large percentages of food products and raw ingredients received daily are those that require temperature control before and after receiving. The food products and raw ingredients should be transferred to proper and designated storage spaces immediately on receipt. The supplies being perishable would deteriorate if they are left at room temperature at the receiving area.

5.4.2   Unauthorized Consumption, Spoilage and Wastage

Due to the edible nature of the food products and raw ingredients, theft by employees is possible post receiving. In addition to being perishable food products and raw ingredients are expensive. Poor preparation styles, incorrect meat fabrication, overproduction, wastage and unauthorized consumption add to the costs of the business.

5.4.3   High Customer Interface

Characteristically, culinary business succeeds due to the high customer interface. Customers are fond of talking to the chefs and operators and vice versa. The relationship between the producer of the culinary products (chef), the service staff (seller) and the customer gradually moves into the realm of personal rapport. This is unlike other industries wherein the producer may never meet the customer.

Chefs take pride in producing special culinary preparations for customers to showcase their skills and/or their affection for the relationship. The special preparations often require ingredients which are not normally purchased by the business. The purchases of such ingredients are categorized as 'emergency purchases' or 'open-market purchases'. Such purchases cannot be controlled by benchmarks such as standard purchase specifications and contracted cost per unit.

5.4.4   Special Events

Special events like food promotions and food festivals help in advertising:

- the diverse talents of the chefs beyond the à la carte menus; and
- the outlet's ability to create fresh culinary products.

The ingredients required for such occasions are procured from 'open-market resources'.

5.4.5 Usage of 'A' Value Products and Raw Ingredients

Culinary business is typical and different from other manufacturing business in the matter of using food products and raw ingredients which are either very expensive, or highly perishable, or those that have subjective accountability. These 'A' value food products and raw ingredients are few in number, but carry high costs. (The reader may revisit complete understanding of 'A' value food products and raw ingredients on **p. 17** in Module 1: "The Culinary Business".)

5.4.6 Subjective Nature of Food Preparation

Manufacturing and other business involve objective and specific use of components to produce the final product and make it ready for sales. All forms of quality conscious culinary business have also moved towards objectivity in food production. However, cuisine would always continue to have an element of subjectivity due to the differences in skills and creative impulses of different chefs.

5.5 BENEFITS OF AND PROFITS FROM CULINARY MATERIALS MANAGEMENT

Over the years, the concept, principles and benchmarks related to culinary materials management have evolved and progressed positively towards profit-orientation for culinary business. Culinary materials management now supports distinct opportunities to improve profits either through reduction of costs or improved productivity or through a combination of both. Additional profits may be obtained through the adoption of a number of methods, for example:

- Purchasing at comparatively low prices, in exchange for either bulk supplies or security of the contract.
- Ensuring the right quality of raw materials in line with standard purchase specifications – through selection and constant communication with selected suppliers.
- Ensuring continuity of supply – particularly service elements.
- Through timely delivery of ordered materials to occur when required for optimum production and minimizing store inventory levels.

Culinary materials management has been presented in the form of modules, as follows:
- Module 6: "Efficient Management of Purchasing Activities"– detailing the purchasing functions.
- Module 7: "Selecting The Right Supplier"– detailing the supplier selection functions.
- Module 8: "Right Receiving"– detailing the receiving functions.
- Module 9: "Efficient Storing, Inventory Management and Right Issuing"– detailing the storing, inventory management and issuing functions.
- Module 10: "Economics of Food Production and Food Service"–detailing the food pre-production, food production and food service functions.

In-depth study and adherence to the guidance provided in different modules of this book would present opportunities to save on costs. Such adherence would relate to efficient handling of food products and ingredients. A flow chart has been provided as **Exhibit 12 between pp. 86-87** to understand the essence of culinary materials management.

5.6 END OF MODULE NOTES

5.6.1 Understanding the Basics of Culinary Materials Management

The **key areas** and **success factors** in relation to understanding of culinary materials management are listed below:

1. Culinary materials management is the cycle of

   (a) identifying requirements,

   (b) the purchase,

   (c) the receipt,

   (d) right storage,

   (e) correct issues,

   (f) scheduled pre-production,

   (g) food production,

   (h) food service, and

   (i) the payments to the supplier.

   Culinary materials management therefore extends to the sale of finished culinary products in the shape of menu items.

2. The culinary business must ensure introduction of processes for continuous market research for superior infrastructure and cost-effective solutions.

3. Culinary materials management deals with purchasing:

   (a) The materials in the right quantities — sufficient for the production, for the immediate future and for safety.

   (b) The materials of the right quality — quality dictated by the outlet's concept, menu, and menu items — governed by standard purchase specifications, neither higher nor lower quality than required by standard recipes and adhering to statutory laws.

   (c) The materials from the right source — from the right supplier for the purchaser's business. Identifying new vendors and fresh supply sources are key enablers of the process.

   (d) At the right time — in time, as scheduled by the process of food production. Investments in inventories and supply-line should be minimum; inventory turnovers into usage/production should be high.

   (e) For the right price — the business should pay an agreed price against the agreed quality defined by standard purchase specifications.

   Any pressure against the above would work contrary to the cost-effectiveness of operations.

6

EFFICIENT MANAGEMENT OF PURCHASING ACTIVITIES

Essence of the Module

The module deals with efficiencies in the management of large number of activities in the purchase department and those linked to it. It establishes the equation between the 'right' purchasing processes and cost-effectiveness of operations. The module also identifies the process to create the quality and quantity parameters of all types of purchases to be made for the culinary business.

Module Objectives and Competencies

After going through this module the reader would be competent to:

1. Define 'right' purchasing.

2. Detail the scope of purchasing activities.

3. Identify the aims and objectives of efficient system for a purchase department.

4. Discuss an efficient system for a purchase department.

5. Determine purchasing needs.

6. Discuss the purchase of products with 'right' quality and in 'right' quantities.

7. Explain the meaning of right quality.

8. Identify the considerations in fixing quality levels of purchase of food products, ingredients and other requirements.

9. Discuss standard purchase specifications, their requirements and their development process.

   (a) Show the process of development of standard purchase specifications for food products, ingredients and other requirements.

   (b) Delineate the role of various departments in developing standard purchase specifications.

   (c) Establish the methodologies of developing standard purchase specifications.

10. Define the term 'right quantity' in respect of ordering of supplies and establish the process of ordering the right quantities of food products, ingredients and other purchases.

   (a) Discuss the role of the menu and the culinary offer in determining quantities to be ordered.

   (b) Discuss the change in quantities to be ordered when the menu introduces fresh items.

   (c) Discuss the change in quantities to be ordered in case menu items lose popularity.

11. Discuss and detail the ordering processes.

   (a) Delineate the process of determination of quantities of perishables and highly perishables and highly perishables to be ordered.

   (b) Discuss and detail the ordering process of perishables and non-perishables.

   (c) Delineate the relevant flow plan for purchase of perishables.

(d) Discuss and delineate the Perishables Order Sheet, and the Butchery Order Sheet and their respective uses.

(e) Delineate the relevant flow plan for purchase of non-perishables.

12. Discuss the Purchase Requisition and delineate its specimen.

13. Discuss the Purchase Order System.

(a) Detail the contents of a Purchase Order and delineate its specimen.

(b) Discuss the Open Purchase Order and identify the reasons for its issue.

14. Discuss the One-Stop Shopping system and its advantages and disadvantages.

15. Discuss the centralized purchasing system and its advantages and disadvantages.

16. Discuss controls in the purchasing functions.

17. Identify common malpractices in the purchasing system and detail the remedial and preventive actions.

18. Detail the various means to reduce the cost of purchasing functions.

19. Identify the primary, secondary and tertiary duties and responsibilities of the purchase department.

6.1 RIGHT PURCHASING: DEFINITION

Purchasing for a culinary business can be defined as functions concerned with the search, selection, purchase, and receipt of food products, ingredients and other requirements for food production and efficient food service.

Right purchasing functions require setting up of benchmarks at each stage and the integration of these benchmarks with an efficient audit trail. The benchmarks should be periodically reviewed based on conclusions from the audit highlights, menu engineering processes, changing business scenario and upgradation of the culinary offers. The benchmarks should be upgraded or maintained.

An efficient purchase activity is a **cost saving programme** and **maximizes profits**. It is also a series of conscious management efforts in an efficient operation leading to customer satisfaction. It is mandatory for culinary business to adhere to the Food Safety and Standards Act. It is prudent to follow industry practices such as HACCP guidelines.

6.2 SCOPE OF PURCHASING ACTIVITIES

The purchase department is a hub of activities for the purposes of the various departments of the business. Right purchasing initiates the processes leading to enhanced values to be provided to the customer. Right purchasing also controls the profitability of the business.

Traditionally, purchasing function was a minimal activity. Operation managers viewed it as a support function to purchase those food products, raw ingredients and other requirements of the culinary business. The focus of cost controls was on food production and thereafter, and not necessarily before the point of food production.

Purchasing has evolved to become a full range of management activities. Purchasing has become a vital back-end operation. Evolved management systems have detected an opportunity to save costs through efficient purchasing functions. The purchasing systems have evolved to create competitive supply markets to ensure satisfaction to the end-customer.

Managements have recognized the need to consider both cost and quality aspects of the purchasing decisions. A price and quality relationship has been established in the purchase system. As an evolution other aspects of purchasing such as price negotiations, creative pricing plans, quality benchmarks and detailed knowledge about the markets are formalized.

All purchasing activities should **suit the business** and should take advantage of:

1. **Efficiency of suppliers** in terms of their price, product quality, and delivery performance.
2. Monthly, quarterly, or yearly **fixed rate** contracts.
3. Computerized property management systems, which take charge of **materials management.**
4. **Analysis based** management systems like Six-Sigma which ensure cost-effectiveness, incorporating efficient methods of management and maximum quality output.
5. Latest **cost accountancy initiatives** or **business application software,** for example, SAP.
6. **Just in time** purchases whenever possible.
7. **Market research.** The research could be for:

   - New products in the market.
   - Higher quality of products of user-friendly characteristics – convenience products.
   - Cost-effective solutions.
   - Products, implements or equipment ensuring greater efficiencies, higher degree of safety of operations, labour and time-saving values and quality output.

Purchases should be made:
- Strictly of what is required in terms of type of supplies and quantities.
- To maintain low inventories in stores.
- To ensure high turnover of stocks from stores.
- To avoid stock-outs and emergency purchases of these items.
- Strictly in accordance with the decided quality standards and strictly as per decided standard purchase specifications – no more and no less.

The focus of purchasing activities should also be to develop, evolve and enforce use of benchmarks. Examples of benchmarks are standard purchase specifications for all materials required by the food production or consuming as well as service departments. The usage of the **right** standard purchase specifications would ensure **maximum yield** and **quality production.**

Purchasing of food products and ingredients required for culinary business is very different from purchasing other non-food products. This is because of the perishability of the food products and raw ingredients. It is vital to maintain different timings for handling of perishables, highly perishables and "stores" products at the receiving department. The purchase department must ensure that selected suppliers agree to the allocated timings and are in a position to supply at these timings.

The aims and objectives of an efficient system for a purchase department have been comprehensively listed in **Exhibit 13 (p. 90)**.

6.3 EFFICIENT SYSTEM FOR A PURCHASE DEPARTMENT (Exhibit 14, p. 91)

The customer is becoming increasingly intelligent and selective. He desires value for money. He is intelligently able to compare products and culinary offerings at different outlets, and reach **his conclusion of value for his money.** The supply markets are becoming increasingly expensive. The continuous additional burden cannot be borne by prospective customers. An efficient purchase system controls

EXHIBIT 13: Aims & Objectives of an Efficient System for a Purchase Department

1.	Material Purchasing	(a) Purchasing of food products, raw ingredients and other requirements for the consuming and service departments – of the right quality, in the right quantity, and in time. (b) Ensuring uninterrupted supplies for the consuming departments.
2.	Quality Improvement and Quality Management	Through evolving standard purchase specifications in line with evolving values of the culinary concept: ▪ Through new sources of supplies. ▪ Through efficient and continuous market research.
3.	Cost Management	(a) Purchasing food products, raw ingredients and other requirements at the right price – lowest total cost against standard purchase specifications. (b) Protecting the cost structure of the business and achieving purchasing activities at the lowest administrative costs.
4.	Supplier Management	(a) Sourcing the right supplier who would meet the requirements of the culinary business, and purchasing from him. (b) Through development of suppliers. Through integration of supplier's strengths with the business objectives. (c) Managing good business relations with suppliers.
5.	Inventory Management	(a) Maintaining low inventories in stores. (b) Ensuring high inventory turnover from stores into food production. (c) Minimizing financial investments in storages and supply line.
6.	Office & Records Management	(a) Keeping of statistical records. (b) Maintaining records for future audits. (c) Timely payment of suppliers enabled through accurate and updated record-keeping and processing of bills. (d) Mandatory adherence to statutory laws through efficient management of records.

all the components of the product purchase process and ensures economic and operational benefits including **higher yields** from purchases. It ensures that the customer is not burdened with costs that can be controlled. Therefore, an efficient purchase system has a direct bearing on the value received by a customer.

Purchase system is a cycle of operations with other components being supplier management, receiving, storing, inventory management, issuing and payments to the supplier. Properly designed purchase systems ensure strengths and report backs from each point of activity. An efficient system for a purchase department supports culinary business:

- On selection of the right supplier.
- On decisions to purchase the right quality products relating to the standard purchase specifications.
- To determine the right quantities to purchase.
- To decide the right time to purchase.
- To maintain effective inventory management.
- To maintain the cost structure.

EXHIBIT 14: Essentials of an Efficient System for a Purchase Department

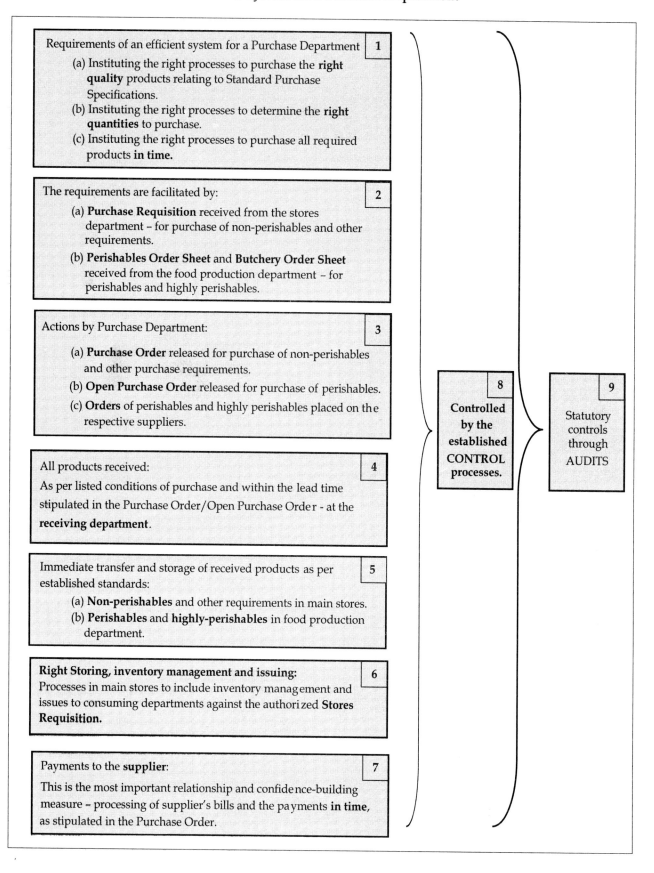

Requirements of an efficient system for a Purchase Department   **1**

(a) Instituting the right processes to purchase the **right quality** products relating to Standard Purchase Specifications.

(b) Instituting the right processes to determine the **right quantities** to purchase.

(c) Instituting the right processes to purchase all required products **in time**.

The requirements are facilitated by: **2**

(a) **Purchase Requisition** received from the stores department – for purchase of non-perishables and other requirements.

(b) **Perishables Order Sheet** and **Butchery Order Sheet** received from the food production department – for perishables and highly perishables.

Actions by Purchase Department: **3**

(a) **Purchase Order** released for purchase of non-perishables and other purchase requirements.

(b) **Open Purchase Order** released for purchase of perishables.

(c) **Orders** of perishables and highly perishables placed on the respective suppliers.

All products received: **4**

As per listed conditions of purchase and within the lead time stipulated in the Purchase Order/Open Purchase Order - at the **receiving department**.

Immediate transfer and storage of received products as per established standards: **5**

(a) **Non-perishables** and other requirements in main stores.

(b) **Perishables** and **highly-perishables** in food production department.

Right Storing, inventory management and issuing: **6**
Processes in main stores to include inventory management and issues to consuming departments against the authorized **Stores Requisition.**

Payments to the **supplier**:   **7**

This is the most important relationship and confidence-building measure – processing of supplier's bills and the payments **in time**, as stipulated in the Purchase Order.

8 Controlled by the established **CONTROL** processes.

9 Statutory controls through AUDITS

- To purchase all the requirements at the right price – lower total cost.
- To achieve purchasing activities at the lowest administrative costs.

Computerization and property management systems aid in reduction of human error. These also enhance efficiency and pace of the purchase system. Controls, guidelines and standard operating procedures are built-in at each step of the purchasing system. These help in matters of efficiency and transparency. In addition, a separate department entitled 'Controls' reviews and checks the purchase as well as consumption activities.

The purchase system is used to purchase food products and ingredients required for the business. It is also used to purchase items of the nature of non-food, for example:

(i) Furniture and at-site equipment.

(ii) Kitchen and kitchenette equipment.

(iii) Glassware, silverware, cutlery and crockery.

(iv) Music gear.

(v) Horticulture related items.

(vi) Stationery items.

(vii) Flowers and decorations.

(viii) Linen and uniforms.

(ix) Cleaning and maintenance supplies.

(x) Solid fuel, cooking gas and charcoal.

6.4 PURCHASING THE RIGHT QUALITY AND QUANTITY

The most important purchasing needs for a culinary business are purchasing the right quality of supplies, purchasing them in the right quantity and purchasing them in time. It is vital for the reader to understand what is meant by right quality and right quantity. Decision on **right quality and right quantity of products** to be purchased ensures standardization in purchasing functions.

6.4.1 Right Quality

A product or ingredient may have varying values of quality. The business must examine its culinary concept and value proposition and decide on the quality of the food products, raw ingredients and non-food items it requires. Establishing required quality levels of food products, ingredients and other requirements involves the following considerations:

- Keeping the overall positioning of the business and competition in view.
- Keeping the expectations of the customer in view.
- Keeping economic concerns of the business in view.
- Keeping statutory requirements (food laws, etc.) in view.

Therefore, quality is never a fixed standard. Quality of a product is dictated by its market demand and its usage and is nurtured with research and development processes.

The quality values of a product or raw ingredient to be purchased are listed through standard purchase specifications. Understanding of the standard purchase specifications, their importance and development are detailed below.

6.4.2 Standard Purchase Specifications

A purchase specification can be defined as a **statement of needs**. Purchase specifications define what the culinary business wants to buy with its quality parameters and consequently what the supplier is required to provide. The success of purchasing activity relies on the specification being a true and accurate statement of the buyer's requirements. Therefore, the specifications should be clearly and logically stated.

Specifications should not over-specify the quality requirements. Over-specification of quality benchmarks can unnecessarily and unintentionally increase costs. Well defined managerial efforts relate to specific quality requirements set forth for every item purchased.

Culinary business can be of any type and size. (The reader can revisit the understanding of the types and sizes of a culinary business in Module 1: "The Culinary Business"). Developing standard purchase specifications is essential for all types and sizes of business.)

The standard purchase specifications are individual to business. A product or ingredient may have varying values of standard purchase specifications from one business to another. This is because standard purchase specifications must match the quality as per the **culinary concept,** the **value proposition** and sometimes the **market conditions.** A fresh business must start with provisional purchase specifications. These provisional purchase specifications may be aligned to the purchasing norms of the culinary industry. The provisional purchase specifications must evolve into standard purchase specifications when all aspects of quality, value proposition and market conditions are checked and built in.

In case a business repositions itself with a different concept or menu offerings it would necessarily mean introduction of new menu items and change in the value proposition. Developing new standard purchase specifications would be vital for the new food products and raw ingredients.

The following are the **aims and objectives** of instituting standard purchase specifications:

(a) For the business to purchase a standard product which would meet the desired quality for further production/usage.

(b) To establish a suitable buying benchmark for a particular product.

(c) To help in setting the price of a product.

(d) To communicate the requirements in specific terms, in writing to the supplier.

(e) To ensure a transparent and ambiguity-free purchase process.

(f) For purposes of control at the receiving department.

(g) To refer to in case of dispute.

Suppliers are required to quote their prices against the standard purchase specifications. In a buyer's market many suppliers quote for the same product. After due negotiations with all possible suppliers, the purchase price of all requirements of the business must be fixed, ideally in relation to a fixed-time supply period.

Apart from being a means of identifying the goods required, a specification will form part of any future contract that might result from offers-to-supply received from suppliers. Standard purchase specifications are therefore part of the financial and quality control systems of a business.

Grouping of standard purchase specifications: A typicality of culinary business is that standard purchase specifications for a range of similar items are bunched together in groups, for example:

- For all categories of vegetables.
- For all categories of fruits.

- For all categories of seafood.
- For all categories of dairy products.
- For all categories of meats.

Suppliers supply the whole range of each category. In other words the needs of the culinary business are grouped.

Purchasing food products and raw ingredients against standard purchase specifications allows for the following **benefits:**

- Uniformity and consistency in raw product quality irrespective of the source of purchase.
- Standard saleable yields.
- Creation of a standard end product.
- Maintenance of desired food cost.
- Removal of ambiguity and arbitrariness.
- Encouragement to many suppliers to quote thereby increasing competitiveness, right quality and reduced costs. This is particularly applicable to culinary business placed in a buyer's market.

In case of non-food items standard purchase specifications contain technical and performance specifications in addition. Technical specifications contain details of fabrication and safety requirements. Scaled drawings are often provided as an extension of the standard purchase specifications especially for equipment and furniture. The drawings indicate the fabrication details along with measurements.

Standard purchase specifications should be made for each item being purchased by the business. The specification should contain the following concise description of the measurable characteristics:

- Definition and/or description.
- Brand name of the product.
- Grade.
- Weight, size, count and colour.
- Unit against which price should be quoted.
- Expiry dates.
- Special note, if any.

In addition to the above measurable characteristics the standard purchase specifications should mention the following information wherever applicable:

- Requirement of hold "safe" guidelines under provisions of the Food Safety and Standards Act of India.
- Inspection and test procedures to determine conformance with the standard purchase specifications – for both food and non-food items.
- Instructions as to packaging and labelling of products.
- Any special methods of production or manufacture that is required at the supplier's end.

Certain specifications of the nature of performance specifications describe the usage for which the specified material or equipment is intended, and how well the material or equipment should perform. The supplier is free to suggest viable alternative brand name or "equal" for the product.

6.4.3 Standard Purchase Specifications: The Development Process

The process of developing standard purchase specifications for a new business often starts with aligning them with prevalent industry practices. There are two important parts of the development process for formation of standard purchase specifications. These two parts synergize with:

1. The pre-launch and launch phase of a new business.
2. The post-launch phase of the business.

The Pre-launch and Launch Phase of a New Business

Development of standard purchase specifications for **new products** often coincides with the launch of a new business. The following are the steps in the process of developing standard purchase specifications for **new products:**

(a) Writing the characteristics of all the requirements and categorizing the same into groups, for example, vegetables, fruits, seafood, meats, dairy, bread products, imported items, delicatessen products, etc. The experience of the chefs and other food service operators is invaluable in writing these characteristics.

(b) Giving a verbal description of the product characteristics to reputed suppliers of similar product line and stressing its use.

(c) Market survey and sample gathering. Observations and vetting the written characteristics.

(d) Writing the specifications using the written characteristics, samples and the supplier's inputs.

(e) Checking the written specifications with suppliers **again** for effectiveness of the written matter. Very often the suppliers are in a position to offer the written standard purchase specifications of similar types of business to which they are supplying.

(f) The specifications are modified as necessary.

Copies of the written standard purchase specifications are forwarded to the eligible suppliers of each category. The suppliers are invited to indicate their quotations based on the specifications. The selected suppliers start supplying the products before the launch of the business and continue the process during the post-launch phase.

The Post-launch Phase of the Business

Conducting yield tests on ingredients is a regular process for the business. Yield tests are conducted to assess the saleable values of each raw item. This is particularly so for the non-vegetarian supplies and other 'A' value products. During the first few weeks of the business, the ingredients are subjected to yield tests. If any ingredient is noticed to be of poor saleable yield as per the specifications, the specifications are amended. Other alternatives are to increase the selling price of the menu item which requires such ingredients. If the menu item loses its popularity due to its increased selling price, it can be removed from the menu.

During the course of the first operating year, the quality of the supplies is observed, and purchase specifications are amended if required. Specifications are firmed up at the next year's contract-awarding opportunity.

In case the menu items change due to change of menu, the process is repeated for any fresh requirements. In case the business repositions itself and/or changes its culinary concept, or enhances its values proposition, the values of these specifications change. The chefs, the purchase department personnel and the food service operators get together again to redo the standard purchase specifications. These are the linkages of these specifications with food production.

All benchmarks are examined periodically. Standard purchase specifications are important benchmarks of a business and are dealt with accordingly. Like any other benchmarks these specifications are either maintained or upgraded.

6.4.4 Standard Purchase Specifications: Role of Different Departments

The process of development of standard purchase specifications involves inputs from many operational and support departments. The main role for the development process is that of the user department. The efforts of the user department are supported by the purchase department and the corporate headquarters in case of chain operations. In addition, the role of the supplier in the development process is often invaluable. (The specific role of the above-mentioned departments is shown in **Exhibit 15, p. 97.**)

Measureable Characteristics for Standard Purchase Specifications

Standard purchase specifications for food products and raw ingredients are developed on the basis of the following **measureable characteristics:**

1. Type.
2. Size.
3. Variety or geographical location.
4. Count per kilogram.
5. Grade.
6. Mandatory temperature when received.
7. Physical characteristics.
8. Physical state when received.
9. Cuts required.
10. Product age.
11. Natural fat percentage.
12. Weight or thickness.
13. Inspection process on receiving.
14. Packing: Size of packing, medium of packing, and drained weight of contents.

(Development of standard purchase specifications has been explained in the **Exhibit 16 on pp. 98-100.**)

Ingredients are represented in the columns. Consolidating the data from each row presents the developed standard purchase specifications, as follows:

Single cream: Cow's milk cream only. Fat content should be above 18%. No fat globules in cream. Should not be yellow in colour or grainy to touch. Should not be sour.

Pomfret whole (large size): Fresh chilled when received. Eyes should be bulging and shiny. Skin should be shiny and smooth. Gills should be bright and red in colour. Tail should be firm and belly should not be swollen and sagging. Weight to be in the range of 350 – 400 gm.

Jumbo prawns: Fresh chilled when received. Firm flesh. Shiny and wet surface. Tail should be springy when touched. Should have a pleasant smell and not bad odour. Shell should be firm and not soggy. The flesh should be bright off white. 5-6 pieces per kilogram.

Crabs: Live with claws tied. Should be heavy and plump. The shell should not be broken in fragments or pieces. 3-4 crabs per kilogram.

EXHIBIT 15: Developing Standard Purchase Specifications: Role of Different Departments

ROLE OF USER DEPARTMENT

(a) For a start-up — the experience values of the Chefs, F&B manager, Outlet manager, Bar manager and team members is vital for the logical setting up of fresh purchase specifications keeping in mind the values of the culinary concept, menu development, menu item identification, recipe development, yield management and continuity of supplies.

(b) For an existing business, the user department examines purchase specifications of an in-use product in the background of supplier performances, changes in the culinary concept or the possibility of cost-reduction in any manner. It is important to re-examine the specification to ascertain if it describes the required quality correctly. The specification should be upgraded, if required, or maintained.

ROLE OF THE PURCHASE DEPARTMENT

The purchase department is responsible for market research and to obtain necessary information to support the process to develop standard purchase specifications. The purchase department contributes by studying market data, procures samples of products for analysis and selection by the user department. The department arranges for trial orders. The samples support firming up of the earlier drafted tentative purchase specifications. The purchase department ensures that the product is available from many sources. This ensures competition, and cost-effectiveness. The department is in direct contact with the suppliers and the market and its experience in working with qualified suppliers, and evaluation of product samples is imperative towards developing the right standard purchase specifications.

ROLE OF SUPPLIERS

Suppliers are not responsible to develop specifications. Suppliers provide the samples and information to assist in the matter of matching standard specifications for same or similar products which they supply to competition. In addition, they inform about new products about to be launched or those that are already in the market. The suppliers help in reviews and critiques of specifications. Whenever practical, specifications should apply to products offered by more than one supplier.

ROLE OF THE CORPORATE HEADQUARTERS

In a chain operation, senior trained and knowledgeable management personnel of all specialist functions are located at the corporate headquarters. The corporate headquarters acts as a guide for new properties in the matter of creating the standard purchase specifications and also other benchmarks.

EXHIBIT 16: Standard Purchase Specifications

Measureable characteristics	Ingredients			
	Single cream	Pomfret whole large	Prawns jumbo	
Type				
Variety or geographical location	Cow's milk cream only.			
Size/Count per kilogram			5-6 pieces per kilogram.	
Grade				
Mandatory temperature when received		Chilled	Chilled	
Physical characteristics	No fat globules in cream. Should not be yellow in colour or grainy to touch. Should not be sour.	Eyes should be bulging and shiny. Skin should be shiny and smooth. Gills should be bright and red in colour. Tail should be firm and belly should not be swollen and sagging.	Firm flesh. Shiny and wet surface. Tail should be springy when touched. Should have a pleasant smell and not bad odour. Shell should be firm and not soggy. The flesh should be bright off white in colour.	
State when received		Fresh	Fresh	
Cuts required				
Product age				
Natural fat percentage	Fat content should be above 18%			
Weight or thickness		Weight 350 gm – 400 gm		
Inspection process at the receiving				
Packing: Size and medium of packing				
Drained weight of contents				

Measureable characteristics	Ingredients	
	Crab	Tandoori chicken
Type		
Variety or geographical location		
Size/Count per kilogram	3-4 crabs per kilogram	Each chicken to be in the weight range of 600 – 700 gm.
Grade		Chilled
Mandatory temperature when received	Ambient temperature	
Physical characteristics	Should be heavy and plump. The shell should not be broken in fragments or pieces.	Without skin. Should not have bad odour. Neck to be 3 inches long from the carcass. Should be free from deformities. Breasts and legs should be free from cuts, tears and missing skin. Birds to be well developed and of even size distribution. Should not have any broken bones. Should be free from discoloured skin and flesh. Flesh to be plump and fat and should not be dark yellow and mushy.
State when received	Live with claws tied	Fresh
Cuts required		
Product age		
Natural fat percentage		
Weight or thickness		
Inspection process at the receiving		Should not have excess quantities of water. Excess water would be drained off at the receiving.
Packing; Size and medium of packing Drained weight of contents		

Measureable characteristics	Ingredients	
	Beef fillet	Beef fillet
Type		
Variety or geographical location		
Size/Count per kilogram	Each fillet to be in the weight range of 1.3 kg – 1.8 kg	Each fillet to be in the weight range of 1.3 kg – 1.8 kg
Grade		
Mandatory temperature when received	Chilled	Frozen
Physical characteristics	Shiny surface with brick red colour. Meat should be firm, tender with no bad odour. No yellowing of tissues and tendons. When pressure is applied to the fillet with the finger and the thumb then they should penetrate the surface. Excess waste meat attached should be trimmed. Side strip should not be present.	Shiny surface with brick red colour. Meat should be firm, tender with no bad odour. No yellowing of tissues and tendons. Excess waste meat attached should be trimmed. Side strip should not be present.
State when received	Fresh	
Cuts required		
Product age		
Natural fat percentage	Trimmed of excessive fat especially at the head.	Trimmed of excessive fat especially at the head.
Weight or thickness		
Inspection process at the receiving		
Packing: Size and medium of packing Drained weight of contents		

Tandoori Chicken: Fresh chilled when received. Without skin. Should not have bad odour. Neck to be 3 inches long from the carcass. Should be free from deformities. Breasts and legs should be free from cuts, tears and missing skin. Birds to be well developed and of even size distribution. Should not have any broken bones. Should be free from discoloured skin and flesh. Flesh to be plump and fat and should not be dark yellow and mushy. Should not have excess quantities of water. Excess water would be drained off at the receiving. Each chicken to be in the weight range of 600 – 700 gm.

Beef fillet: There are two specifications of beef fillet below - just to illustrate the minute difference. One specification is for fresh beef fillet and the second is for the same in a frozen form.

First specification: Fresh, chilled when received. Shiny surface with brick red colour. Meat should be firm, tender with no bad odour. No yellowing of tissues and tendons. When pressure is applied to the fillet with the finger and the thumb then they should penetrate the surface. Excess waste meat attached should be trimmed. Side strip should not be present. Trimmed of excessive fat especially at the head. Each fillet to be in the weight range of 1.3 – 1.8 kg.

Second specification: Frozen when received. Shiny surface with brick red colour. Meat should be firm, tender with no bad odour. No yellowing of tissues and tendons. Excess waste meat attached should be trimmed. Side strip should not be present. Trimmed of excessive fat especially at the head. Each fillet to be in the weight range of 1.3 – 1.8 kg.

6.4.5 Right Quantity

It is vital for culinary business to safeguard the health of the customers. Food products and raw ingredients are perishable. All food products and raw ingredients deteriorate with the passage of time. Some foods do not exhibit noticeable signs of deterioration. Display of date of expiry on ingredients helps in their timely consumption. Displaying the date of expiry on groceries is mandatory as per the provisions of the Food Safety and Standards Act.

The culinary business should therefore adopt a system that would ensure that only those quantities of food products and raw ingredients are purchased that will be needed immediately or in the immediate future. The useful life of the commodity is one consideration when considering the quantities to purchase.

Purchasing the right quantity of food products and raw ingredients is as essential as purchasing their right quality. Over-ordering results in monies tied up in inventory and unavailable for other operational requirements. Purchasing the right quantities and maintaining of minimum stock levels for perishables, highly perishables as well as for non-perishables is an ideal situation to:

- Reduce food costs – less spoilage, wastage and pilferage.
- Eliminate possibilities of employee theft.
- Reduce required storage space.
- Reduce number of staff to manage food inventories.
- Reduce operational expenses.
- Ensure optimum product quality due to right movement of stocks into food production and usage within the product's shelf life.
- Allow otherwise blocked capital to be used for other operational expenses.

Ordering insufficient quantities of food products and raw ingredients may result in "stock-out" situations, which, in turn, would result in "non-available" menu items and customer dissonance. The purpose of stocking is to allow for:

- Increased popularity of menu items and therefore increase in requirements of its ingredients.
- Delivery delays due to market conditions.
- Other inefficiencies of the supplier.

Role of the Menu and the Culinary Offer in Determining Quantities to Order

The nature, complexity and size of a menu decide the requirements of ingredients and their intended use. The popularity of menu items decides the quantities of raw ingredients to be purchased. As sale of menu items increases, additional quantities of ingredients are required. The reverse is also true.

Food products and raw ingredients of the nature of perishables, highly perishables and groceries are governed by the following:

- The menu inherently holds the concept of the culinary business.
- The menu items are listed under the sub-menu headings.
- Quality of production of menu items is decided by the standard recipes.
- Standard recipes list the ingredients required.
- Ingredients of the nature of perishables are ordered through a Perishable Order Sheet. Ingredients of the nature of highly perishables are ordered through a Butchery Order Sheet.
- Perishables and highly perishables are ordered by the chef to the supplier through the purchase department, but received directly in the food production department from the receiving area.
- The maintenance of sufficient inventories of the perishables and their right usage is the responsibility of the chef.
- Ingredients of the nature of non-perishables are managed by the stores department. This includes their issues to the food production department. It is the responsibility of stores personnel to maintain sufficient quantities of items in the stores. When stocks in stores deplete and reach the ordering point, the stores department raises a Purchase Requisition.

Quantities to Order When the Culinary Concept or the Menu Items Change

When menu items change the purchase quantities also change. Some food products and raw ingredients would be required in additional quantities, some in reduced quantities, and some not required at all. Whenever there is a **change of the menu**, the food products or raw ingredients needed for the earlier menu's demands are sometimes unutilized, and remain in the stores. Sometimes the sale of a particular menu item is lower than expected. Excess stock of food products and ingredients in stores results due to changes in the menu or lower-than-expected popularity of menu items.

Non-moving or slow-moving stocks of such ingredients are utilized by chefs through:

- Special preparations of the day.
- On buffets.
- In banquets.

Chefs should keep the stores and purchase managements informed about the prospect of a menu change, and also the quantities of new ingredients that would be required. To arrive at consumption patterns of food products and raw ingredients and their replenishment through fresh purchases, a collaborative approach is required.

Maintaining a safety or minimum level of food product or ingredient on hand requires buying a quantity above what is actually needed. The purpose of stocking is to allow for delivery delays due to market conditions and other unexpected inefficiencies of the supplier as well as to provide for increased popularity of menu items."

Effect of Reduced Popularity of Menu Items on Quantities to Order

Many factors including market dynamics and increasing per portion selling price of menu items may reduce their popularity and their sale. This would result in lesser production of those menu items and lesser quantities to be purchased. The following are some of the reasons for reduced popularity of menu items:

- Customers come in with expectations of menu items prepared as per their own understanding of preparation styles, and also of the menu item's accompaniments and embellishments. In cases when expectations differ from the menu items served to them, they switch their loyalties to other preparations on the menu on their repeat visits, suiting their "taste imprinting".

- A typicality of culinary business is that most customers do not complain about lowered quality of the ingredients used or the preparation style. On many occasions customers do not appreciate a correctly prepared menu item. However, they switch their ordering preferences to other menu items on their repeat visits. In addition, they often advise their family members, colleagues and friends accordingly.

- Customers perceive other menu items to offer higher values for monies spent by them.

- Customers prefer other menu items with seasonal ingredients.

- Customers notice an increase in per portion selling price of menu items and order other items.

6.5   THE ORDERING PROCESS

Food products and ingredients are divided into two main categories:

1. Perishables.
2. Non-perishables.

6.5.1   Ordering of Perishables

Ingredients of the genre of vegetables, fruits, milk products, etc., are classified as **perishables.** Ingredients of the genre of seafoods, meats, meat products, and preserved meats, etc., are classified as **highly perishables.**

Traditionally, in India, the chefs control the perishables and highly perishables and also their care, usage and ordering. As per the hospitality industry trends perishables and highly perishables are purchased on a daily basis or several times each week.

Receiving and supplier's functions are often limited to six days a week. In addition, markets often close down due to local or political requirements. Extra quantities of perishables are purchased in advance to provide for such **non-supply days.**

Certain culinary business units, depending upon their geographical location, as well as upon whether they are in buyer's market or seller's market, often schedule purchase of **highly** perishables on designated or alternate days. This is specially so for culinary business in hotels. Ordering highly perishables on designated or alternate days supports convenience of their further fabrication into ready-to-use à la carte or banquet portions. The process also allows stock accumulation, which is desirable for a hotel's culinary business. In addition, fabricating highly perishables on designated days supports hygiene and HACCP conditions.

Chefs are responsible to take a daily inventory of perishables and highly perishables, use them strictly on first-in-first-out basis and to decide on the quantities to be ordered. The determination of quantities to be ordered is based on:

- Volume of business on hand and in the immediate future. This is supported by:
  (a) The knowledge of the menus.
  (b) The menu engineering processes.
  (c) Noticing and analyzing trends in business volumes.
  (d) Data and worksheets, for example, the banquet prospectus.

- Quantities in stock checked through physical stock-taking, observation and experience of the chefs.

- Other factors unique to the order period.

The difference in between the quantities the chefs require and the quantities on hand is ordered through the use of Perishables Order Sheet. (The determination of quantities of perishables and highly perishables has been explained in the **Exhibit 17.**)

> **Note:** The chefs normally maintain safety stocks of all perishables and highly perishables. The safety level for each ingredient allows for delays of supplies due to market conditions or/and delivery performances of the supplier. The safety level also allows for unusual and higher-than-estimated consumption, for example, requirements of unannounced banquets.

6.5.2 Ordering of Non-perishables

All food products and ingredients perish with time, and are subject to expiry dates. However, food products and ingredients with a longer shelf life, for example, canned items, spices, oils, staples, etc., are classified as non-perishables. These are considered non-perishables as it is assumed that these would be ordered in just that much quantity as is required by the business, and would be consumed before their expiry dates. It is further assumed that with the right handling, non-perishables won't perish and their full value would be utilized.

The stocking, issuing and ordering of non-perishables is handled by the stores. (The processes of determination of quantities of non-perishables have been taken up in Module 9: "Efficient Storing, Inventory Management and Right Issuing".)

6.5.3 Perishables Order Sheet

Culinary business requires perishables and highly perishables. The Perishables Order Sheet acts as the Purchase Requisition for the food production department. It lists the requirements of the perishables for food production activities of the immediate future.

Quantities of perishables to be ordered are calculated by taking into account normal or increased business, availability of safety-level stocks and the stock-in hand.

Culinary business with many food production units use Perishables Order Sheet with columns assigned for the requirements of each food production unit. The individual requirements are consolidated and the total quantities of each item are communicated to the purchase department for further communication to the suppliers. (The reader can go through a sample of the Perishables Order Sheet **Exhibit 17 between pp. 104-105**).

6.5.4 Butchery Order Sheet

The butchery is called the meat fabrication department in today's business world. However, the department's basic functions remain the same:

- Efficient dissection of all non-vegetarian raw ingredients.
- Yield testing.
- Packing with date and priority tags.
- Issuing to different kitchens.
- Maintaining of sufficient inventory and reordering.
- HACCP controls of all ingredients.
- Maintaining records and answering accountability and audit issues.

To support the purchase process the department prepares a Butchery Order Sheet. (The reader can go through a sample of the Butchery Order Sheet **Exhibit 18 between pp. 106-107**)

6.5.5 Purchase Cycle for Perishables and Highly Perishables

As per the established practices of the Indian hospitality industry, perishables and highly perishables are stored in the food production areas. It is the responsibility of the chef and the kitchen brigade to handle these perishables and highly perishables in terms of:

(a) Their receipt from the receiving department.

(b) Their storage in designated storage places under the right storage conditions.

(c) Their authorized issue within the generic kitchen and speciality kitchens.

(d) Maintaining their stocks as per requirements of the business.

(e) Ordering in time and in the right quantities that are required for the business for the immediate future.

The eight stages in the purchase cycle for perishables and highly perishables are explained below.

(a) **Creation of the 'need' to purchase:** Food pre-production and food production processes have forward integration with expected or actual customer orders of menu items. Large numbers of food pre-production or food production processes take place in a single working day. On initiating these processes existing inventory of perishables and highly perishables depletes. The depletion creates a 'need' to re-stock.

(b) **Assessment of quantities:** Food production department determines the requirements and quantities of perishables and highly perishables to order in a systematic manner. The methodology has been explained earlier in the current module. The perishables and highly perishables are of all types – vegetables and fruits, dairy products, ice creams, eggs & poultry, meats, processed meats, seafood, river fishes.

(c) **The document of requirements:** A Perishables Order Sheet and Butchery Order Sheet are prepared by the food production department. In smaller establishments the Perishables and Butchery Order Sheets are combined.

(d) **The transfer of the Order Sheets:** The Perishables Order Sheet and the Butchery Order Sheet are transferred to the purchase department, with a copy for the receiving department to facilitate the process of receiving. A copy is marked to the finance department for control purposes. The Internet and property management systems have facilitated the preparation as well as e-mail transfer of the order sheets to the purchase department. The purchasing cycle determines the frequency at which products are purchased. The Indian hospitality industry largely follows the six-days-a-week ordering system for perishables and highly perishables. Quantities to order take charge of non-supply days.

(e) **The ordering process:** The designated purchase assistant telephonically announces the requirements and quantities of various perishables and highly perishables to respective suppliers-on-contract. The order sheets are also transferred to designated suppliers through the e-mail system. The supplier has the option of collecting a physical copy of the orders personally or through his employee from the purchase department.

The contract between the culinary business and the supplier is for a designated period of time. Most contracts are for yearly duration. The contract documents constitute the statement of agreed upon parameters of quality, price, the payment schedule, the supply timings and other terms and conditions. The contract documents also specify the inherent authorization of the culinary business to the supplier, specifically for the supplies under his contract. The contract documents include:

- The agreed-to standard purchase specifications of every item of supply.
- The agreed rates per unit of perishables and highly perishables.
- An Open Purchase Order for the supply for the entire contract period.

Each day's order for perishables and highly perishables therefore becomes a contract.

(f) **The delivery of ordered supplies:** On designated days and at designated timings, different suppliers supply the perishables and highly perishables to the receiving department, along with a delivery invoice.

At the receiving department the supplies are checked for quality against the standard purchase specifications for quantity as per the Perishables Order Sheet or Butchery Order Sheet.

Once the supplies are accepted, copies of the delivery invoice of the supplier are signed. The original is retained by the receiving department. The approval of supplier's delivery invoice indicates transfer of ownership and responsibility from the supplier to the purchaser.

(g) **The transfer of supplies:** The perishables and highly perishables are immediately transferred to the food production department directly. These are stored in the designated places/racks in the cold stores/deep freezers or as per the ideal storage conditions for each. Fresh chilled raw meats are dissected immediately, and portion or bulk-packed with date tags to facilitate their issue for food production on a first-in-first-out basis. Frozen raw meats are handled as per the production schedule of the meat fabrication department.

(h) **Records, approval and payments:** The Daily Receiving Report (DRR) and the approved invoices of the supplier are clubbed together and sent to the chef for his acknowledgement. Once countersigned by the chef the DRR and the invoices are sent to the finance department. Property management systems have enabled the DRR to be sent through the e-mail.

The controls section of the finance department cross checks, and authorizes the Bills Payment section of the finance department to make payments. The payments are made to the supplier. The supplier can collect his payment cheque directly from the finance department. The cheque is often routed to the supplier through the purchase department. Contemporary practices include electronic fund transfers to the supplier, directly crediting to his bank account. Records are updated.

Note 1: Controls and audit trail are in-built at each stage of the purchase cycle for perishables and highly perishables.

Note 2: The flowchart for the purchase cycle of perishables and highly perishables is presented on p. 107.

EXHIBIT 20: Purchase Cycle of Non-Perishable Food Products, Raw Ingredients and Other Requirements

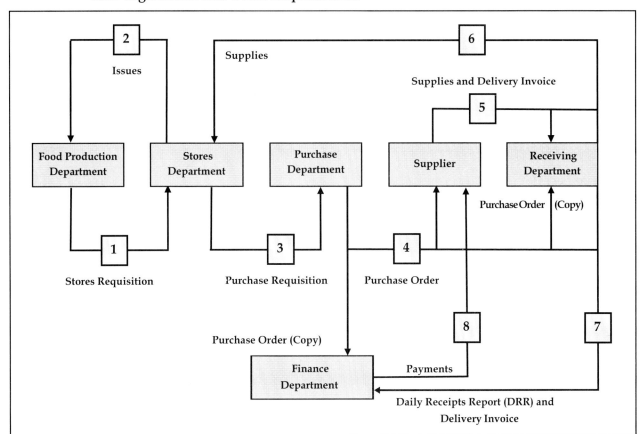

Note 1: The reader may read about the Daily Receiving Report in Module 8: "Right Receiving".

Note 2: Controls and audit trail are in-built at each stage of the purchase cycle for non-perishables.

Note 3: Generic control measures have been detailed in this book in modules related to each stage.

6.6 PURCHASE REQUISITION

Stocks of various items deplete in stores due to issues. It is vital to maintain adequate stock and avoid stock-out situations. Various methods are used to check the quantities in stock and place orders for the replenishment. There are many systems to identify the quantities in stock. These systems are:

- The physical inventory system.
- The perpetual inventory system.
- The bin-card system.
- The minimum/maximum inventory and ordering system.
- Property management systems.
- The SAP system.

EXHIBIT 21: Format of Purchase Requisition

RG Riverside Grill

Purchase Requisition

Serial No. _____

Date _____

Code _____

Budget _____

Budget utilized to date _____

Budget available _____

Ordered by _____

Please arrange to purchase the following items by _____

Item Code	Qty. To Be Purchased	Unit	Description of Item (Brand Name, Size, Colour, Etc.)	Average Consumption	Present Stock	Unit Price	Total Value	Remarks

_____ _____ _____
Prepared By   Stores Incharge   Authorized By

(The reader would study the systems of identifying quantities in stock in Module 9: "Efficient Storing, Inventory Management and Right Issuing".)

The Purchase Requisition is an internal document of the business and is generated by the stores department. When the stock levels of any item reach the ordering point, the stores personnel list the required items and the required quantities in the Purchase Requisition. The requisition is sent to the purchase department to inform the purchase personnel to purchase the requirements mentioned, within the time frame, as per the established purchase system.

"Purchase Requisition" is part of the audit trail. The purchase requisition is individual to the use of a business and its format can be modified to suit the requirements. However, it is not used as a purchase order. Depending on the total monetary value of the purchase requisition it is endorsed by an authorized person. A copy is retained in the stores and one is marked to the finance department for control and audit purposes.

Property management systems or the SAP system manage the activity of preparation of the purchase requisition and its transfer to the purchase department by e-mail and computer software system.

6.7 PURCHASE ORDER

A Purchase Order (PO) is the record of the specifics of order for all incoming supplies. Purchase order is written by the purchaser listing a purchase transaction and sent to a supplier. It is a formal document listing various values of an item which the purchaser intends to purchase. Purchase orders allow purchasers to clearly and explicitly communicate their intentions to suppliers.

The purchase order details items and their quantities to be purchased. The PO is prepared in the name of specific suppliers. The details of items and their quantities are transferred from the Purchase Requisition.

When the seller agrees to supply the requirements, under the conditions written in the purchase order, it becomes a legally binding contract on both parties and cannot be changed without the consent of both parties. Suppliers are protected in case of a buyer's refusal to pay for goods or services.

The supplier raises his invoice once he supplies the goods, quoting the purchase order. The purchaser must pay the agreed-upon price for no less than the agreed-upon quality, for the quantities ordered in a specific time frame. The purchase order therefore is a tool to minimize the problems arising out of insufficient communication and ambiguity.

The original or top-copy of the purchase order is meant for the supplier and is sent through post. The supplier has the option of collecting his copy personally or through his representative from the business premises of the purchaser. Copies of the purchase order are circulated internally among the receiving and finance departments and a copy is retained in the purchase department. This is the essence of the purchase order system. Purchase orders can be used by suppliers to source financial assistance from commercial lenders or financial institutions.

6.7.1 Contents of Purchase Order

(a) **Purchase order no:**   This is the number that is assigned to the purchase order. Numbering of the purchase order helps in the process of record-keeping, for payments and computerization of the purchase orders. Purchase orders are generally pre-printed, numbered documents generated by the purchaser's purchasing system. For purchase requirements of multiple culinary outlets or for different departments within the same business, for example, in a hotel, individual sets of purchase orders may be used. This is especially so with large hotels. Some organizations maintain different colours of purchase orders for different departments.

(b) **The date of the purchase order:**   The date helps in future correspondence and follow-up.

(c) **Purchaser's name and business address:**   This would be the address to which the goods are to be supplied. In case the delivery is to be made at another address the same should be mentioned.

(d) **Delivery date:**

(e) **Name of the supplier and/or the company and the address:**   Purchase orders are often released on the e-mail system. In addition to the postal address, the e-mail address should be added to the contact information about the supplier.

(f) **Payment terms, discount terms, freight terms, etc.:**   These may include the modalities of bill submission and payments receivable.

(g) **Any other terms and conditions, if applicable:**   These may be the inspection rights of the purchaser, for example, for HACCP checks, disclaimers and "hold harmless" provisions and other legal and contractual terms.

EXHIBIT 22: Format of Purchase Order

RG Riverside Grill				
Purchase Order				

To	Date:
_____	Purchase Order No.:
(Supplier/Company)	Supply To :
_____	**Riverside Grill**
(Supplier's Address)	
_____	Address:
(Pin Code)	_____
_____	Pin Code :
(E-Mail Address)	_____
	E-Mail:

Delivery Through	Delivery Terms	Delivery Date

Please Supply:

S. No.	Product Name & Description	Quantity	Unit Cost	Total Cost

Notes & Instructions:	Subtotal	
	Discount	
	Tax	
	Total	
Contact Person & Address		
	Authorised Signatory/Date	

(h) **Brief description:** This section often corresponds with the defined standard purchase specifications.

(i) **Quantity ordered:**

(j) **Unit of Purchase:** This information could be in terms of numbers, measurements, boxes, etc.

(k) **Unit Cost:**

(l) **Total Cost of each item:** If there are many items being ordered to the same supplier in the same purchase order, this information represents the total of the quantity of the item multiplied by its unit price.

(m) **Total value of the entire purchase order:**

(n) **Contact details:** When large number of purchase orders are issued in the course of a working period, for example, for large hotels, the contact details of the contact person representing the purchaser are also provided. The contact person is responsible to attend to all the queries of the suppliers.

> **Note:** For culinary business the standard purchase specifications are grouped as explained on **p. 93**. These specifications are handed over to the suppliers along with the fixed term contract which can be of monthly, quarterly, half-yearly or yearly duration. An open purchase order is also issued.

6.7.2 Electronic Purchase Orders

Many purchase orders are no longer paper-based, but rather transmitted electronically over the e-mail system. These are also controlled by property management systems or computerization.

6.7.3 Open Purchase Order

A typicality of culinary business is that a contract for supply of food products and raw ingredients is contracted for at a fixed rate for a fixed period. These are called **fixed-rate contracts**. The following is the process of such a contract:

- Tenders for supply of a class of products or ingredients, for example, for vegetables, fruits, spices, table condiments, meats, seafood, dairy products, etc., are advertised.

- In a typical buyer's market, many suppliers show interest in supplying the required class of products.

- They collect the documents containing standard purchase specifications developed by the purchaser for the class of products or ingredients which they wish to supply.

- They quote their prices for a fixed term – for example, a month, a quarter, half-year or a year for each of the items of the class of products or ingredients.

- The suppliers are called for negotiations.

- Rates are negotiated and fixed for supply for the forthcoming period.

- An open or standing purchase order is issued by the purchaser to the supplier listing the general conditions for supplies, and listing the standard purchase specifications, once again as an attachment to the purchase order.

All the values of the purchase order remain same throughout the period of supply except the date of supply and quantities ordered and receivable. The date changes and records are maintained for the same. This is called an open or standing purchase order. The open purchase order is often used in case of for purchase of contracted items.

6.8 CONTROLS IN THE PURCHASING FUNCTIONS

Culinary business presents singularly typical circumstances, unlike any other business. This is the perishable and highly perishable nature of food products and raw ingredients. Right handling processes ensure safety and well-being of consumers of the business's products – the customers, as well as staff members.

Certain statutory controls are built in to control the hygiene aspects of the business. Contemporary requirements and the need to be competitive in the market further oblige business managements to identify the HACCP processes related to each menu item's production and service.

The perishability of ingredients allows for certain malpractices in the purchasing systems. Often it is difficult to prove a malpractice having taken place minutes after receiving takes place. Intelligent managements ensure adequate in-built control measures so that losses are eliminated. The control processes should ideally be of the **preventive** genre instead of the **corrective** genre. However, remedial actions have also been detailed for complete understanding.

6.9   MALPRACTICES AND SAFEGUARDS

Losses to the culinary business due to malpractices in the purchasing system and the **preventive and remedial actions.**

Financial losses are attributed to poor management and lack of supervision. Employees and suppliers take advantage of the gaps in controls and supervision and resort to malpractices. Instead of remedial action post losses, it is important to set up specific benchmarks, control and audit systems. Benchmarks help culinary business to trim down costs and add to the profitability. Human beings are always wary of being caught. Benchmarks would act as preventive actions when followed and eliminate **malpractices.**

Suppliers often offer inducements to personnel in the purchase system to increase their business and/or their profits. These inducements could be in the form of cash, or in kind. Examples are gifts, entertainment, or services to the personnel's family, or allowing the personnel to pick up personal items from the business premises of the supplier, or a combination of these inducements.

The following are just a few of the examples of **malpractices and preventive actions**:

6.9.1   Bribes

The supplier manages to influence and control an employee of the purchase or receiving department. The supplier inflates the price quotations on the basis of inside information. Very often the supplier's quotations are not even negotiated. He also gets to supply a larger number of products, in addition to the products that are part of his core competence, often at inflated prices, due to his 'inside' contacts. If the supplier manages to influence the receiving personnel also, than items not even supplied are billed for. The supplier and the 'inside' personnel benefit from these malpractices and share the extra profits that the supplier earns.

To enable the business to safeguard itself from bribes to its personnel, the following are some of the preventive or remedial actions:

- An employee acting alone can develop a bribe system with the connivance of the supplier. In most organizations, the purchasing, receiving, stores and controls personnel are part of the finance department. Ensuring separate personnel for receiving and storing functions is one preventive measure.

- Regularly interchanging of duties of the purchase, receiving, stores, and controls personnel acts as a deterrent and is another preventive measure.

- Introduction of the system of **'blind receiving'** is another preventive measure. Blind receiving is a term used in the stores, and involves transferring the materials received by the stores, without the accompanying DRR (daily receiving report) and the supplier's invoice. The stores personnel check the material for quantities in terms of weight and count.

- Strengthening the control and audit processes is another preventive measure. Inherently, the strengthening would ensure questioning of orders for many products placed on the same supplier.

- Similar purchase specifications for same or similar products as those of the market and random checking of their market prices would throw up any irregularity in fixing the rates for supplies in respect of a supplier. Re-negotiating of suspect rates is a remedial measure.

- Examining the process of selection of the suppliers is a remedial measure. In case large number of orders are flowing to one supplier, examining the process of selection of the supplier would bring out any irregularities or preferential treatment.

6.9.2   Payments Made for Products Not Received

With negligent systems and poor supervision a supplier may get away with payments for products that he has not supplied. This is often when the supplier is able to control the receiving personnel.

To safeguard itself from this malpractice the following preventive actions can be adopted:

- Crosschecking of supplies and quantities.
- Blind receiving system.
- Strong controls and audits.

A combination of the above actions would eliminate the possibilities of payments made for products not received. Payments are made to a supplier on the basis of his invoice, the acceptance of the products, and records in the daily receiving report (DRR). For non-perishables, an important control measure is checking the entries of the daily receiving report against those in the inventory system of the stores. In case of perishables a preventive action would be random checking of the quantities by the consuming and/or controls department.

6.9.3   Intentional Errors in the Delivery Invoice

Deliberate arithmetical errors, writing invoices for higher quality or higher cost products and supplying lower quality or lower cost products are some malpractices that suppliers engage in often. They are supported in these malpractices by the receiving personnel. An example is the supply of prawns and tomatoes. Large prawns and large tomatoes are expensive in comparison to small prawns and small tomatoes. If the respective supplier supplies the smaller variety of either of the two, and makes the invoice for the larger variety, the business would incur losses.

To enable the business to safeguard itself from this malpractice the following preventive action can be adopted:

- Modifying the standard purchase specifications to link the size with numbers per kg.
- Double-checks of quality with the active involvement of the user department in the receiving process and through their endorsement of the quality of products received.

6.9.4   Shortfalls in Quantities Received

In these cases the supplier himself is not always the culprit. Many supplies are sent by the supplier through his agent or his employees or through courier. The quantities delivered at the receiving area of the business are lesser than those mentioned in the accompanying invoice. In some cases the supplier's agent or his employee or the courier service or the courier service's employee are to be blamed. Couriers are often received at post-receiving timings. Many times these couriers are collected from the landing port by the purchaser's personnel and also by non-operators like airport representatives, lobby personnel or clearing agents. Prepayment is made to the supplier in for certain supplies.

To enable the business to safeguard itself from this malpractice the following remedial action can be adopted:

- Clearly amending the supplier's invoice in a legible manner, adding a note-on-file for the discrepancy, notifying the purchase, the receiving, and the finance department about the same, and informing the supplier immediately or at the earliest available opportunity.

- In case prepayment has been made for the supplies the purchase department should ask for a credit memo from the supplier.

> **Note:** In case the supply has been received during post-receiving timings, a witness should sign the discrepancy in the invoice.

6.9.5 Presenting Duplicate Invoices for Supplies Paid For

In such cases, a supplier sensing lack of effective controls and payment procedures presents an invoice for which he has already received payment. If he is caught he pretends the same to be a mistake. If he is not caught, he takes payments for the second time.

To enable the business to safeguard itself from this malpractice the following preventive action can be adopted:

- This type of malpractice is eliminated by use of computerization and also by cancelling invoices which have been paid for. Business must place a "paid" stamp on the invoice for which payment has been made.

6.9.6 Purchasing Items for Personal Use

This type of malpractice has many variations:

(a) Purchasing items for personal use and allowing the business to pay for it. In this case the supplier may or may not be aware of the malpractice.

(b) Purchasing larger than necessary quantities of items to allow the supplier to make larger profits.

The crooked employee then picks up personal items from the supplier's premises at no cost or at heavily discounted prices.

To enable the business to safeguard itself from this malpractice the following preventive actions can be adopted:

- Creation of an effective purchase system and design control procedures at each stage.
- Randomly asking questions about odd purchases – those that are not in the line of the business's requirements.
- Having an efficient audit trail. All purchases should actualize only with requirements from stores or consuming departments and should have authorization.

6.9.7 Quality Substitution

In this type of malpractice supplier quotations are for products of higher quality. However, the supplier supplies products of lower quality or of alternate brands.

To enable the business to safeguard itself from this malpractice the following preventive action can be adopted:

- Involving the representatives of the user department in addition to the receiving personnel as a practice while receiving supplies. The experience of the representatives of the user department and their familiarization with the product quality is of immense value in checking the products against standard purchase specifications at the receiving department.

- Training the receiving personnel to match products with standard purchase specifications.
- Removing ambiguity of the receiving process through ready access to the standard purchase specifications, along with their coloured photographs.
- Cross-checking yields of successive supplies against Standard Yields, wherever applicable.

6.10 REDUCING THE COST OF PURCHASE

An important aim and objective of an efficient purchasing system is cost management. Each business has individual characteristics. It is vital for the survival of the business for it to discover fresh management initiatives, applications and inputs to reduce cost. Continuous examination of the business, business needs, and the benchmarks; aided by the zeal of the operators to save on costs, their alertness and **application of mind** can do the needful. Operators should spend monies wisely.

A few strategies to reduce the cost of purchase are explained below.

6.10.1 Reducing the Cost of Purchase through the Process of Competitive Bidding

The goal of competitive bidding is to reduce costs of purchase through the process of creating competition amongst suppliers. All suppliers have a fair chance of winning the contract. To create competition, larger number of prospective suppliers are attracted through placing of advertisements in newspapers or regular information sources of the hospitality industry. The requirements could be for a once-only supply or for a purchase period of a year or a month, etc.

The purchaser issues documents listing the standard purchase specifications for each food product, ingredient, or equipment that it wishes to purchase. For purchase of specific items like furniture or equipment technical specifications and accurate drawings are also issued. In addition the supplier has to fulfil certain criteria for evaluation of the bids. Examples of the criteria are:

- Listing of current clients of the supplier for same or similar products.
- Detailing of supplier's financial strength to carry out the supplies during the purchase period.

Through fulfilment of the above criteria the prospective supplier confirms that his delivery performance would be of high standards. The supplier quotes for the supply keeping in view the desired quality specifications. Sealed bids are opened simultaneously in the presence of the designated personnel of the hotel who initial the quotations. Only such bids which are countersigned by designated personnel representing the purchaser are considered for evaluation and negotiations. This practice ensures that there is no manipulation of quotations which can vitiate the bidding process.

All other conditions being equal, the supplier with the lowest bid is awarded the contract for supplies. However, if for some reason, the contract is awarded to a supplier with a higher bid, the reasons for such decision are recorded and signed by the designated authorities.

6.10.2 Reducing the Cost of Purchase through Negotiations

Negotiating and reducing supplier quotations is not always achieved by pitching prices quoted by different suppliers against one another. Negotiations of supplier quotations are also done when only one trusted and existing supplier quotes. Negotiations involve a patient and thorough study of the market, the market conditions and offering payments to suppliers in time. Negotiations are also done on the basis of discussions on standard purchase specifications and reducing number of deliveries per week, if possible. It is vital for the negotiators to develop healthy relations with the suppliers. The suppliers should feel proud of their association with the purchaser's business. Combination of tangible and intangible approaches results in the supplier agreeing to reduce the quotations.

6.10.3 Reducing the Cost of Purchase through Larger Combined Orders

Cost of purchase can be reduced by placing combined orders for a larger variety of requirements, for example, on a one-stop shop. The one-stop shop offers large discounts for some products and lesser discounts for other products. The overall result is that the culinary business gains and the cost of its purchases are reduced. However, combining orders through the one-stop shop can be an on-and-off strategy. Culinary business cannot depend only on a one-stop shop system. The essential operating systems of a one-stop shop are varying prices, often changing on daily basis. Daily changes in prices lead to other inaccuracies and inefficiencies in operations including total collapse of the menu engineering system.

6.10.4 Reducing the Cost of Purchase through Purchasing Larger Quantities of Individual Items

Suppliers and manufacturers often offer promotional discounts on purchase of larger quantities of the same product. This can be due to introduction of a new product or a new brand in the market. Offer of promotional discounts and larger purchase of a product is often done as a strategy to prevent purchase of similar products manufactured by competitors. The larger discounts are also given to reduce overstocked items in the business premises of the supplier.

Operators must measure potential savings from volume purchases against cost incurred in:

- blocking money and storage space;
- possibilities of thefts by employees; and
- possibilities of spoilage.

It is better to purchase larger quantities of selected items on specific occasions if the negative factors are controllable or within limits.

6.10.5 Reducing the Cost of Purchase through Availing of Cash Discounts

Some suppliers, especially of the genre of stockists offer cash discounts on immediate payments or payments within stipulated time period. Culinary business should take advantage of such discounts.

6.10.6 Reducing the Cost of Purchase through Changing Standard Purchase Specifications

It is important to review quality benchmarks of purchase requirements against the:

- business concept;
- value proposition;
- service guarantees;
- standard recipes; and
- yield tests.

Purchase of products of higher quality more than necessary and those which are not easily available in the market increases the cost. Using items of the right quality would lower costs.

Depending on the volume of usage of individual food products and raw ingredients, a few can be purchased in larger packing size to save on costs.

6.10.7 Reducing the Cost of Purchase through Central Purchase

For chain operations, purchasing through the Central Purchase system presents possibilities of reduction of costs.

6.10.8 Reducing the Cost of Purchase through Use of Scratch Foods

Scratch foods are commercially available products that help in constituting a recipe and reducing the time and efforts of production. Manufacturers of scratch foods use contract farming to reduce their costs. With fluctuating markets in terms of availability of food products and raw ingredients, and also continuity in requirements of seasonal products for food production, scratch foods present possibilities to reduce costs of purchase.

> **Note:** Scratch foods are not always cost-effective. The reader may read further on purchasing of scratch foods as "End of Module Notes".

6.11 CENTRALIZED PURCHASING

Culinary business can be on a stand-alone model or part of a hotel's services. The size of the operations can be different. On the path towards success these operations develop their own:

- standard purchase specifications;
- standard yields;
- standard recipes;
- benchmarks of food service; and
- standard operating procedures governing operations of different departments.

All of the above standards have bearing on purchase policies and systems.

Successful stand-alone culinary business have an inherent potential to grow into chain operations. Many business operations add the values of experience of their officers and other personnel to the above and build an all encompassing and successful business model. This business model is made into a template to establish fresh business units at different geographical locations.

The operation can grow bigger either with its own investments or through the franchise route. Franchising is often the approach with which chain operations grow. The individual franchisee operator follows the quality benchmarks as well as other standard operating procedures of the franchisor. The technical proprietary knowledge and processes allow the franchisee to sell the culinary product under the business name of the franchisor. The franchisee therefore uses the franchisor's successful business model and the inherent intellectual property values.

6.11.1 Understanding Centralized Purchasing

For the chain model, purchasing of number of requirements is often actualized at a centralized location. Centralized purchasing refers to purchasing at a central, geographical location, products common to requirements of all units of a chain. Total requirements of individual units of the chain are conveyed to a central office. The quotations from various suppliers are sought for bulk quantities. Suppliers supply their products to a centralized point or to individual units at diverse geographical locations as per the agreement at a fixed cost per unit.

The **centralized purchase system** gives strength and support to individual units of a chain by:

(a) being **cost effective**;

(b) bringing **centralized evaluation** of product line by number of technical persons and specialists;

(c) bringing the benefit of **centralized research** and development of products;

(d) bringing **standardization** of product line greater choice of markets;

(e) introducing fresh product line for upgradation of the culinary concept and its service design;

(f) bringing **reduction in gaps of service and delivery** requirements;

(g) ensuring greater control over **dishonesty** of individual unit food purchases; and

(h) allowing **crosscheck** of **quality** of food products, ingredients and other requirements of the business by units of a chain as well as the central purchase department.

6.11.3 Disadvantages of Centralized Purchasing

The centralized purchasing is **not** advantageous in all working conditions. It has its **disadvantages** also. These are:

(a) The chefs of individual units lose independence in determination of quality. They are unable to take decisions contrary to those taken by the central purchase.

(b) In certain product ranges the advantage of local product or local specials is lost, especially at reduced prices.

(c) The suppliers focus their service, loyalty and attention to central purchase. The units lose out.

(d) The individual unit's operators need to set aside their own creativity and competitive urges in so far as a product line is priced and it is mandatory on them to fall in line.

(e) The centralized purchasing depends on orders being placed on them by individual operating unit weeks in advance of their actual requirement. Sometimes these are done on monthly basis and sometimes on quarterly basis. For imported goods the orders are placed on central purchase on yearly basis.

(f) Individual units are worried about the next supply in case they miss the current ones. The forecasted requirement therefore is wrong sometimes, the activity resulting in **over-procurement.**

(g) The central purchase system can be slow at times.

When a supplier or manufacturer can supply only to a limited geographical area, decentralized purchasing is a better option.

6.12 ONE-STOP SHOPPING SYSTEMS

Normally, culinary business gets its supplies from suppliers of specific product lines. These product lines are for example: seafood, poultry, meats, fruits, vegetables, groceries, dairy products and imported goods. The non-food requirements of the business are met by specific suppliers in a similar fashion.

Products subject to a 'buyer's market' are delivered at the doorstep of the business. For products subject to 'seller's market, the purchaser is often obliged to visit the seller, purchase the requirements and bring these back to his business premises at his cost.

Due to globalization of products, a new class of 'suppliers' has evolved. This is a supplier who can procure a wide range of products for a culinary business and has the economic power to maintain a large inventory of each of these products. This 'supplier' is the one-stop shopping system.

However, selection of goods and quantities to be purchased has to be done by the culinary business at the business premises of this one-stop shop. The one-stop shop advertises its product lines and the matching photographs through the format of catalogues. The catalogues can be used by the purchaser to order the requirements on telephone or through the e-mail. The selected requirements are delivered at the doorstep of the purchaser.

One-stop shops provide many products and efficient services to customers at single point of contact. Compared to visiting a separate institution for each area of need, the "one-stop shop" is convenient and saves the consumer a lot of time and effort.

One-stop shops are commercial establishments which are in a position to provide large number of day-to-day food and non-food requirements of culinary business. One-stop shops are business-to-business (B2B) models and are meant to serve only other business. They do not encourage the business-to-customers (B2C) model of retail sales to individual customers, for example, housewives. During the purchase visits of customers the one-stop shop recommends and is able to sell additional products to them.

The one-stop shop business model has become commonplace and is growing in popularity due to variety of reasons. The one-stop shop has economic powers to purchase food products and raw ingredients as well as non-food items in large quantities. Globally, the one-stop shops keep every possible brand of food, beverages and non-food items with **huge individual inventories in their portfolio**.

Large farmers, dairies, breeders, fisheries, and manufacturers are ready to supply and reward one-stop shops with large discounts and high quality products. Delivery costs become minimal due to the large inventories ordered by the one-stop shops. The one-stop shops are able to control their own supplier's production in terms of conditions of hygiene and HACCP controls. Audits done by these one-stop shops at the production stage ensure that quality and food safety standards are strictly adhered to.

Customers are encouraged to pick their requirements themselves. Store guides are available to help the customers. The customer pays a highly competitive price, selection of available products is huge, the products are available in immediate stock and the store's operations run within customer-friendly hours.

Statutory laws require food products and raw ingredients to be supplied to culinary business with warranties related to shelf life and quality. Warranties are also required to assure the food service operator for unadulterated food products, and those which are safe for human consumption in terms of pest infestation.

Conscientious one-stop shops arrange for customers to be provided with guarantees of quality product with provision of expiry dates, warranties of food products and raw ingredients as explained above and for those products that may require after-sales service.

Food safety being the priority, these shopping systems also ensure that they have provision for controlling the temperature of food products and raw ingredients as desired under HACCP guidelines. Under this requirement, one-stop shops ensure provisions of the cold store chain. The cold chain ensures that those food items which are supposed to be refrigerated or frozen are continuously stored at the correct temperature. This includes supplies to the one-stop shop and, in turn, supplies to the culinary business. On delivery to the culinary business, the cold stores of the business take over to ensure maintenance of correct temperatures.

The one-stop shops place computer readable bar codes on stored food products and ingredients as well as non-food items. These bar codes help in inventory management. The computer presents data about each of the stored food products and ingredients to ensure that these are sold before their expiry dates, either directly or through special promotional sale.

One-stop shopping systems often develop their own brands, with products of food and non-food on sale. These are called **personal brands**. These personal brands offer cost-effective solutions. Culinary business can benefit from purchase of these personal brands. These personal brands are on offer only at the one-stop shop obliging purchasers to visit them and purchase other products. One-stop shops often act as inspiration and encouragement for specialist food products to be made and exhibited for sale.

The one-stop shopping system has its advantages as well as disadvantages. The business needs and priorities of each operation are different from another. Each culinary business must examine and weigh the advantages and disadvantages of any one-stop shop that it deals with to suit its operations. An "off and on" usage of one-stop shopping service is ideal.

6.12.1   Advantages of the One-stop Shopping System

- Provides convenient and efficient service.
- Allows for wide range of products.
- Offers food items at the correct temperature and ensures maintenance of the cold store chain.
- Presents immediate warranties required under statutory laws – in respect of provisions of the Food Safety and Standards Act as well as for after-sales service.
- Can offer highly competitive prices.
- Offers products in immediately available stock.
- Operates with customer-friendly hours of operations.
- Offers market research for new products on an immediate basis.
- Eliminates the potentially time consuming process of selecting individual suppliers.
- Reduces time necessary to negotiate with different suppliers; process and issue purchase orders, and follow up on the ordered goods.
- Provides for volume efficiencies received by consolidating orders from a single source. This results in protecting the cost structure of the purchasers and achieving purchasing activities at the lowest administrative costs.
- Being a single source of supplies, offers purchasing leverage for the purchaser.
- Supports "Just-in-time" purchases.
- Stocks in-house brands.

6.12.2   Disadvantages of the One-stop Shopping System

- Prepares its own standard purchase specifications in respect of its own purchases. Very often these specifications are not suited to individual culinary business. Standard purchase specifications are individual to an organization. As a rule, the specifications should match the quality of products desired in relation to the culinary concept and the value proposition. One-stop shopping system deals with large number of customers. The standard purchase specifications followed in respect of its own purchases often over-specify quality. As a consequence the product becomes more expensive on the shelf.
- Changes its selling prices very often. This is because of its own purchases at prevalent rates. Changing selling rates prevents the purchasing culinary business to form a standard recipe cost and standard food cost.
- Is not a specialist supplier. With the increased number of product lines there is a decreased likelihood that the one-stop shopping system is an expert in each of the many food products, ingredients and non-food items that a culinary business purchases.
- Having already stocked sufficient quantities of a particular item is forced to offload the stock, before stocking a new version or fresh product-line or different stock-keeping unit.

> **Note:** In India, an example of an extraordinary efficient one-stop shopping system is the **Metro-Cash-And- Carry** in operations at multiple geographical locations.

6.13 ROLE OF THE PURCHASE DEPARTMENT AND ITS PERSONNEL

Managing available resources or those likely to be available is the prime managerial role of the purchase department. Efficient purchasing management continuously assesses needs of consuming departments, evolves itself in line with the requirements and satisfies the needs in a manner which maximizes value for the operation and its customers. Efficiency of the purchase department relates directly to the ultimate satisfaction of the customer and the profitability of the business.

Food production requires continuous creativity. The requirements of freshness and product appeal can be accomplished through interactions and touch-points with the customers and the markets.

On most purchase occasions **economies of scale** is the key to good purchasing, and to get better terms while sourcing raw materials.

6.13.1 Primary Duties and Responsibilities

1. Identification and selection of suppliers, in association with consuming departments.
2. Locating new sources of supplies and developing vendors.
3. Negotiating prices for a purchase period – lowest prices without sacrificing product quality or supplier's services. This involves intelligent interpretation of the market, the supplier, and the needs of the business.
4. Accomplishing the purchasing objectives at the lowest possible administrative costs.
5. Purchasing required products and ingredients at lowest total cost.
6. Maintaining continuity of regular stores supplies and in time. It is the responsibility of the purchase department to actualize the purchase of the items required by the stores in an uninterrupted manner. Actualization means dealing with suppliers already contracted for supply of various food products, ingredients and other requirements of the business.
7. Actualization of purchase requirements of the nature of perishables and in time. The requirements of these perishables are placed by the **chef** on the purchase department using the Perishable Order Sheet.
8. Purchasing of the **right quality** of food products, ingredients and other requirements of the business in line with their standard purchase specifications.
9. Purchasing of the **right quantities** of food products, ingredients and other requirements of the business. Quantities to be stocked are governed by the consumption pattern, the lead time taken by the supplier to service a Purchase Order, sometimes by the financial capacities of the business and the storage capacities.
10. Expediting and follow-up to ensure ordered supplies reach business facility at the right time. Some suppliers being more conscientious require fewer follow-ups than others.
11. Supporting Just-in-Time purchasing whenever possible.
12. Developing suppliers and managing good business relationships with suppliers. This involves identifying competent suppliers and establishing productive relationships with them for efficient and uninterrupted supplies.
13. Maintaining records for future audits.

6.13.2 Support Duties and Responsibilities

The purchase department remains in regular dialogue with the consumer department, which is primarily the food production department in case of culinary business. The purchase department has the following **support** duties and responsibilities towards the consumer department:

1. Establishing quality value of food products, ingredients and other requirements of the business.

2. Establishing standard purchase specifications of all food products, ingredients and other requirements of the business for a purchasing period.

3. Evolving standard purchase specifications, if necessary in line with changing business scenario, and careful evaluation of food products, ingredients and other requirements of the business. Business scenario changes due to changes in the business concept, evolving benchmarks of service guarantees, upgradation and repositioning of culinary product line.

4. Ensuring efficient, continuous and evolving market research to support the consumer department. Informing and transferring details of market research of specific nature to the consuming department supports the business retaining market competitiveness. Market research also supports the purchase function of negotiating prices.

5. Highlighting, evaluating and sourcing new products and ingredients in the market.

6. Researching for, evaluating and purchasing new equipment and fresh technologies.

7. Highlighting market and price trends, and cost-effective solutions.

8. Highlighting possible shortages of food products, ingredients and other requirements of the business in the market in the future – immediate or distant and sourcing alternate source products.

9. Coordinating purchase requirements of emergency nature.

10. Coordinating requirements of special food products or raw ingredients required rarely. This happens due to special requirements of customers.

11. Analyzing and coordinating requirements of food products or raw ingredients of the nature of enhanced consumption. Unusual consumption is not factored while listing consumption patterns.

12. Evaluating and achieving operational efficiencies in outsourcing ready-to-use food products, if required by the food production department in line with defined business model. For example: outsourcing of ready-to-serve desserts and boulangerie items.

6.13.3 Tertiary Coordination Duties and Responsibilities

1. **Coordination with the Bills and Payments department:** The purchase department coordinates with the Bills and Payments department for the payment of suppliers, as per the payment schedules.

2. **Coordination with the Food & Beverages Controls:** The purchase department coordinates with the Food & Beverages Controls for diverse needs including processing of supplier's bills for payments. (The reader may like to visit Module 11: "Controls" for details.)

   In conjunction with the control department the purchase department sells scrap of various types, for example: obsolete or irreparable equipment, reusable packing material, recyclable products like empty bottles or empty oil tins. This activity produces non-forecasted revenues and freeing of valuable storage space.

3. **Coordination with the receiving department:** The purchase department coordinates with the receiving department for quality and quantity inspection of food products, ingredients and other requirements.

4. **Coordination with stores department:** The coordination in between the purchase and stores departments involves:

- Updating consumption pattern of commodities.

- Assessing unusual consumption.

- Reducing stores inventories and investments in stocks-in-hand. Actualizing reduced stocking positions in stores (low inventories), thereby keeping investments in inventory to a minimum. This also means maintaining high inventory turnover.

- Updating list of slow and non-moving commodities. The purchase department takes active interest in energising consumption of slow-moving and non-moving commodities in stores. All food products and raw ingredients are perishable. Such consumption ensures prevention of loss due to spoilage or due to product-life-cycle expiry.

- Minimizing losses in quality of commodities, and their faster consumption.

5. **Coordination with senior management:** The purchase department coordinates with senior management for audits and for conveying:

- Market trends.

- Cost-effective solutions.

- Possible shortages of commodities in the market.

6.14   END OF MODULE NOTES

6.14.1   Cost-effectiveness in Purchasing Functions

The understanding, **key areas** and **success factors** in relation to an efficient system for a purchase department are listed below. The culinary business must:

1. establish purchasing needs;

2. set up benchmarks of the purchasing functions and integrate these with an efficient audit trail;

3. formalize price negotiations, creative pricing plans and regular market research;

4. avoid over-specifying quality benchmarks. The quality benchmarks must be in line with the culinary concept;

5. purchase the 'right quality' of requirements, and purchase these in the 'right' quantities;

6. purchase specific infrastructure, culinary products and ingredients centrally, if within chain operations, for higher efficiency and economies of scale;

7. use one-stop shopping systems only for select purchases;

8. ensure effective controls, preventive and remedial actions against malpractices in the purchasing system;

9. take advantage efficiency of the supplier and just-in-time purchases whenever possible;

10. reduce subjective purchasing through fixed rate contracts;

11. avoid stock-outs and emergency purchases;

12. purchase requirements at the right price – lowest total cost against standard purchase specifications of each item to be purchased;

13. ensure maximum yields through standard purchase specifications which match business concept;

14. ensure quality and regular interaction between the purchase personnel, the chef, the chef's representatives, and other users/operators;

15. eliminate arbitrary decisions and implement a committee approach towards higher objectivity of operations; and

16. modify menu/menu items to eliminate/reduce items of a seller's market.

6.14.2 Purchase Period

The period of contract between the purchaser and the supplier is known as the purchase period. The start of the purchase period corresponds with:

- the standard purchase specifications in respect of each item to be ordered accepted by the supplier;

- a formal communication from the purchaser to the supplier through a contract, a purchase order or an open purchase order;

- acceptance of delivery schedules by the supplier; and

- acceptance of other conditions of supply, for example, the payment cycle, timings of delivery, hygiene and HACCP standards to be maintained by the supplier.

Once a purchase period comes to an end, the next purchase period corresponds with re-establishing of the processes mentioned above, afresh.

6.14.3 Purchasing "Scratch Foods"

Scratch foods are commercially available products that help in constituting a recipe and reducing the time and efforts of production. Scratch foods are not always cost-effective.

Indian market conditions fluctuate with seasons. Due to this fluctuation the continuity in food production of promised menu items often requires scratch foods. Scratch foods are useful also in circumstances where the basic ingredient used in their manufacture is not available in a geographical location. An example is carcass of prawns required for preparation of prawn sauce or prawn-infused butter. It would be appropriate for a culinary business placed in a non-coastal area to use a ready-to-use prawn sauce or prawn-infused butter. At certain geographical locations, it is wise and economical to use scratch foods at certain times of the year and not economical at other times of the year.

Food processing in developed countries is highly evolved in terms of food processing standards. Food processing in these countries is often controlled or/and sponsored by their government. Most of these developed countries have very large coastal front/ in proportion to landlocked areas. Extremely inflexible statutory laws govern the food processing industry in these countries. These laws include those relating to hygiene and HACCP standards. Usage of scratch foods or other processed foods by chefs of such countries is very much the norm of their hospitality industry. This is due to 'convenience-factor', top quality of the scratch foods as well as the high labour costs in these countries.

The Indian food processing industry is still underdeveloped in terms of reach, variety, creativity and usefulness of the processed item to the hospitality industry. Delivery of frozen processed foods in diverse geographical locations is disadvantaged due to insufficient extent of cold-store chain.

Indian chefs have mastered the arts of food production not only of ethnic cuisines but also of Euro-American and Asian cuisines. A chef must weigh the option of using the scratch food against producing the same within his premises in the light of losing the culinary skills.

Customers are encouraged to inform the culinary business if they suffer from any food-related allergies. Commercial scratch food manufacturers do not disclose the complete list of ingredients which go into the production of such items. Usage of scratch foods for preparation of food for customer who suffer from food-related allergies is risky.

The decision of whether to use scratch foods or not in certain geographical locations or during certain periods is essentially individual to each culinary business. The decision often depends on the business needs of the day as well as on policy decisions. The path to arrive at a decision is to do a cost-benefit analysis. In respect of scratch foods, a cost benefit analysis would list all costs as well as the tangible and intangible benefits of using the same as against its identical production in own kitchen. The identical production would work as an alternative and allow for the right comparison.

If the culinary business decides to go in for usage of any scratch food, its purchase must be controlled by listing its standard purchase specifications, at least for whichever scratch food it is possible.

EXHIBIT 23: Efficient Management of Purchasing Activities

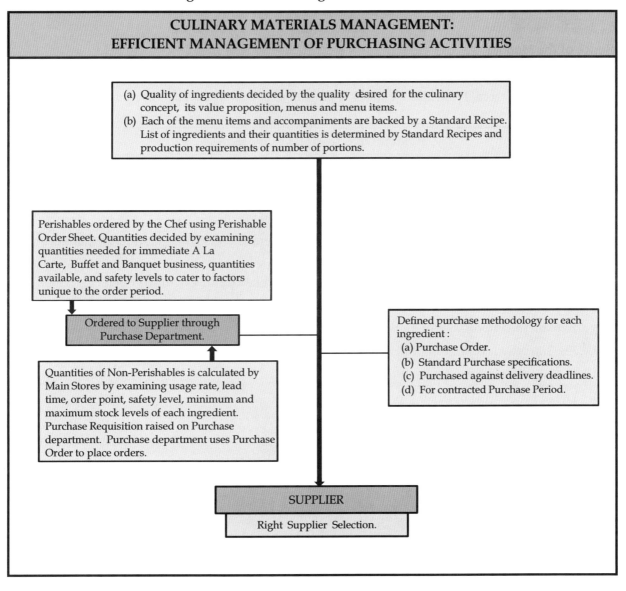

CULINARY MATERIALS MANAGEMENT: EFFICIENT MANAGEMENT OF PURCHASING ACTIVITIES

(a) Quality of ingredients decided by the quality desired for the culinary concept, its value proposition, menus and menu items.
(b) Each of the menu items and accompaniments are backed by a Standard Recipe. List of ingredients and their quantities is determined by Standard Recipes and production requirements of number of portions.

Perishables ordered by the Chef using Perishable Order Sheet. Quantities decided by examining quantities needed for immediate A La Carte, Buffet and Banquet business, quantities available, and safety levels to cater to factors unique to the order period.

Ordered to Supplier through Purchase Department.

Quantities of Non-Perishables is calculated by Main Stores by examining usage rate, lead time, order point, safety level, minimum and maximum stock levels of each ingredient. Purchase Requisition raised on Purchase department. Purchase department uses Purchase Order to place orders.

Defined purchase methodology for each ingredient :
(a) Purchase Order.
(b) Standard Purchase specifications.
(c) Purchased against delivery deadlines.
(d) For contracted Purchase Period.

SUPPLIER

Right Supplier Selection.

7

SELECTING THE RIGHT SUPPLIER

Essence of the Module

This module explains the process of selecting the right supplier to support cost-effectiveness of operations. In addition, the module would enlighten the reader of the reasons of treating suppliers as partners of the culinary business.

Module Objectives and Competencies
After going through this module the reader would be competent to:

1. Understand market conditions. In addition, understand a seller's market and a buyer's market.

2. Show how the right supplier would add value to the business.

3. Show how to develop a supplier towards higher performances, and enumerate parameters of supplier training.

4. Discuss why it is important to have good working relationships with suppliers.

5. Differentiate the ways of identifying supply sources—number of suppliers.

6. Explain the importance of market information received through suppliers.

7. Explain why it is important to select the right supplier.

8. Explain the process of selecting the right supplier.

9. Detail the process of evaluation of a supplier's performance.

   - Quality performance.
   - Price performance.
   - Delivery performance.
   - Relationship performance.

10. Evaluate suppliers of new products.

11. Examine the importance of moments-of-truth in re-selection process of a supplier of in-use products.

12. List the qualifications of a good supplier.

13. Evaluate the individual conditions of the culinary business which dictate the selection of suppliers. In continuation, understand why one supplier is not good enough for one business and is the right one for another.

7.1   UNDERSTANDING MARKET CONDITIONS

It is important for the culinary business to keep developing suppliers for various requirements of products and ingredients. To select the right supplier it is essential to understand market conditions. There are two types of supply markets:

- Seller's market.
- Buyer's market.

For any business, some material requirements may be subject to seller's markets, and others may be subject to buyer's market. Especially in India, culinary business is fortunately placed in a predominantly buyer's market in current market scenario and are likely to remain in such circumstances.

7.1.1   Seller's Market

In certain market conditions, especially in non-metro and resort locations, identifying suppliers is difficult. Supplier selection options are limited. This market condition is known as a seller's market.

A seller's market for the culinary business is often characterized by high prices and supplies falling short of demand.

In a seller's market, the culinary business is unable to exercise its complete control over:

1. Quality in terms of compliance of the supplier with the standard purchase specifications of the culinary business.
2. Cost-effectiveness of product or ingredient supplies.
3. Timely delivery as instructed in the purchase order or daily perishables order sheet.
4. Total supplies in one lot.
5. Delivery at its business premises. The purchaser is often obliged to visit the seller, purchase his requirements and carry them back to his premises at his cost.

From the above it is clear that in a seller's market the objectives of purchasing correctly are sacrificed in terms of quality, price, time, quantities and convenience. The culinary business is unable to take a rigid position over supplies and suppliers in a seller's market.

Another type of seller's market is one in which manufacturers appoint distributors. The branded food products and raw ingredients have their own pricing structures and the price point has to be acceptable to the culinary business. Sales of large or small branded equipment required for a culinary business often falls under the category of seller's market.

In such a seller's market, decision has to be taken whether to buy the product or not. A culinary business can take a menu item off from the menu offer if an ingredient is subject to a seller's market.

7.1.2   Buyer's Market

Buyer's market is one where there are a number of suppliers offering food products and raw ingredients of same values. The services of the suppliers are also efficient and they are able to meet demands in terms of:

1. Quality of supplies – food products or raw ingredients in line with the standard purchase specifications.
2. Delivery benchmarks – timely and efficient delivery each time and at the designated receiving area of the purchaser.
3. Quantities of supplies – in line with demands.

The following are some of the characteristics of a buyer's market:

(a) The suppliers are located at a nearby and / or convenient place.

(b) There are possibilities for culinary business to use the competition amongst the different suppliers in the market and enforce lowering of prices.

(c) The objectives of effective purchasing are met.

A culinary business is therefore supported most efficiently if it is placed in a buyer's market.

7.2 DEVELOPMENT OF SUPPLIERS

A good supplier is an asset to culinary business. Just as employees are trained for higher performances, suppliers are also educated, trained and developed for greater performance. It is important to develop suppliers who exhibit some measure of promise.

Culinary business must keep developing existing and potential suppliers through structured sessions. The most important requirement is for the supplier to be trained in a manner that he is in total understanding of the purchasing organisation's business, and its vision and mission. This training would support the supplier taking pride in the organisation to which he supplies.

The process of development of a supplier includes:

(a) Visual familiarization with product or ingredient through existing samples.

(b) Training of actual use of the product or ingredient. Understanding of the end use of a product supports better understanding of the culinary business and its business benchmarks with the supplier.

(c) Training of the standard purchase specifications of each product or ingredient. This can be eminently achieved through photographic binders detailing quality specifications with corresponding photographs.

(d) HACCP training. A supplier should have thorough knowledge of the requirements of HACCP.

(e) Training of the supplier's delivery and handling personnel on matters of personal hygiene and grooming.

(f) Training of mandatory standards of sanitation of the supplier's premises and delivery vehicles.

(g) Training of the temperatures at which different commodities should be brought into the business.

(h) Training of safety requirements applicable to the supplier in relation to his supplies to the business.

(i) Training of supplier's responsibilities towards environment in terms of recycling, returnable packaging, energy efficiencies, reduced water usage, vehicle efficiency, and usage of e-procurement system, etc.

(j) Knowledge of food laws.

(k) Knowledge of the purchaser's corporate social responsibility and the inherent responsibility of the supplier.

The relationship between the culinary business and supplier should be a win-win situation for both. Suppliers should always be regarded as partners to the business. For the supplier the culinary business should become a key account.

Good working relationships with a supplier works towards satisfaction of the customer of the culinary business. A good working relationship also ensures the supplier to develop pride in the business.

7.3 NUMBER OF SUPPLIERS

Many factors decide the number of suppliers for a food product or raw ingredient or a group of ingredients. It is ideal for some culinary business to have just one supplier for selected purchase requirements. For other purchase requirements, however, two suppliers would be the right solution. Very often an alternate supplier is also selected. By consolidating buying efforts of a particular period, ordering is simplified and the operator has an opportunity for volume discounts. This is especially so for grocery and other non-perishable items.

Depending on a single supplier often means lack of competition which may set in uncalled for comfort levels and complacency amongst the personnel of the purchaser and gradual increase in costs. In addition, a single supply source may cause supply shortages and gradual deterioration in quality of supplies. In certain markets however, a single supplier for a product is beneficial. This is basically because of the supplier's risk-taking capacity and efficiency of delivery.

The overall goal of any culinary business is reduction of costs and **profit maximization.** Creation of value in purchase functions is important. In certain circumstances a good business relationship results from at least two suppliers for most of the products. Non-perishables are best purchased in bulk from one supplier. Orders for perishables are often split among several suppliers, with a primary and secondary supplier for each category.

It is for the business to decide the number of suppliers for each category. Very often having one supplier for a category of food products or raw ingredients is better. The decision totally depends on the chefs and managers of the business. The following are some considerations while deciding the number of suppliers for each category:

1. The product category.
2. Stocking capacity of the business unit.
3. The type of market.
4. The type and quantum of the orders.
5. The geographical location of the supplier in relation to the business premises.
6. Working relationship with the supplier.
7. The performances of the supplier.
8. Financial and technical capability of the supplier.

7.4 MARKET INFORMATION

Two important and on-going activities of any business are to increase revenues and cost-effectiveness of operations. Both activities mandate the operators to remain abreast with market conditions. Operators adopt diverse methods to source market information relating to their specific requirements. Specialist external agencies are available to source market information as per the parameters individual to each area of operations. However, most forms of hospitality business prefer to source the market information through own employees.

The market information described in this module relates to cost-effectiveness in the purchase processes through market surveys. Market information is sourced through a process of regular and formal market surveys. Market surveys are normally done for each group of supplies. (The reader may like to revisit p. 84 to refresh understanding about group of supplies.)

A committee approach is taken to assess market conditions in an objective and systematic manner. The committee normally consists of:

(a) the chef and the food & beverages manager or their representatives;

(b) the purchase personnel responsible for purchases of food & beverages; and

(c) the food & beverages controller.

The committee surveys rates offered by various suppliers. The survey identifies new and applicable food products, ingredients, and scratch foods as well as labour and cost saving devices. An important agenda of a market survey is to identify and approve manufacturers and suppliers of ready-to-serve food items, which can then be outsourced.

The market survey helps in identifying possibilities of any disruptive activity – positive or negative in the immediate future. The survey also identifies possibilities of reducing the inventories within the purchaser's storage systems through enhanced supplier-efficiency.

Data is recorded and analyzed at the end of the market survey. The interpretations from this data provide fresh insights into the market conditions. An important study is on the difference of the rates in the market and that paid by the business as part of a fixed-term contract with individual suppliers. Such interpretation minimizes risks for future operations. Exhaustive reports and checklists are filed at the end of each market survey. These reports are useful while negotiating rates with existing and prospective suppliers for the next supply period.

To compete in a buyer's market suppliers endeavour to remain dynamic in their approach to their specialist supply line. Some suppliers automatically provide formal, written market information each month to the purchaser. In certain instances, suppliers contact the purchase or consumer department with market updates, as and when conditions of supply change.

Market information also emanates from sales representatives of manufacturing and procuring companies. On certain occasions this information is inadequate as the representative would not recommend a new product with technological improvements that is not part of his portfolio.

It has become easy to keep abreast of the market for new products through the help of the Internet search engines. A regular visit to trade events supports intelligent interaction with suppliers and manufacturers of new food products, raw ingredients, scratch foods and devices.

Expected use: Due to the mention of the standard purchase specifications in the Purchase Order or Open Purchase Order, the expected use of the product is accurately defined. Yields of products enhance due to the supplier's understanding the expected use. In case of short-fall in the quality of the product, due to market conditions, the supplier would usually offer additional benefits or discounts. He may offer additional portions and/or products to meet up with the original quality and yield requirement, and also give substitutes. In India, this is regularly done for fish supplies during certain periods.

7.5 SELECTION OF A SUPPLIER

A supplier is selected by the Finance department after a due process of negotiations, etc.

1. A supplier can be one who has **supplied earlier** to the institution.

2. A **new supplier** can be selected.

7.5.1 Existing Supplier

An existing supplier is one who has supplied same or similar goods to the business already. There is, therefore an awareness of the quality of goods that he has supplied, the price that he charged, and the type of service – conscientious or otherwise; that the supplier has provided. These include the speed of response and requirements for follow-up.

7.5.2 Evaluating and Selecting a New Supplier

The process of selecting a new supplier starts with evaluation of potential suppliers. When selecting a new supplier, caution must be exercised and detailed enquiries made to establish credentials of the potential supplier. These enquiries should include:

1. Full details of the potential supplier's firm and the **range of items** they are selling.
2. Copies of their **recent price lists.**
3. Details of **their trading terms.**
4. Details of **other customers.**

In addition, the prospective supplier must present his existing portfolio. These would include:

(a) Copies of the purchase orders that the supplier has executed for customers requiring similar general items or food products or raw ingredients.

(b) Copies of the standard purchase specifications of general items or food products or ingredients that the supplier has dealt with for customers with similar business.

A potential supplier is also required to submit samples of his food products or raw ingredients.

Subsequent to the study of the above, a visit to the premises of a potential supplier is made. The visit is vital and supports first hand:

- Understanding the size of the potential supplier's organization.
- Understanding the range of products the potential supplier is marketing.
- Examining the storage facilities of the potential supplier.
- Examining the processing facilities (if any) of the potential supplier. This is important while selecting suppliers who are manufacturers and packers of scratch foods, spices and ready-to-use products like desserts and bread products.
- Examining the transport owned by the potential supplier.
- Evaluating the quality of personal hygiene of the potential supplier's workers.
- Evaluating the HACCP systems of the potential supplier in relation to:
- The supplier's procurement processes.
- The supplier's storage systems.
- The supplier's supply systems.
- Examining the procurement processes and the storage systems of the potential supplier.

The visit requires spending time with a prospective supplier, but worth it to:

- initiate a healthy and satisfactory business relationship;
- develop a supplier who is willing and financially capable to stock the quality and quantity of products that the culinary business purchases;
- develop a supplier who is knowledgeable about the products that he is likely to supply; and
- develop a supplier who is able to offer a satisfactory delivery performance, within acceptable price range.

Subsequent to the success of the above process, the selected suppliers are considered **approved suppliers** and trial orders are given to them to further judge their services.

7.5.3 Evaluation of an Existing Supplier's Performances

After having purchased from the supplier their performance is periodically evaluated. The performance is recorded regularly, and evaluation is done once a year. This evaluation is done in time for the yearly contract process. Experiences of the culinary business with the supplier at various moments of truth, wherein contacts are direct or indirect, are listed and a supplier's performance evaluated. A system of evaluating supplier's performance during a performance period is to give percentage ratings.

The evaluation is based upon the supplier's tangible and intangible performances such as:

1. Quality performance.
2. Price performance.
3. Delivery performance.
4. Relationship performance.

1. **Quality performance:** Consistency is the keyword. A supplier should be consistent with the quality of **each of his** supplies. To ensure this consistency and to obtain the desired quality, the culinary business sets and follows up on standard purchase specifications. Consistency in delivering supplies which meet the standard purchase specifications would give a high quality performance rating.

   The performance is calculated as percentage of the total orders placed on the supplier. The majority of deliveries meeting standard purchase specifications would give a high rating figure. Poor quality or regular rejection of supplies would lower the rating figure.

2. **Price performance:** Suppliers have different business strengths. One supplier is capable of supplying a product of **lower quality at a lower price** and the other supplier is capable of supplying a product of **superior quality at higher rates**. Both suppliers are selling their products. It depends on the culinary business to choose the **quality** that it requires.

   Price performance is measured by comparison of prices of each supplier of the same product with the **same** standard purchase specifications in a known trading period. It is possible to do a comparative study of the prices of different suppliers for supply of the same product line and arrive at a conclusion in advance of the award of the contract. The lower the price per unit of product or ingredient the better would be the price performance of that supplier.

3. **Delivery performance:** The services of a supplier are of no use if his supplies are products of good quality against laid down standard purchase specifications, are price competitive, but supplies are not made in time.

   Parameters of delivery performance like the time, day and date of deliveries are set up through the Purchase Order or through notes exchanged on the subject, or through the e-mail system. The ability of the supplier to meet agreed delivering times and dates with the business is called delivery performance.

   Food products and raw ingredients should be delivered when required, and also, when staff qualified to check these goods are available. Late deliveries add to pressures of work at the purchaser's receiving and consumption department. The nearer the scheduled delivery date and time, the higher the delivery performance rating. Delivery performance also includes the need for regular follow-up in varying degrees on orders placed.

   Delivery performance is calculated against the percentage of deliveries made on time. The majority of deliveries made on time would give a high rating figure.

4. **Relationship performance:** Relationship performance is typically an intangible performance parameter. It is very important for the success of a culinary business to have a great working relationship with its suppliers.

In addition, evaluation of the **supplier's efforts** towards maintenance of working relationships even under difficult market conditions is an essential element of performance evaluation at the end of a business period, mostly a year.

The above are methods for evaluating suppliers of in-use products. In case of new products, evaluation of a supplier is done through observation of the supplier's zeal to support the culinary business's requirements. It is the combination of a supplier's resourcefulness, and the action he takes to focus on the quality, and timely delivery of the new products. It is often difficult for the supplier to control the price factor in the initial stages of procurement of new products.

7.5.4 The Right Supplier

The right supplier for a business is one with whom the culinary business can have a long term relationship. He is one who:

(a) provides the proper quality and quantity of products;

(b) is capable and committed to provide good service;

(c) has an understanding of the market of the culinary business and one who contributes through positive ideas of how best to meet this market's needs;

(d) has technical ability to handle supplies, and has trained personnel working under him well;

(e) meets requirements of statutory laws including food laws;

(f) meets requirements of HACCP including personal hygiene and sanitation of people, premises and delivery vehicles under his control;

(g) informs the culinary business about new, improved or cheaper products, which may be applicable to the operations;

(h) is able to involve in processes of development of new products for the culinary business.

(i) provides timely information regarding price changes to ensure price competitiveness;

(j) follows up on problems, resolves difficulties that arise, and negotiates any concerns of the culinary business;

(k) has an ongoing interest in improving products and services provided;

(l) has the financial capability to stock up products required by the culinary business. This, in turn, ensures that monies are not blocked unnecessarily in stocks in the stores of the purchaser. Stocking by the supplier also ensures that lead time for deliveries is reduced;

(m) is financially capable of growing with the culinary business;

(n) is aware and duty-bound towards requirements of safety; and

(o) is aware of his duties towards environment.

The requisite qualities of a good supplier have been provided above. Cost-effectiveness in supplier selection, the economic corollary of the above, has been taken up in the section "End of Module Notes" below.

The culinary business should examine its consumption patterns for a business period. This would allow identification of purchase quantities. The supplier can then be given commitments of quantities required. This would allow the supplier to determine and plan his own stocking levels, and reduce his inventories. This is an example of how the culinary business and supplier could work towards mutual benefits.

The interests of the purchaser and the supplier are served when a cooperative working relationship exists.

7.6 END OF MODULE NOTES

7.6.1 Cost-effectiveness in Supplier Selection

The exercise of selecting a good supplier is a key factor towards cost-effectiveness of culinary operations. The interests of the purchaser and the supplier are served when a cooperative working relationship exists. The understanding, **key areas** and **success factors** in relation to the process of selecting suppliers are listed below. The culinary business must select a supplier:

1. Who is knowledgeable about his products, has an understanding of the market of the culinary business and one who contributes through positive ideas about how best to meet this market's needs.

2. Who can ensure that his tangible and intangible services are performances of quality, delivery and relationship within an acceptable price range.

3. Who has the financial capability to grow with the purchaser's business and to stock up required products.

4. Who informs the culinary business about new, improved or cheaper products, which may be applicable to the operations.

5. Who provides timely information regarding price changes to ensure price competitiveness.

EXHIBIT 24: Selecting the Right Supplier

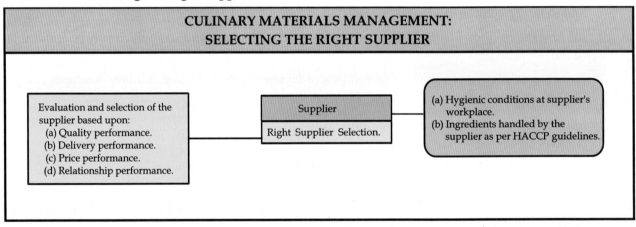

8

RIGHT RECEIVING

Essence of the Module

This module explains the importance of right receiving, the receiving processes and linkages of right receiving to customer satisfaction. Once the delivery invoice is signed by the receiving personnel, the responsibility of the corresponding commodities is transferred from the supplier to the purchaser. This is a dominant guiding principle of the receiving activities. The module also deals with the integration of the receiving process with robust controls to prevent malpractices in the system.

Module Objectives and Competencies
After going through this module the reader would be competent to: 1. Understand, identify and describe management of the receiving department.   2. Enumerate the basic steps involved in receiving products and receiving procedures.   3. Detail the post-receiving activities.   4. Establish the system of payment of suppliers' bills.   5. Discuss the importance of receiving department as an area of cost control.   6. Relate efficient receiving activities to the satisfaction of the customers.

8.1 INTRODUCTION TO RIGHT RECEIVING

Culinary business requires food products, ingredients and also items of other operational requirements. The requirements of the business are received under properly managed benchmarks of quality, quantity and time frames and overcoming possible malpractices. (For nature of non-food items **see p. 92.**)

8.2 MANAGEMENT OF THE RECEIVING DEPARTMENT

Efficient management of the receiving department requires thorough knowledge of and clarity about:

(a) The sequential process of receiving.

(b) The standard purchase specifications – defining quality parameters - in relation to each of the incoming products.

(c) Purchase procedures and purchase documents such as Purchase Order and the Perishables Order Sheet. In addition, the receiving personnel should have clarity of details regarding price and quantities to be received in respect of each incoming product.

(d) Selected vendors and committed timings to receive supplies from each supplier.

(e) Operation of equipment placed at the receiving.

(f) Documents to be completed at the receiving department and other post-receiving activities.

(g) Minimum standards of personal hygiene of staff, as well as hygiene and sanitation of the receiving area. In addition, knowledge of HACCP requirements at the receiving.

(h) The malpractices that suppliers could resort to in respect of incoming products and preventive measures against such malpractices.

The following is the sequential activities of a day at the receiving department:

1. Setting up of the receiving department for the day.
2. The process of receiving supplies.
3. Transfer of the supplies to their right storage place.
4. Thorough cleaning and sanitising of the receiving area.
5. Completing documentation.
6. Getting ready for the next day's activities.
7. Training and knowledge upgradation activities.

8.2.1 Setting Up of the Receiving Department for the Day

The important activities for setting up the receiving department for the day are:

(a) Keeping copies of the purchase orders and perishables order sheet ready for the receiving business of the day. These documents indicate the nature of supplies expected for the day. These documents are sourced at the end of the previous day's receiving activities from the purchase and food production department, either in physical format or through the property management system.

(b) Listing up the receiving schedule of the day.

(c) Keeping the photographic binders of standard purchase specifications of each commodity ready.

(d) Checking of weighing scales and other measuring equipment and their readiness for business.

> **Note:** Regular checking of the weighing scales for correct weights is done post-receiving through outsourced expertise.

(e) Checking of other equipment at the receiving, for example, the vegetable washing machine.

(f) Sanitizing of all equipment once again before start of operations. Strict sanitation benchmarks are part of all food receiving and handling processes.

(g) Checking of all HACCP requirements involving equipment, area, etc.

8.2.2 The Process of Receiving Supplies

The business should pay for an agreed price against an agreed quality. Checking incoming food products, ingredients and other operational items against the Purchase Order or Daily Perishables Order Sheet removes possibilities of error.

The important steps for receiving products are:

(a) **Checking incoming items for quality:**

- Contracts are made with suppliers for supplies of diverse nature for a period called **purchase period**. The rates of each item in respect of each unit of measurement are decided against quality parameters known as standard purchase specifications. Very often the rate of each incoming product remains constant for the duration of the purchase period. (The reader can read details on the subject of standard purchase specifications within Module 6: "Efficient Management of Purchasing Activities".)

- The standard purchase specifications for all food products, ingredients and other operational items are placed in binders. This is an important activity of the finance department. It is wise to remove ambiguity for all concerned by creating photographic binders for all food related specifications. This enables all to "speak the same language" in relation to the quality parameters of the supplies. Copies of such binders should be given to the supplier, to the receiving, to the purchase department and to the consuming departments.

- Checking incoming products against standard purchase specifications requires trained receiving personnel. A representative of the consumer department is also deputed to check the quality of the supplies. The representative recognizes the quality characteristics of every item which are required for the business.

- Certain culinary ingredients are measured for their true quality characteristics through testing procedures. Checking the milk for fat content is an example. Similarly, checking the commodity's temperature at the time of delivery is essential for perishables like meats, seafood, frozen processed foods, mandated to be delivered at the receiving department either fresh-chilled or frozen.

- For certain commodities, for example the supply of prawns the number of pieces per kilogram decides the quality and is paid for accordingly.

- In case of pre-portioned meat products, percentage of natural fat allowed is checked against the quality parameters agreed to as part of standard purchase specifications.

- For certain weight-range bound commodities, for example, the supply of chicken, quality is checked by counting the number of chickens received and checking these against the total weight of chicken received. In addition, individual bird is checked for conformance to the weight specification.

(b) **Checking incoming items for quantities:** The supply is also checked carefully for quantities in terms of weight or volume through the usage of weighing scales or calibrated measuring jugs for liquids. Only those quantities should be received which are ordered through the Perishables Order Sheet, the Butchery Order Sheet, and through the Purchase Order/Open Purchase Order.

(c) **Accepting the supplies:** The basis for payment to the supplier is the delivery invoice. The supplier is expected to provide a delivery invoice for each of his supplies for each event of delivery. The delivery invoice is part of the audit trail. Once the receiving personnel and the user department's representative signs the delivery invoice, the ownership and responsibility of the commodity is transferred to the business in all respects.

Once the product quality and quantity are verified as mentioned in the delivery invoice, the invoice can be signed. A typicality of most of the supplies in respect of culinary business is that invoices are often made by the supplier or his representative at the receiving area once the supplies are quantified and accepted. This is due to possibility of rejections of certain quantities of supplies as not conforming to the agreed standard purchase specifications.

8.2.3   Transfer of the Supplies to their Right Storage Place

Due to the edible nature of the food products and raw ingredients, theft by employees is possible post-receiving. Large percentages of products received daily are those that require temperature control before and after receiving. The supplies being perishable would deteriorate if they are left at room temperature at the receiving area. The food products and raw ingredients should be transferred to proper and designated storage spaces immediately. The practice adopted by the Indian hospitality industry is to transfer the perishables to the food production areas and the non-perishables to main stores.

8.2.4 Thorough Cleaning and Sanitising of the Receiving Area

The predominant supplies for culinary business are of the perishable and highly-perishable nature. (Supplies for culinary business are grouped as explained on **p. 137**). All types of food products and ingredients – raw, cooked, frozen, fresh chilled, dry and proprietary are received in an average day. The receiving area presents the greatest possible risk of cross-contamination, spoilage and infestation of food supplies and it is imperative to prevent the same.

Receipt of supplies is regulated through explicit observance of delivery timings, allowing for a gap between supplies belonging to two different groups or suppliers. An important activity of the receiving department throughout the day is to keep cleaning and sanitizing of the area and the equipment used after each supply. Once all the supplies for the day have been received, the equipment and the receiving areas are once again sanitized before closing the operations for the day.

8.2.5 Completing Documentation: Post Receiving Activities

The post-receiving activities are as important to the culinary business as are the receiving activities. These are:

(a) **Preparation of the Daily Receiving Report (DRR):** Post-receiving activities in terms of documentation are very important to confirm that "right" products have been received. The important document to prepare by the receiving personnel is the Daily Receiving Report (DRR), which is a part of the audit trail. The DRR includes information about the received items. This information is taken from the supplier's invoice, the perishable/butchery order sheet and/or the purchase order. Separate DRRs are made for different consuming departments.

Non-perishables are not received on a daily basis. A large component of the DRR represents receipt of perishables. The chef retains a copy of the Daily Perishables Sheet through which the perishables were ordered.

The DRR, along with the corresponding supplier's delivery invoice, is presented to the chef or other consuming department heads on the following day. This helps to confirm that types and quantities of received products fit the quality and quantity requirements of the business. The chef's signatures on the DRR are indication to the food & beverages control department to process the invoices for payment.

The industry practice is for the DRR to be routed to the chef and the finance department through the purchase department. The finance department is responsible for final processing of the bills and also release the payment.

In certain operations, the receiving personnel are responsible for an initial verification of the calculations. They ensure that the number of units purchased when multiplied by the agreed-upon purchase price, equals the supplier's total charges.

For certain other operations, the suppliers need not mention the costs in the delivery invoice. This is so because all the rates are contractually agreed, and the total amount that the supplier is to be paid for is effected through the supplier's statement, as further explained below.

(b) **Preparation of the short-supply note:** In case the ordered supplies have not been received or they have been supplied in quantities short of the required, the receiving department writes the shortfall on a document called the "short supply note". This is sent to the head of the respective consuming department. If required, the shortfall of supplies is sourced by the purchase department directly from the open market at the cost of the supplier.

(c) **Processing supplier's bills for payment:** The finance department processes the bills of the suppliers for payments. Copies of the purchase orders are sent by the purchase department to the finance department in advance of the receipt of supplies. The DRR and the respective delivery invoices are transferred to the finance department on a daily basis. The supplier submits a statement of supplies for each of the billing period. The statement covers all the deliveries of the billing period and mentions the respective delivery invoices. The finance department checks the statement in relation to quantities and rates contracted earlier. All documents are filed properly for the purposes of maintaining the audit trail.

Another method to process payment is through the inputs of delivery invoices. This is the general method to adopt for food products or raw ingredients which are not purchased regularly or are non-contractual in nature. In such cases the supplier does not send a statement. The delivery invoices are checked for the contracted or agreed price. The payments are made.

Except for petty cash expenses and rare purchases all payments are paid through cheques. Information regarding payment date, cheque number and cheque amount is recorded.

8.2.6 Getting Ready for the Next Day's Activities

Once the documentation of the day's receipts is complete and the receiving area sanitized; it is time to get ready for the next day's activities. This involves accessing copies of the purchase orders, the Perishables Order Sheet and the Butchery Order Sheet for the next day's supplies. These documents indicate the quantum and nature of supplies expected for the next day. Another important activity is to safeguard the photographic binders and the tools used during the day for receiving. The weighing scales are checked for their accuracy during this period, and very often external expertise is sought for this activity.

8.2.7 Training and Knowledge Upgradation Activities

Each organisation defines the standard operating procedures for its business. Personnel of the receiving department should be trained to carry out receiving procedures efficiently.

Effective receiving requires knowledgeable personnel. In addition, there are many post-receiving activities at the receiving area. Receiving personnel must understand all receiving procedures and know how to complete internal receiving records. The internal receiving records are part of the audit trail. The receiving personnel should be literate and have some experience of similar operations.

The personnel should be trained on the standard purchase specifications of all the commodities and general items of the operation's requirements. A representative of the consuming department is deputed for the quality check. However, instead of remaining mute spectator to the quality check process, it is important that receiving personnel should act intelligently and knowingly about the incoming products to be received.

Systematic training of commodity identification, commodity usage, and defining of quality characteristics is important. The binders of standard purchase specifications, along with their photographs help in the matter. The systematic training would help the personnel to recognise the product quality standards when food products and raw ingredients are received.

Receiving personnel should also be trained on their personal hygiene, general hygiene of the receiving area and HACCP aspect of receiving operations. This training is made mandatory in culinary business. As far as the receiving of culinary ingredients is concerned, training is vital in the matter of food safety and standards. This training safeguards the business's interests.

Equipment which support the receiving functions like transportation equipment, computers, and thermometers, etc., should be available at the receiving department and the receiving personnel should be trained to use these.

Documents like formats and document recording systems for example physical or computerized files should be available and the personnel trained to use them.

8.3 COST CONTROLS IN THE RECEIVING FUNCTIONS

Receiving is an important part of the product cost control system. The processes of right purchasing and right supplier selection would be wasted if no one makes sure that the products delivered meet the standard purchase specifications of the business.

Only selected and trained employees should be permitted to receive food products and raw ingredients. Properly trained receivers would know how to act when there is a problem with product deliveries.

The receiving area should be near the delivery door. Proper receiving requires that most items would be weighed or counted. Therefore, proper measuring scales for dry items and measuring jugs for liquid supplies should be available.

Marking and tagging of food products and raw ingredients places information of the delivery invoice on to the items or their packing material. This supports stock rotation. The tags can be used when calculating the value of the store's inventory. The recording of the unit price on the tag helps in creating cost connotations and awareness of the product for personnel.

Marking and tagging is often used for receiving supplies of meats, seafood and non-perishables. Handy tagging machines are available to facilitate the process. Marking and tagging helps in food cost control matters. The information from the tag can be entered onto a requisition form when the product is issued. Theft and pilferage are controlled as the tag helps to identify the products that should be in storage. The physical inventory becomes easier and speedier. Stock rotation can be maintained easily.

Marking and tagging supports understanding of yields and per kilogram product costs especially in case of raw meat products. Culinary supplies should be checked thoroughly for quality. Once the supplies are accepted the possibilities of recovering from accidental or purposeful theft by suppliers is very difficult.

Some of the ways the **suppliers cheat** are as follows:

- Supplying meat products like chicken, lamb, beef, etc., with higher percentage of fat than agreed for.
- Supplying thawed out products in place of fresh items. Very often the 'fresh-chilled' quality of supplies is more expensive than frozen quality of the same. An example is fish supplies.
- Supplying chicken with excess water content. It is easy to fill water in a just-butchered chicken. The bird retains large percentage of this water till the time of pre-portioning prior to cooking. The business pays for water at the rate of chicken.
- Supplying ground meat products in which finely crushed ice is mixed. The business pays for ice at the rate of ground meat. In addition, there is no way to find out at the receiving if inferior/cheaper meats have been ground and charged for ground meat of superior quality. Most culinary outlets do not purchase ground meat products for this reason, as well as the possibilities of faster contamination of the ground meat.
- Weight of ice or packing material may be included in the product weight.
- Supplying seafood which has lost its prime freshness. The business pays for top quality of seafood.
- Supplying expensive steak meat mixed with inexpensive cuts of meat in one supply basket. The business pays for the entire supply at the rate of steak meat.
- Supplying ready-to-cook cuts of lamb with a mix of baby lamb meat and that of an aged animal and charging for baby lamb meat, which is more expensive.
- Supplying a case of bottled products in which one bottle is broken. The contents of the bottle cannot be used. The business pays for the entire case.

Very often the suppliers manage to bribe receiving personnel and get away with inferior quality, get excess weight recorded and accepted in the delivery invoice, or commit purposeful thefts such as the above examples. These are **common malpractices** at the receiving.

The business can **safeguard its interests by**:

- changing receiving personnel often;

- training the receiving personnel to receive properly;

- regular committee approach for receiving and ensuring that knowledgeable persons from the consumer department are available to check product quality. The schedules for receiving should be planned at timings of low operational activity;

- the process of in-house meat fabrication and avoiding purchase of ready-to-cook meat cuts;

- checking the weighing scales and measuring equipment regularly for accuracy;

- removing the possibilities of employee theft. This can be achieved by transferring supplies immediately to designated storages; and

- keeping the delivery personnel of the supplier under constant watch. Representatives of the supplier including their delivery personnel should not be allowed beyond the receiving area. They should not be utilised for transfer of supplies to designated storage areas. All precautions should be taken to ensure that they have no opportunity to steal or pilfer part of their products for personal consumption, once the delivery process is complete.

8.4 SCHEDULING OF DELIVERIES

Scheduling deliveries is a management exercise. Supplies of diverse nature arriving at any and all timings/days would create chaos at the receiving area. The user department which is required to depute knowledgeable personnel for quality check of supplies would not be in a position to spare the personnel at all times. The deliveries should be in line with the purchasing schedules set by the receiving department. Scheduling deliveries of perishables go in line with the market conditions. Traditionally in India, delivery of perishables and highly perishables is scheduled for mornings and pre-lunch period.

Supplies of non-perishable food products and raw ingredients are scheduled for specific days and always post-lunch. In a similar manner deliveries of other needs are scheduled on specific days and always post-lunch. Once agreed upon, the schedule of deliveries must be maintained.

8.5 TIMINGS OF DELIVERY

Receiving of supplies involves time-consuming but important tasks. Right receiving of supplies supports the satisfaction of the customer. The receiving personnel need cooperation from the consuming departments. A representative of the chef is deputed to check supplies for quality characteristics along with the receiving personnel who check the quantities received. The receiving personnel also have other duties at the receiving area.

Culinary business has typical peak periods and low periods of work load on each day. An example of low periods of workload in the food production department is from 1000 hours till 1130 hours. This period corresponds to the end of the breakfast session and up to an hour before the lunch session starts at 1230 hours.

Receiving of supplies should take place ideally during comparatively low periods of workload, so that the chef's representative can give undivided attention to the receiving duties. As an industry practice the perishables are received during this period. In a similar fashion, non-perishables are received post-1500 hours, when another low period of workload for culinary professionals starts. This period corresponds to post-lunch session.

Non-acceptance of deliveries at certain times of the day is common in culinary business. The delivery timings are communicated to the supplier in writing along with the contract documents at the start of a purchase period. These are also communicated to all concerned by displaying a schedule of delivery timings in respect of all deliveries in the receiving area.

8.6   E-RECEIVING

Computerization helps in rapid generation of important control information with minimal chances of error. Each food product or ingredient which is purchased is allotted a computer code. Computer codes are given for:

- delivery size;
- shape;
- volume;
- quantity;
- price;
- date; and
- time of receipt.

The DRR and the short supply notice are made and sent on e-mail to the required persons. The continuity in the system is ensured till payments are made to the supplier. For example, on receipt of the DRR on e-mail, the chef checks the documents, and if found correct, forwards it to the food and beverages controls department. If the chef has any comment, the same is made in the body of the forwarding note. Similarly, after checking, and making their own entries, the food and beverages controls department forwards it to the Bills and Payments Department for payments to the supplier.

The Perishables Order Sheet, the Butchery Order Sheet, the Purchase Requisition, and the Purchase Order are also transferred through the computerized system and e-mails to the respective users and to respective suppliers.

8.7   END OF MODULE NOTES

8.7.1   Cost-effectiveness in Receiving Functions

It is the responsibility of receiving personnel and the user department's representative to receive supplies. They must check supplies for quality and quantity. The ownership and responsibility of the supplies in all respects is transferred from the supplier to the purchaser, immediately on signing the supplier's delivery invoice. The **key four areas** and **success factors** in relation to the cost-effectiveness of receiving operations are listed below. The culinary business must:

1. receive quantities of supplies in conformation to orders placed. The quantities of perishables/ highly perishables should be checked against the Perishables Order Sheet/Butchery Order Sheet. The quantities of non-perishables should be checked against the Purchase Order. Other supplies for the culinary business should be checked against Purchase Order;

2. receive supplies in conformation to quality benchmarks as prescribed by standard purchase specifications;

3. ensure support from user department for quality check of supplies;

4. ensure knowledgeable and trained personnel are available to receive ordered supplies;

5. ensure effective control of malpractices;

6. transfer accepted supplies immediately to their right storages; and

7. ensure availability and usage of correctly calibrated weighing scales and measuring equipment.

8.7.2 Delivery Invoice

Delivery invoice is a document made by the supplier in respect of any product that he supplies to the business. The delivery invoice lists all the values and quantities of items that were ordered, and has references of the Purchase Order, or the daily Perishable Order Sheet. The delivery invoice serves as a proof of delivery and is attached to the bill prepared by the supplier for each billing period, and submitted to the purchaser.

Once the delivery invoice is signed by the receiving personnel, the ownership and responsibility of the corresponding commodities is immediately transferred from the supplier to the purchaser.

8.7.3 Bill /Billing

Billing corresponds to a period of time. Depending on convenience, billing can be done for a week, or for a fortnight or for a month. The bill is a document prepared by the supplier. It lists the supplies executed in the preceding period or on the same day. The bill also lists the price per unit which was agreed to at the start of the purchase period, the total value of supplies of that particular bill, and taxes if any.

8.7.4 Billing Period

This is the period between two billings. Sale price agreed between the culinary business and the supplier is recovered by the supplier through the process of billing. The billing period is mentioned in the contract made with the supplier. The billing period is mostly a fortnight or a month.

Billing period is decided to suit the business's administrative convenience. This decision is often based on the quantum of supplies in the period, the funds available and also the amounts that the supplier is able and willing to keep invested in the purchaser's business. However, the billing period is communicated to the supplier so that he can arrange his finances accordingly.

EXHIBIT 25: Right Receiving

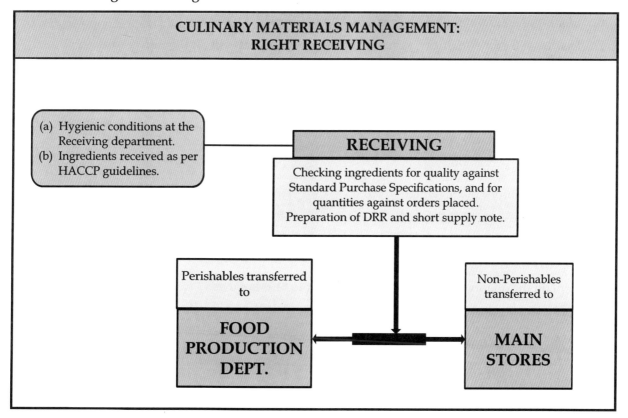

9

EFFICIENT STORING, INVENTORY MANAGEMENT AND RIGHT ISSUING

Essence of the Module

This module presents cost-effectiveness through efficient stores management. It explains why it is imperative to maintain low inventory and high turnover from stores. The module further describes the process of issues from stores.

Module Objectives and Competencies
After going through this module the reader would be competent to:

1. Explain the broad contents of the systems of an efficient storing, inventory management and issuing system.

2. Explain maintenance of quality of foods during storage.

3. Discuss the just-in-time purchasing process.

4. Understand the difficulties in prediction of quantities of ingredients.

5. Understand the management of stores.

6. Identify the aims and objectives of efficient storing.

7. Discuss the Euro-American format of storing perishables and highly perishables.

8. Explain "stock-outs".

9. Understand the reasons of grouping stored products. Identify the two important tools of grouping of food products and raw ingredients:

   (a) Relative cost per portion.

   (b) Relative perishability.

10. Detail inventory management.

11. Identify the aims and objectives of efficient inventory management.

12. Identify the 'golden' rule of inventory management.

13. Discuss the control of inventories.

14. Explain the qualification of a commodity for it to be treated as a "stores" item or a "direct" item.

15. Understand inventory record keeping systems:

   (a) Physical inventory system. In addition, understand the Bin Card system as a support function.

   (b) Perpetual inventory system.

16. Showcase the process and techniques of assigning values to inventories in stores and to issues for food production. In the process understand average inventory and its calculations.

17. Understand inventory turnover, inventory turnover rates and their possibilities thereof.

18. Detail the inventory turnover calculations.

19. Establish inventory turnover trends.

20. Explain the Minimum/Maximum Inventory and Ordering System and its nomenclature. Detail the advantages and disadvantages of the system.

21. Discuss computerization of stores.

22. Discuss the process of 'Right issues'.

23. Identify the aims and objectives of 'Right issues'.

24. Explain the stores requisition process and form.

25. Identify the duties and responsibilities of the storekeeper.

9.1 INTRODUCTION TO EFFICIENT STORING, INVENTORY MANAGEMENT AND RIGHT ISSUING

Materials management is the optimum utilization of materials, their maintenance and safety. Storing is keeping materials in hand for future requirements. Materials are considered to be "stored" when these are transferred from the receiving department and are entered into the store's inventory.

The majority of materials handled by culinary business are related to food products and raw ingredients. The processes of efficient storing, inventory management and right issuing of food materials for food production are important links in the culinary materials management chain.

Management of food materials is a cyclic activity as well as an on-going process. Overordering of food materials would result in materials not consumed as regularly as desired. It would also result in possibilities of unauthorized consumption, pilferage, wastage, etc. Right ordering patterns have to be evolved by operators to ensure that the right quantities are ordered. All activities involved in materials management must happen as per requirements, and in time. The materials should be handled in prescribed manner, with the help of benchmarks, at different stages.

In culinary business the main stores typically deals with storing of non-perishable food materials. For the purposes of this module therefore, storing, inventory management and issuing would represent dealing with non-perishables. The principles of materials management enumerated in the present module can be successfully applied to materials of the perishable and highly perishable nature also. However, the values explained in present module are limited to the "raw" or "as-purchased" status of food materials – as stored in main stores; and not necessarily to semi-prepared or ready-to-serve menu items or those at the holding stage – handled by the food production department.

It is vital for culinary business to safeguard the health of their customers. All food materials are perishable and deteriorate with passage of time. Irresponsibility in handling food materials can result in food poisoning and damage to the reputation of the outlet.

Quality of food products and raw ingredients must be **maintained** during storage. Efficient materials management in the stores ensures that the quality of the food materials is kept at optimum levels. Some foods do not exhibit noticeable signs of deterioration. Display of date of expiry on ingredients helps in their timely consumption. Displaying the date of expiry on non-perishables is mandatory as per the statutory food safety and standards act.

Useful life of the food materials is an important consideration. Maintaining quality of materials in storage depends upon the right ordering and purchasing processes. Food materials should be received and stored immediately under the right storage conditions. Stored food materials must regularly move out for consumption. Once materials are issued from stores for food production, the management of these materials is immediately transferred to the food production department and its chefs.

The main stores must check the quality of non-perishables on receipt from the receiving department.

While in the main stores the quality of food should be maintained through:

- planned handling and stacking of supplies;
- control of temperature of food items in storage. Different food items require different temperatures for maintenance of their optimum quality;
- ensuring proper ventilation and humidity control of the stores;
- issuing of supplies strictly in the order of first-in-first-out;
- utilization of otherwise non-moving and slow moving items, before their expiry;
- stores cleaning, sanitation and observation of HACCP principles; and
- regular inspection of stocks for pest infestation and physical damage.

The personnel of the main stores must check the quantities of non-perishables. Blind receiving, explained below is a process of cross-checking the correctness of the quantities.

Blind receiving is a form of Quantity Control. Supplies for a culinary business are mostly in the genre of food products and raw ingredients. All these supplies are perishable or highly perishable. Once received, minimum time should be spent in transferring the supplies to their right places of storage and placed under the right conditions of temperature control.

On receipt at the main stores, the personnel of the food stores immediately check the quantities of various supplies through a process of physical inventory and record these quantities. The stores personnel do not access the supplier's invoice or any other document while performing this quantity check. This process is called blind receiving. Materials which are received in this manner are cross-checked for quantities immediately afterwards with the documents prepared by the receiving department.

9.2   JUST-IN-TIME PURCHASING

On receipt the perishables are transferred to the food production department and non-perishables are transferred to the main stores. Just-in-time purchasing means purchasing food products and raw ingredients just when they are required. These are then transferred straight from the receiving area to the food production department for immediate requirements and usage. Therefore, for culinary business just-in-time purchasing usually refers to purchase of non-perishables.

This technique circumvents the need for the food product or ingredient to be sent to stores on receipt, and requirements of their subsequent issues to food production department when required against stores requisitions. Just-in-time purchasing requires efficient coordination among the:

- food production department;
- purchase department; and
- the supplier.

Just-in-time purchasing supports minimum inventory in stores and also inventory costs to be kept minimum. Just-in-time purchasing process also saves on requirements of storage space. The typicality of the system is to order frequently, for example, once daily, but in relatively smaller quantities. Available monies can be utilized for other operational requirements of the business. This improves the return on investments.

Just-in-time purchasing is a common methodology to save on inventory costs in manufacturing business. It is not an ideal purchase system for purchases of all requirements of culinary business. Just-in-time purchasing can be exercised for selected ingredients. The totality of the culinary business **cannot** be subjected to just-in-time purchasing. Just-in-time purchase system is also used to purchase requirements of emergency nature. These emergencies could be to honour the special requests of customers. The system is useful in such cases.

9.3 FORECASTING THE QUANTITIES OF INGREDIENTS REQUIRED

The typicality of culinary business is that **demand of food cannot be firmly and accurately established.** In a hotel scenario there are a number of cuisine outlets. This encourages customers to try out different cuisines on different occasions. In addition, the customers are not captive to the hotel, and are free to enjoy variety of cuisines in the market where the hotel is located. The same is true for other stand-alone culinary business.

Even a highly successful stand-alone culinary outlet cannot predict the type of à la carte orders that it would execute in a day. Using the weighted average method and other methods of controlling food production quantities, the outlet can come closer to the expected number of portions of different à la carte **menu items** which would be required for a particular business day. (The reader can understand the methods of forecasting quantities of food production in Module 10: "Economics of Food production and Food Service".)

In continuation of this understanding and its relationship to efficiencies in management of stores it is difficult to forecast the exact quantities of ingredients that would be required each day.

In a scenario where fixed number of customer footfalls come into the business and the menu offering is strictly *table d' hôte*, requirements of food products and raw ingredients can be predicted. This is possible in resort type of business while dealing with tourists in a group with fixed rates per meal, and guaranteed customers for a particular meal. This type of business is becoming rarer.

Quantum of food to be produced for buffets for a day can be established by closely observing trends of consumption as well as expected business. However, there is no guarantee that such forecasting would be absolutely accurate.

The essence of the above discussion is that **quantities of food production** and **demand do not perfectly match.** In addition, operating deficiencies in the system of the culinary business may result in the food product or ingredients to be unavailable. These deficiencies can also be due to inconsistent delivery performance of the supplier or due to market conditions. **Eliminating inventories** in the culinary business is therefore **not wise and practical.**

9.4 MANAGEMENT OF STORES

Management of stores is an important task of the business of a culinary outlet. Correct management practices would result in a cost-effective operation. Maintaining low inventories, quality inventory recording system, ordering fresh supplies through a minimum/maximum inventory and ordering system, and right issue procedures would ensure that the right financial results accrue to the business and the quality results accrue to the customer. A storekeeper is an important person to ensure results.

Management of stores involves three major activities, as follows:

1. Efficient storing.
2. Efficient inventory management.
3. Right issuing process.

9.4.1 Efficient Storing

The **aims and objectives** of efficient storing are as follows:

1. To enable the production to be planned and executed as per schedules.
2. To analyze and coordinate unusual consumptions.
3. To control the environments to maintain the optimum material quality.
4. To ensure in-built control measures within stores management, for example access control.
5. To prevent unauthorized consumption and opportunities of theft of materials.
6. To maintain links with the production and purchase departments.
7. To manage employee safety while handling materials.
8. To maintain store timings strictly. Exclusive time should be devoted to each function in the management of stores – storing, inventory management and issues.

9.4.2 The Euro-American Format of Storing Perishables and Highly Perishables

Euro-American culinary business choose to place their perishables and highly perishables in stores after receiving, and issue these to food production department against authorized stores requisition, in a similar manner as groceries are issued. In such cases the perishables and highly perishables also become "stores" items. The trend is nascent in India. In this format of stocking food products and raw ingredients, the quantum of purchase and stocking levels of these perishables and highly perishables are guided by the chef, while the management including financial accountability and inventory control remains with the stores management.

The non-perishables are stored and managed by the stores management. The essence of the Euro-American format of storing perishables therefore is that **every food product and ingredient** purchased is stored and managed by the stores management.

9.4.3 Stock-out

Stock-out is a situation in stores when a food product or ingredient required by the food production department is not available due to market conditions and / or due to poor management of the stores or purchase department.

Purchasing insufficient quantities of food products and raw ingredients has disadvantages. Insufficient quantities may result in "stock-out" situations. Stock-out of ingredients results in delay in food production and necessitates rescheduling of food production. "Stock-out" in stores may result in "not-available menu items" which, in turn, would result in customer dissonance. In the event of "stock-out" emergency open-market purchases may have to be made. These open-market purchases not being subject to contractual rates – would be expensive and time consuming. In certain cases discounts otherwise available for volume purchases would be lost. These are administrative inefficiencies.

Food products and raw ingredients are perishable. Non-perishable foods do not deteriorate rapidly. However, monies are invested in "stores". **The items should be purchased in minimum quantities.** Maintaining of "minimum stock levels" for non-perishables is an ideal situation to:

- eliminate possibilities of employee theft;
- reduce required storage space;
- reduce number of staff to manage food inventories;
- reduce operational expenses;
- ensure optimum product quality due to right movement of stocks into food production; and
- reduce spoilage.

9.4.4 Storing of Purchased Items

The culinary business purchases products of the nature of food and those of the nature of non-food. (Examples of purchases of non-food items have been provided in Module 6: "Efficient Management of Purchasing Activities".)

On receipt, non-food but perishable items, for example, flowers are immediately transferred to the user department. Non-food items of the nature of capital expenditure are placed in their designated stores. To maintain continuity of quality of items of the nature of capital expenditure, extra quantities are ordered. A typical example is the purchase of furniture items. The extra quantities are stored in back-of-the-house areas in special stores. Kitchenette equipment is handed over to the chef. Extra quantities of kitchenette equipment, glassware, silverware, cutlery and crockery are maintained in kitchen stewarding stores. In a similar manner every non-food item is stored in a designated store.

9.4.5 Storing of Food Products and Raw Ingredients

Food products and raw ingredients require independent storage. A 'food-store' is used for the purpose. Every food product and ingredient must have a place of its own. In addition every food product and ingredient must always be stored in its own place. The storage racks, bins and other containers should be designed and positioned accordingly.

Marking and tagging of food products and raw ingredients while being received and while being stored supports right storing. Marking and tagging helps in avoidance of spoilage of food products and raw ingredients and their issue and consumption well before their expiry dates.

Organizing stored items is an important activity. Food products and raw ingredients require separate storage and must be stored in groups. The grouping is done for many reasons, as follows:

(a) To avoid cross-contamination.

(b) To maintain accountability of expensive and easily stolen items, for example, saffron sachets.

(c) For convenience of storing, issuing and stock-taking. Food products and raw ingredients which show a high consumption pattern should be nearer to the issuing area.

(d) To maintain their quality.

9.4.6 Grouping of Stored Food Products and Raw Ingredients

Food products and raw ingredients display two important features, i.e., they are perishable and they are purchased at different price points.

Food products and raw ingredients are subject to statutory laws, which dictate their "usage-within" dates and other quality parameters. In culinary business quality parameters are defined by the standard purchase specifications. All food products and ingredients have prescribed shelf life and must display their dates of expiry. Extreme care is required in handling food products and raw ingredients. Irresponsibility in handling food materials can result in food poisoning and damage to the reputation of the culinary business.

How should food store personnel group food products and raw ingredients?

The tools to evaluate food products and raw ingredients for grouping are the relative perishability and relative cost as explained below:

(a) **Relative perishability of food products and raw ingredients:** All food products and ingredients deteriorate with passage of time. Some deteriorate more quickly than others. In other words perishability of food products and raw ingredients is **relative.** Therefore, one tool of evaluation for **grouping** of food products and raw ingredients is their **relative perishability.**

(b) **Relative cost price of food products and raw ingredients:** Food products and raw ingredients are purchased at different price points. Culinary business with variety of culinary offers purchase food products and raw ingredients with a very wide range of cost prices.

Raw ingredients, as purchased, cannot be sold, as a finished menu item. Ingredients are processed and cooked as directed by the standard recipes formulated for each menu item. The cost of each ingredient as per its measurement is listed in the standard recipe. The cost of recipe is calculated on the basis of the number of portions that it would produce. The standard recipe is based on number of portions of the menu item. Standard recipe costs can be worked out for one portion of menu item. This cost is known as the **cost of per portion sale** in respect of the particular menu item.

The above relates to "stored" ingredients. In a similar manner cost of sales of perishables and highly perishables can be calculated. Cost of sales of perishables and highly perishables is represented by the cost of issues from the cold stores in the food production areas, etc. The issued ingredients require combination with other ingredients in a step-by-step method to formulate into the standard recipe of a particular menu item. The sale price of each portion of the menu item is known from the menu.

Through the method of costing standard recipes, the costs of "as-purchased" food products or raw ingredients can be evolved in the form of cost per portion of each menu item. Each standard recipe, in respect of individual menu item would produce different costs per portion. The second tool of evaluation for **grouping** of food products and ingredients is their **relative cost per portion.**

The two tools of evaluation for **grouping** of food products and raw ingredients are listed below:

- Relative perishability.
- Relative cost per portion.

Food products and raw ingredients are grouped in a way to present an immediate and clear picture of their **perishable nature** and their **costs per portion.**

Grouping of food products and raw ingredients is essential in the stores as well as in the food production area. **Grouping** of food products and raw ingredients facilitates controls in operations. The system also governs theft prone items in relation to their costs. It is for individual culinary business to group their own food products and raw ingredients in stores and in food production areas as per this system. The **groups** of food products and raw ingredients are presented below:

Group 1: This group consists of food products and raw ingredients which are **high in perishability and high in cost of sales per portion.** Examples are fresh shellfish, fresh fish, and fresh meats. The supply of these food products and raw ingredients to the culinary business should be done via a cold store chain. The cold store chain must start from their catchment or source area. These food products and raw ingredients perish fast and exhibit spoilage. Inappropriate care can result in fast deterioration of quality and the items can easily become unfit for human consumption. These food products and ingredients are very expensive.

Group 2: This group consists of food products and raw ingredients which are **low in perishability and high in cost of sales per portion.** Examples are frozen seafood, frozen meats, canned seafood, canned meats, frozen vegetables, preserved specialty items and canned imported goods. The inherent perishability of the items is reduced due to the use of different preservation methods. While the perishability is low, they continue to be very expensive. Costs per unit rise due to the costs of preservation and packaging.

Group 3: This group consists of food products and raw ingredients which are **comparatively low in perishability and comparatively low in cost of sales per portion.** Examples are fresh poultry, dairy products, and fresh produce. The perishability of fresh poultry, dairy products and fresh produce is not as high as seafood. In addition, the cost per unit of these items is not as high as seafood or meats.

Group 4: This group consists of food products and raw ingredients which are **low in perishability and low in cost of sales per portion.** Examples are spices and seasonings, condiments and staples. These food products and raw ingredients also spoil and perish with time, but the process of spoilage is slower. In addition, these food products and ingredients are comparatively quite low in their costs.

> **Note: Grouping** of food products and raw ingredients is easier when the culinary business adopts the Euro-American format of storing perishables, explained earlier in the current module. The stores management must maintain visual and written checklists to ensure the grouping of food products and raw ingredients. The stores assistants must be trained for the requirements of grouping.

9.5 EFFICIENT INVENTORY MANAGEMENT

Inventory management ensures synergies of operations through:

- Planning and scheduling of storage, issues and reordering activities.
- Actual storage, upkeep and maintenance of materials.
- Facilitating issues.

9.5.1 Aims and Objectives of Efficient Inventory Management

1. To stock sufficiently to honour the requirements put up to the stores.
2. To ensure that the right material quantities are ordered and replenished and in time.
3. To ensure high inventory turnover.
4. To ensure as low inventories as is possible.
5. To enable regular inventory-taking processes.
6. To maintain records in an audit-friendly manner. Efficiencies in stores and inventory management require up-to-date knowledge of inventory levels.
7. To facilitate stock valuation. Stock valuation at any point of time is possible through computerization or usage of property management systems.

9.5.2 Golden Rule of Inventory Management

Higher efficiencies in inventory management are directly related to:

- The lesser materials in stores in terms of individual stock keeping units (SKUs).
- The lesser space (often premium space) required to stock the materials.
- The lesser manpower required to handle the materials.
- The lesser capital investments in purchasing the materials.

9.5.3 Controls of Inventories

Control and reduction in inventories to lowest possible levels can be achieved through:

- Improved forecasting through efforts and systematic approaches like closer monitoring of food products and raw ingredients.
- Improved delivery performance of suppliers.
- Usages of technology like bar coding systems, computerization, and specific property management systems.

As quantities of food production and demand are not perfectly matched in culinary business, a need to introduce buffer in the storage system arises.

The ingredients in stores have to be issued for food production. Issuing of ingredients is also called **stock rotation** or **stock turning**. To replenish stocks of ingredients depleted due to issues, fresh ingredients are purchased and placed in stores. This is a continuous process.

For purpose of inventory, food products and raw ingredients are often separated into two categories: **stores and directs**.

9.5.4 Stores and Direct Items

Stores items: Stores items are those food products and raw ingredients which after receiving are sent to the stores for safe-keeping and systematic issues to the food production department against authorized Stores Requisition. Stores items are predominantly non-perishables. These are also known as groceries.

Stores items are:

(a) Part of the stock replenishment system like the Minimum / Maximum Inventory and Ordering System, explained within the current module.

(b) Part of the financial reporting system.

(c) Part of the audit-trail.

(d) Part of the statutory tax structure. The inventory valuation is taken as part of "stock-in-trade", for purposes of preparing the final accounts.

(e) Controlled on the basis of weight, volume, unit or count. "Stores" items can be easily computerized.

Direct items: **Direct items** are perishable and highly perishable food products and raw ingredients. These are purchased for relatively immediate use in comparison to groceries. Perishables and highly perishables are purchased several times a week. Some examples are fresh fruits, vegetables, dairy products, etc. With Indian culinary business opting to use perishable food products and raw ingredients from global sources, many perishables are very expensive per unit of purchase.

These products are called "**direct**" because they are transferred immediately to the food production areas after receiving. The products can be held in workstation storage areas. The primary concern with "**direct**" is proper receiving against standard purchase specifications.

(a) These are items of perishable and highly perishable nature and include milk products, local and imported meat products, seafood, speciality products and goods meant for special occasions.

(b) Not entered into storage records as these are not considered part of the store's inventory system.

(c) Considered part of the food costs of the day on which they are received.

(d) Considered the responsibility of the chef and the food production personnel.

> **Note:** The above is as per the current industry practice within Indian culinary business. The Euro-American format has been explained on **pp. 45, 152**.

9.5.5 Inventory Record Keeping Systems

Inventory control is part of the control of storage activities by finance personnel. The finance department discourages theft and pilferage by being closely involved with storage activities and accountability thereof. **Inventory recording systems are aids to identify the right inventory values.**

There are two basic kinds of inventory record keeping systems for products in storage. These are:

1. The physical inventory system.
2. The perpetual inventory system.

1. **The Physical inventory system:** Calculations of inventory value at the beginning and end of a month is important to understand inventory turnover and to calculate food and beverages costs. In addition, for any culinary business, stocks in stores represent investments in absolute terms of money. Balance of stocks at the end of a financial year represents assets which are entered in the balance sheets of the business. Therefore, stocks in stores are governed by statutory laws and require close monitoring. Once-a-year physical inventory of all stock balances in stores is mandatory for all forms business.

In addition to once-a-year format for conducting physical inventories, business may decide upon its own chronological schedule. The physical inventories are usually conducted monthly, or at the end of each quarter (three-month period) for the entire stocks in the stores. Reconciliation of the stock balances with the ledger figures is done, and differences ascertained. Actual stock balances accurately matching the figures in the books point to:

- accurate inventory accounting records;
- an efficient system;
- efficiency of the store personnel; and
- every item found in the stores is recorded and every recorded item in the books is found in the stores.

    A physical inventory involves actual observation, counting, weighing and volume measuring of each item in the stores. The storage unit is the basis on which costs of inventories is assessed. A serious shortcoming of a physical inventory system is that it does not indicate how much of each product should be available.

While this physical inventory is being conducted, normal business activity of the stores in terms of issues and receipts is avoided. In case of large size of business the food products and raw ingredients are stored in many stores. The responsibility of physical verification of the entire stocks is shared by personnel deputed from consuming and finance departments. Two people can make independent counts and compare results before entering information on the physical inventory form.

While making a physical inventory check, products can be listed in the same order as the store ledger or as they are found in the storage area on the shelves or bins. Listing food products or raw ingredients in this sequence makes the task of locating items on the physical inventory form easier. It also reduces the likelihood that products will be missed when inventory is taken. Maintenance of the bin card supports efficient functioning of the physical inventory system.

Bin Card is a stock-status recording document of stores. **Each stored** food product or ingredient is considered a stock-keeping unit (SKU) and assigned a bin card. In case an ingredient is stored in two different weights or volumes packing then both packings have different stock-keeping units assigned to them. The most important responsibility of the management of stores is to manage supplies. Supplies come into stores from the receiving department, are stored and issued to the food production department against Stores Requisition.

Based on various factors, discussed above, the following are decided:

(a) Maximum quantity of the ingredient to be maintained in stores.

(b) Minimum quantity of the ingredient to be maintained in stores.

(c) Ordering point.

The bin card is devised to keep the above in check. Issuing the requisitioned ingredients to the food production department depletes quantities in stores. The supplies are ordered again. The ordering of ingredients, their receipt, transfer to stores, storing, and issuing is a cyclic process.

Exhibit 26: Format of Bin Card

RG Riverside Grill

Bin Card

Bin Card No. _____

Bin No. _____   Maximum Quantity _____

Stores Ledger Folio _____   Minimum Quantity _____

Name of the Food Ingredient _____   Ordering Quantity _____

Date	Receipts		Issues		Balance	Date of Checking	Remarks	Ingredient ordered		
	Goods Received Note No.	Quantity	Stores Requisition No.	Quantity	Quantity			Purchase Requisition No.	Quantity	Date of Receipt

Storekeeper

The bin card assists the storekeeper to control the stock. The bin card keeps a running record of receipts, issues and balances on hand. The physical balance of any stored item should match the quantity shown in the bin card. If it matches, it proves the accuracy in management of stocks. Bin card is maintained by the storekeeper. He is answerable for any difference between physical stock in stores and the balance shown in the bin card.

Bin card is also called a cardex or tag card. Bin cards are hung up or placed on the shelf, rack or bin where the ingredient has been kept. Bin cards are also maintained in a ledger kept in stores. Computerisation has changed the requirements of maintaining bin cards in physical format. A specimen of a Bin Card is shown in **Exhibit 26 above**.

2. **The Perpetual inventory system:** Perpetual inventory system is a continuous inventory system. Perpetual inventory is a format of taking inventory on a daily or regular basis. The inventory system records balances of stock brought forward, purchases, issues to food production department and the daily balance of the stock.

   Perpetual inventory system is an important control tool. The essence of the system is related to quantities of stock in terms of numbers, or weight or volume measurements, and not in terms of costs.

As stocks are purchased, received and stored, the quantity is recorded on the perpetual inventory record, to show an increase in inventory. As stocks are issued to the food production department, the depleted balance is recorded. The process is repeated for each item of the store's stock on each day. This enables the storekeeper, as well as the food & beverages controller, through physical observation and count, to match how much product is available to how much should be available. Difference between these figures give a measure of the effectiveness of inventory control systems.

Each stock keeping unit has a separate inventory card. The same process is used in a computerised format.

(Specimen of Perpetual Inventory is shown in **Exhibit 27 below.**)

EXHIBIT 27: Format of Perpetual Inventory

 Riverside Grill

Perpetual Inventory

Name of the Stock Unit Pineapple Slices "DEL MONTE" Brand

Stock Unit Size Tin of 836 gm

Inventory Period November 2011

Date	Purchase Quantity	Issues	Balance Quantity	Remarks	Date	Purchase Quantity	Issues	Balance Quantity	Remarks
			28 Tins	Brought forward				131 Tins	Brought forward
1		8 Tins	20 Tins		17		7 Tins	124 Tins	
2	96 Tins	6 Tins	110 Tins		18		8 Tins	116 Tins	
3		7 Tins	103 Tins		19		13 Tins	103 Tins	
4		8 Tins	95 Tins		20			103 Tins	
5		13 Tins	82 Tins		21		6 Tins	97 Tins	
6			82 Tins		22		8 Tins	89 Tins	
7		8 Tins	74 Tins		23		7 Tins	82 Tins	
8		7 Tins	67 Tins		24		6 Tins	76 Tins	
9		6 Tins	61 Tins		25		8 Tins	68 Tins	
10		8 Tins	53 Tins		26		13 Tins	55 Tins	
11		7 Tins	46 Tins		27			55 Tins	
12		14 Tins	32 Tins		28		8 Tins	47 Tins	
13			32 Tins		29		7 Tins	40 Tins	
14	120 Tins	7 Tins	145 Tins		30		8 Tins	32 Tins	
15		6 Tins	139 Tins		31				
16		8 Tins	131 Tins						
			131 Tins	Carried				32 Tins	Carried
				Forward					Forward
							Storekeeper		

9.5.6 Inventory Valuations

Costs have to be assigned to ingredients in stores and those issued for food production. Inventory turnover rates are not calculated for **individual** food products or raw ingredients in store. Calculations are done for their bulk in store. Calculations of inventory costs are typically made when once-a-month physical inventories are done.

Prices of ingredients change often. In addition, it is possible that during the same inventory period ingredients are purchased more than once. Different supplies within the same inventory period may cost differently. The **valuations of the issued stocks** and the **valuations of the physical inventory of in-store stocks** are done through:

(a) actually costing the stocks on the basis of supplier's invoices and records of DRR;

(b) averaging purchase costs over a time period;

(c) the FIFO (First In First Out) technique of stock valuation; and

(d) the LIFO (Last-In-First-Out) technique of stock valuation.

(a) **Actually costing the stocks:** This is the industry practice for valuation of the inventories in stores. The calculations are easy due to computerized entries of values of stocks coming into the stores on each purchase occasion. Marking and tagging of stock items helps the process of valuation. (The process of marking and tagging has been explained in Module 8: "Right Receiving".)

(b) **Averaging purchasing costs over a period of time:** This method is adopted by many culinary business. Many supplies with different purchase prices are received in the same inventory period. The calculations of inventory value are done by averaging. This is done by adding the values of each stock and taking an average. This average figure, often in weighted format is used for inventory valuations of stocks issued from stores and those remaining in the stores.

(c) **The FIFO (First-In-First-Out) technique of stock valuation:** FIFO is a technique of costing of inventories of in-store stocks. Under this technique food products and raw ingredients that are purchased first or earliest and brought into stock first, form the **basis of costing of issues from the stores**. The costs assigned to the ingredients issued from the stores are equal to their **as-purchased price**.

These costs reflect in the calculations of standard recipes. These costs per unit of the ingredients **may** be lower than the **recently purchased** stocks of the same ingredients. As the valuation of issued ingredients is lower, it would mean low cost of standard recipe and lower cost of sales.

The FIFO technique of stock valuation supports the principle that issued ingredients should be **assigned the cost of the ingredient unit incurred.**

The more recent purchases **may** be higher in costs per unit. Under the FIFO technique the stored items with more recent (and **if** higher) costs remain in inventory. This creates a higher total inventory value of food products and raw ingredients remaining in inventory. The valuation of the food ingredients remaining in the inventory would be what has been paid for them (**if** higher). Dating and tagging of food products and raw ingredients help in identifying which units are older.

Inventory turnover rates are not calculated for **individual** food products or raw ingredients in store. Calculations are done for the bulk of them in store.

FIFO inventory costing technique is best when most of the ingredient units in stock have been purchased through a yearly fixed-rate contract. The FIFO inventory costing technique is difficult to operate if frequent purchases are made at different prices and if ingredient units from different purchases are on hand in the stores at the same time.

> **Note:** The above is the first-in first-out (FIFO) inventory valuation system and should not be confused with last-in-first-out (LIFO) stock turning method, explained below.

The action desired for the **physical movement** of the ingredients is to issue for food production those which were purchased first and stocked first. This is known as first-in-first-out (FIFO) stock turning method.

(d) **The LIFO (Last-In-First-Out) technique of stock valuation:** Under the LIFO technique of stock valuation, the valuation of food products and raw ingredients issued for food production (first out) is equal to the costs of the most recent purchase (last in).

The valuation of issued stocks is used to cost standard recipes. The cost of the standard recipes goes up. This means higher cost of sales.

Under the LIFO (Last-In-First-Out) technique of stock valuation, the cost of sales per portion more accurately reflects **current replacement costs**. Under the LIFO technique of stock valuation, the inventory remaining in stores has **a smaller monetary value**.

The issued ingredients carry the most recent and usually higher costs. The inventory remaining in stores is made up of the stocks of ingredients which are costed at earlier and usually lower costs.

9.5.7 Average Inventory

As mentioned earlier physical inventories for culinary business are done once a month. Average inventory is the averages of inventory at the beginning and at the end of the month.

The average inventory is therefore:

$$\frac{\text{Average}}{\text{inventory}} = \frac{\text{Inventory at the beginning of the month} + \text{Inventory at the end of the mont}}{2}$$

Average inventory is useful for understanding the inventory turnover or stock turnover.

9.5.8 Inventory Turnover or Stock Turnover

It is a financial term to measure the number of times inventory is used in a time period. It is an equation between the cost of ingredients issued (used) for production (cost of sales) used by the average inventory. In effect, inventory turnover or stock turnover means movement from stores to the food production department for profitable and sales oriented food production. The equation of inventory turnover can be represented as follows:

$$\text{Inventory turnover} = \frac{\text{Total cost of food used for the month}}{\text{Average inventory for the month}}$$

Inventory turnover rates can be calculated for food products and raw ingredients in storage.

Inventory management in respect of food products and raw ingredients is an effort to reduce higher than necessary holding costs. Managers measure the inventory turnover rate to determine how much money is tied up in non-productive inventory. The inventory turnover rate shows the number of times in a given period that inventory is turned into revenue. In financial nomenclature it measures the rate at which inventory is turned into food costs required to generate income. Stores management must determine the "just-right" levels of food products and raw ingredients in inventory.

Store inventory turnover **rates** can have three possibilities in terms of their turnover (movement from stores to food production department), as follows:

(a) Low inventory turnover rate.

(b) High inventory turnover rate.

(c) Ideal inventory turnover rate – hospitality industry benchmark.

9.5.9 Inventory Turnover and Inventory Turnover Rates

(a) **Low inventory turnover rate:** **Low inventory turnover rate** may mean higher inventory levels. In simple language low inventory turnover rate would mean that stores inventory is not moving out of stores for food production **fast enough**. For food products or raw ingredients a **low inventory turnover rate** or inventories turning over slowly may result in:

- overstocking;

- obsolescence (their "expiry" in relation to "use-before" date);

- spoilage; and

- unauthorized consumption.

Low inventory turnover rate also means that more monies are being invested in purchasing and stocking of food products and raw ingredients, than necessary.

The above situation would mean a higher-than-necessary cash investment in store stocks. It would also mean blockage of funds which can otherwise be suitably utilized elsewhere in the operations.

(b) **High inventory turnover rate:** **High inventory turnover rate may** indicate inadequate inventory levels. In simple language high inventory turnover rate would mean that stores inventory is moving out of stores for food production very fast. This may lead to "stock-out" situations.

High inventory turnover rate would mean the other opposite of a low-inventory turnover rate. It would mean that insufficient monies are invested in purchasing and stocking of food products and raw ingredients, than necessary.

In between the two possibilities is the ideal benchmark of inventories to adopt, and an ideal inventory turnover rate. Two extreme parameters of ordering would further clarify the inventory turnover rates.

1. If at one extreme sufficient food products and raw ingredients to last **one full season** are purchased **at once** and stored, the inventories in store would be excessive and would lead to wastage, spoilage, inefficiency, and greater than necessary costs.

   The food production department would requisition the items as per **its requirements**. Stocks would continue to be on hand in the stores, causing continuous high inventories meaning **low inventory turnover. Purchasing in smaller quantities would bring in efficiencies in this case.**

2. On the other extreme, **if** food products and raw ingredients are purchased to last only for a few days, **stock-outs** would result. Stores would not be able to honour the requisitions of the food production department. This would be a case of low inventories, and **high inventory turnover. Purchasing in larger quantities would bring in efficiencies in this case.**

Somewhere in between the two extremes is an idealized amount of food to have on hand for a specific period. This idealized amount would depend on the menu and the number of **"Star" and "Standard" menu items** as the ingredients used for these categories of menu items would turn over faster. It would vary from place to place, and would be determined by many factors, including the amount of cash available for such purposes, the space available for storage, efficiencies of the suppliers and the lead time necessary to receive food once it is ordered.

(c) **Ideal inventory turnover rate – hospitality industry benchmark:** If a culinary business orders and uses an inventory two times each month, it is considered an ideal situation. **This is the hospitality industry benchmark.** This means that if the inventory turns 24 times a year, the inventory management is correctly situated in terms of:

- consumption patterns;

- ordering of supplies;

- supplier performance; and

- issues from the stores.

All food products and raw ingredients **are not turned over** during the prescribed period of time. In case of groceries, the ingredients used for Star menu items would turn over faster. Depending on the type of the culinary business, tinned and bottled food products may turn over much less frequently. Some perishables are handled by the stores management. These perishables would turn over daily.

For all forms of culinary business it is acceptable to have higher store inventory levels for a few food products or raw ingredients. This happens when the source market presents a scenario of rapidly rising prices or shortages for these food products and raw ingredients and it is vital for the business to have them on hand. Storekeeping for these items is characterised by low inventory turnover rate.

On the other hand food products or raw ingredients including proprietary products, which are available in plenty in the markets, can be grouped. Low or very low store inventory levels can be maintained for such a group of supplies. Just-in-time purchases can be considered for these supplies. Storekeeping for these items is characterised by high inventory turnover rate.

Understanding of the correctness of inventory turnover rate for the business – whether low, high or ideal can only be done through valuations of the stock-in-stores actualized through once-a-month inventories.

9.5.10 Inventory Turnover Calculations

The inventory turnover rate and its calculations support the stores management or the chef to decide if the inventory turnover rate is right for their business or not. The inventory turnover rate is therefore an important cost-device to use in the inventory management process.

For example, to calculate the inventory turnover rate of food products and raw ingredients for a month, assume the following data:

Food inventory value at the beginning of month = Rs. 1,02,000

Food inventory value at the end of the month = Rs. 1,14,000

Therefore, average food inventory for month =

$$\text{Average food inventory} = \frac{\text{Beginning inventory} + \text{Ending inventory}}{2}$$

$$= \frac{1,02,000 + 1,14,000}{2} = \text{Rs. } 1,08,000$$

Assume cost of food (issued or used) for the month = Rs. 2,73,000

Therefore,

$$\text{Food inventory turnover} = \frac{\text{Cost of food used for month}}{\text{Average food inventory for month}}$$

$$= \frac{2,73,000}{1,08,000} = 2.53 \text{ times.}$$

This means that the value of inventory has turned into revenue during the month at 2.53 times. This falls in line with the understanding of the industry benchmark for ideal inventory turnover rate.

9.5.11 Inventory Turnover Trends

Costs of operation can be controlled by effective purchasing, storing and management of issues from stores. Ordering groceries required in the correct quantity can have far reaching effects in terms of product costs, product quality, operating profits, shelf life, storage capacity and reordering of supplies.

Close monitoring of inventories and inventory turnover rates help operators to establish the best turnover rate suitable for **their** business. Quantum of business changes with each business month. Due to the monthly calculation of turnover rate the store management and chefs can make assessment of increases or decreases in inventory turnover and make corrections in their purchasing activities accordingly. This method of monitoring detects **turnover trends.**

The questions that arise are:

1. How should a culinary business arrive at an ideal inventory turnover rate?

2. How should food products and raw ingredients be ordered to prevent over-stocking or under-stocking?

The answer is to adopt the minimum-maximum inventory and ordering system.

9.6 MINIMUM/MAXIMUM INVENTORY AND ORDERING SYSTEM

To **determine** the quantities of stocked items to be ordered by the stores management to the purchase department, culinary business can use the minimum/maximum inventory and ordering system. The system also guides the stores management to order required stock items **in time.** The units to be ordered are the normal packing size or units of weight and volume.

The system supports the **right inventory turnover rate** desired by the culinary business. The system prevents over-stocking of the ingredients beyond a certain predetermined quantity. This is called maximum stock. The system also prevents reduction of stocks below a fixed quantity. This is called the safety level. The system therefore ensures maintenance of the right quantities of stored items. Each stock item in stores is assigned minimum and maximum quantity levels.

With the help of computers, it is feasible to develop the minimum/maximum inventory and ordering system for all items in stores. High cost items should definitely be subjected to the system if computerization is not possible.

The following terminology is used in the system:

(a) The quantum of least stocks that must always remain in inventory is the **safety level** and is known as **minimum** stock. The safety level for each stock item allows for delays of supplies due to market conditions or/and poor delivery performance of the supplier. The safety level also allows for unusual consumption, for example, requirements of unannounced banquets.

(b) **The order period:** As a practice in the hospitality industry, orders of stored items are placed on suppliers for supply at regular intervals. The order period relates to weekly or fortnightly or monthly intervals.

(c) **The usage rate/usage quantity:** The usage rate/usage quantity is the number of stock units issued to the food production department during a day or a particular period. Different stock items are required by user department in different quantities on different days. The usage rate/ usage quantity for a day is often arrived at by averaging the quantities used over a longer period, for example, quantities used in a month or in a season. The usage rate/usage quantity for a day arrived at through this exercise is used in addition to the usage rates/usage quantities in respect of order period, safety levels, and lead time.

(d) The quantum of maximum stock level of any stored item allowed in the stores is called the **maximum** stock. The maximum number of units allowed to be stored will be the usage quantities of that item for the order period plus the minimum (safety level) stock.

(e) **The lead time quantities:** The stores management also determines lead-time quantities for each stored item. This is done in consultation with the purchase department, and involves study of a supplier's delivery performance. The lead time quantities are the number of units of each stocked item issued to the food production department between the time the order is placed to the supplier by the purchase department and when it is delivered, and placed in stock. Different suppliers supply different stock items. Therefore, lead time quantities are often different for different stock items.

> **Note:** The lead-time quantity is **not** the safety (minimum) level of units kept in inventory. Depending on the market conditions and supplier's efficiency in respect of each stored item, the store management may decide to maintain the safety level quantities equal to the lead time quantities. In addition, the lead time quantities could be higher or lower than the safety level quantities in respect of each stored item.

(f) **Order point:** The order point for any stock item is defined as the number of stock-keeping units in stores when an order for its purchase is placed. The order point is triggered when the number of stock-keeping units of any stored item reaches a combined stock level of safety and lead time quantities.

It means that the lead time quantities of stock would keep depleting till the stocks are replenished. By the time the inventory pares to the minimum (safety level) of quantities, the supplies would be received and the inventory levels would again become equal to the maximum stock level.

> **Note:** Suppliers undertake supplies of a group of food products and ingredients, for example, dry fruits, spices, lentils, proprietary sauces, and canned products, etc. Orders for purchase of different stock items forming part of a group are released together. This facilitates the purchase and receiving processes.

(g) **Quantities to order:** When ordering at the order point, the **quantity to order is the usage rate of the order period.**

The **minimum/maximum inventory and ordering system** supports the management of stores to order the "right" quantity of the required items at all times of the year. The system has several advantages as well as disadvantages. The advantages of using the system outweigh its disadvantages. The system is therefore here to stay. Computerization of the system often aided by integrated property management systems is supportive to the cause of cost-effectiveness of the operation of stores. The advantages and disadvantages of the system are listed below:

9.6.1 Advantages and Disadvantages of Minimum/Maximum Inventory and Ordering System

Advantages

(a) Culinary business predominantly stocks food products and non-perishable raw ingredients in stores. These stock items are governed by the statutory laws and expiry dates. The minimum/maximum inventory and ordering system in combination with the FIFO (first-in-first-out) system of issues ensures that all food products and raw ingredients are consumed well before the stipulated expiry date.

(b) Excessive inventory is prevented. This helps in reduction in the quantum of valuable storage space.

(c) Minimum inventory is ensured. It is possible to ensure the right inventory turnover rate. Possibilities of **stock-outs** are reduced.

(d) An important aim & objective for an efficient purchase department is to order the "right quantities". The minimum/maximum inventory and ordering systems ensures the same.

(e) The system is easy to use.

(f) It is possible to measure actual performance against expected (budgeted) performance through the usage of this system.

(g) The business is able to utilize cash for its other operational requirements and need not block funds in excessive inventories.

Disadvantages

(a) Assumptions and historical data are used to calculate the lead time quantities of stock items. The system could generate inaccuracies of stocking quantities if these assumptions are wrong.

(b) The processes of developing minimum/maximum inventory levels to manage individual stock items are initially time consuming. Fresh efforts to develop the same would be required with change in season and business outlook.

(c) Food product or ingredient based sales promotions by suppliers are unaccounted under the system.

(d) Suppliers often announce time and quantity based discounts which the culinary business cannot avail of.

(e) The business often encourages retail suppliers only. Manufacturers or bulk stockists are unable to become suppliers and quote. This is because the manufacturer or bulk stockists are unable to supply lesser quantities that may be more appropriate to the culinary business.

(f) The supplier's contract to supply is often exclusive of delivery charges in respect of specific stock keeping units. In such cases, the culinary business through stores and purchase department may place orders for purchase of such specific stock keeping units less frequently and in higher quantities.

   If the costs to process purchases (administrative costs) are high at a geographical location the culinary business may place orders for purchase less frequently and in higher quantities. In such cases the minimum/maximum inventory and ordering system can only be a guideline.

Example of the minimum/maximum inventory and ordering system:

For an assumed stocking of bakery flour:

Purchase unit = kg

Usage quantities = 15 kg per day

Order period = 30 days.

Order period usage quantities = 15 kg per day × 30 days

$$= 450 \text{ kg}$$

Lead time = 5 days.

Lead time usage quantities = 15 kg per day × 5 days = 75 kg

Safety level quantities = minimum stock

$$= \text{stock of 7 days}$$

$$= 15 \text{ kg per day} \times 7 \text{ days} = 105 \text{ kg}$$

Order point = lead time usage quantities + safety level stock

$$= 75 \text{ kg} + 105 \text{ kg} = 180 \text{ kg}$$

Quantities to order = order period quantities = 450 kg

Maximum level = order period usage quantities + safety level stock

$$= 450 \text{ kg} + 105 \text{ kg} = 555 \text{ kg}$$

Note 1: The above example assumes that the safety level quantities of 7 days of stock in respect of bakery flour are good enough for the business considering market conditions and supplier's efficiencies. The safety level could be different for different stock items, as it would again depend on market conditions for the same as well as the supplier's efficiency. The suppliers for different items are often different.

Note 2: 450 kg of bakery flour would be ordered. This amount equals the order period usage quantities.

Note 3: Orders for purchase of fresh supplies of bakery flour would be placed when the stock pares down to the order point, which is 180 kg in the above example.

Note 4: As per the understanding of this example the supplier would take 5 days to supply the quantities ordered. That would mean that between the ordering and receiving 75 kg of bakery flour would be indented and used. The stock levels at the end of 5 days would therefore reduce by 75 kg to a level of 105 kg from a level of 180 kg. The decided safety level quantity in this example are 105 kg.

Note 5: On the day the stock in the stores reaches 105 kg the supplies of bakery flour would be received.

Note 6: Due to the receipt of 450 kg of bakery flour, the stock level in stores would rise to 555 kg. This is the maximum level of stock that is allowed in this example.

9.7 RIGHT ISSUING PROCESS

The following are the **aims and objectives** of the process of issuing:

1. To issue just what is requisitioned for.
2. To effect immediate entries of issues in the books of stores or in the property management system.
3. To transfer the responsibility of the materials being issued to the consuming department.
4. To control the issue process chronologically.

9.7.1 Stores Requisition

The 'purchase process' is a cyclic process. The first part of the process is the generation of 'demand' of materials for production as well as for other necessary operations. On receipt, the perishables are sent directly to the food production department and the non-perishables to the stores.

The requisitioned quantities should be sufficient for the production planned for the day and of the immediate future. A tight-fisted approach to authorization of consumption is desirable, and this is most effectively done with a stores requisition. The stores requisition is used to identify the type and quantity of food products and raw ingredients to be removed from the store's inventory. Checklists are useful for the process of preparing the stores requisition. The requisition is authorized by the chef or the department head. The consuming department forwards the requisition to the stores department. Based upon this **authorized** requisition, items are issued from stores to the requisitioning department.

Calculation of daily food cost is based partly on the value of daily issues. The entries in the inventory management system should be made immediately on issuing. Evolved inventory management systems do not allow materials to move out of the stores premises without a corresponding entry. Updating records with issues ensures the necessary provision of information to the controls department.

In case of culinary business the products used are of predominantly perishable nature. Mistakes in issuing – by oversight or by design reduce the operational profitability. Excess issues – if noticed later cannot be taken back into stock again. The representative of the consuming department has to accept the responsibility of having checked all issues against the stores requisition and sign for the receipts. Afterwards the responsibility shifts to the consuming department. The issuing function is a link between the storing and production functions. A specimen of the **Stores Requisition is shown on p. 169.**

9.8 ROLE OF THE STOREKEEPER

The processes of right storing, inventory control and issuing ensures **cost-effectiveness** of the operations and must be run as per laid down benchmarks. The storekeeper should be a trained and skilled person. He should have technical knowledge and experience in the management of stores.

Food products and raw ingredients may be spoilt and lost while being delivered to stores, in actual storage and during issues. The duties and responsibilities of the storekeeper are to safeguard the investments made in the purchase and storage of these commodities through excellence in handling and efficient stores management. The storekeeper has a wide range of duties and responsibilities. A storekeeper is duty bound and responsible for:

1. receiving of the supplies from the receiving department;

2. checking of the supplies on receipt from the receiving department for:

    (a) Damage   (b) Signs of rust   (c) Pest infestation

    (d) Swelling of tins   (e) Leakages   (f) Lumps in items like flour

    (g) Expiry dates. Just received foods should not be near their expiry dates;

3. handling and stacking of supplies in a planned manner and ensuring easy access to these. All supplies should have bin cards next to them;

4. issuing of supplies to consuming departments, against authorized stores requisitions, strictly in the order of first-in-first-out;

5. ensuring product and employee safety in handling of stores items;

EXHIBIT 28: Format of Stores Requisition

RG Riverside Grill

Store Room Requisition - For Food Production

Serial No. _____

Department _____   Date _____

S. No.	Item	Material Code	Quantity Requested	Unit of Measure	Quantity Issued	Unit Cost	Total Cost

Authorised By: _____ Issued By: _____ Received By _____ Cost Controller: _____

6. maintaining adequate stock balances in stores with the lowest possible inventory levels and preventing stock-outs;

7. reporting of non-moving and slow moving stock items to consuming departments and ensuring that the same are utilized. All food products and raw ingredients must be consumed before their expiry dates;

8. responsible for documentation and record keeping. Documentation and record keeping provides the information and statistical data to enable the management to make correct decisions. Without an effective documentation and reporting system, management decisions will be impaired or made impossible. Documentation and record keeping includes maintenance of bin cards, stock ledgers, filing of store-room requisitions, purchase requisitions and physical/perpetual inventory records;

9. changing purchase quantities of ingredients in line with change of menus;

10. liaising with the consuming departments and purchase department for unusually high consumption;

11. regular inspection of stocks for pest infestation or physical damage. A sampling spade can be used to check food items like flour, grains, lentils, etc. Food supplies may attract various kinds of pests, for example:

    (a) Insects

    (b) Rodents

    (c) Cockroaches

    (d) Beetles

    (e) Moths

    (f) Birds

    Insecticides and fumigants to control insects and rodenticides to control rats and mice are dangerous to human health. Storekeeper should ensure that pest control activities are handled by trained staff;

12. maintenance, cleaning and sanitizing of stores. The storekeeper is responsible for the HACCP issues of stores;

13. maintaining the quality of the food products and raw ingredients in storage through:

    (a) first-in-first-out issues to the food production department.

    (b) maintaining temperature control of stored foods. Different food items require different temperatures for maintenance of optimum quality, for example:

    - Dry storage items are required to be kept in a temperature range of 10°C to 21°C.

    - Refrigerated items are required to be kept in a temperature range of 4°C to 5°C.

    - Deep frozen items are required to be kept in a temperature range of –18°C to – 20°C.

14. ensuring proper ventilation and humidity control. Special care is required to take care of food products and raw ingredients in coastal areas;

15. ensuring compliance to all standard operating procedures benchmarked for stores operations;

16. assisting stock taking and auditing processes. The storekeeper is responsible for any variation found in stock inventories; and

17. ensuring that all weighing scales and measurement tools are in correct working order.

> **Note:** The designing of the stores and its facility planning is not part of the current module. The essence of this module focuses on the economics of stores, inventory management and issues.

9.9 COMPUTERIZATION OF STORES

Software applications allow faster and accurate statistics and also a larger chronological base. Applications allow for forward and backward integration of demand and supply of consumables and items of general operational requirements. Computerization also records the flow of information through various departments involved in subject materials management. Computerization of stores aids to efficiency in storing, inventory management and right issuing. Computerization of stores supports the audit trail, as well as instant inventory valuation.

9.10   END OF MODULE NOTES

9.10.1   Cost-effectiveness in Stores & Inventory Management

The perishable nature of the stored items necessitates strict control in the management of stores and inventories. The **key areas** and **success factors** which work towards cost-effectiveness of the stores and inventory management are listed below. The culinary business must:

1. store the food materials immediately on receipt;

2. maintain optimum quality of stored items through environment control;

3. use the minimum/maximum inventory and ordering system to order fresh supplies;

4. maintain low inventories to:

    (a) ensure optimum product quality;

    (b) reduce spoilage;

    (c) reduce operational expenses;

    (d) reduce storage space;

    (e) reduce number of handling personnel; and

    (f) eliminate theft by staff;

5. achieve control and reduction in inventories to lowest possible levels through:

    (a) improved forecasting;

    (b) closer monitoring; and

    (c) improved delivery performance of suppliers.

6. maintain high inventory turnover rate. Prevent low inventory turnover rate. Ordering and using inventory twice monthly is ideal for culinary business;

7. maintain quality inventory recording system including computerization. Closely monitor inventories; and

8. introduce higher accountability through segmentation of stored items as per their storage conditions, frequency of issues, accessibility and costs.

9.10.2   Cost-effectiveness in Issuing Functions

The right issuing benchmarks also contribute to the cost-effectiveness of the culinary business. The **key areas** and **success factors** in relation to issuing standards are given below. The stores management must:

1. issue **just what** is requisitioned-for through the authorized Stores Requisition. Mistakes in issuing, by oversight or by design, reduce the operational profitability;

2. not allow materials to move out of the stores without a corresponding entry of the issues in the books or in the computer system of stores;

3. prevent theft of stored items. Maintain access control. Allow issues only at the entrance of the stores; and

4. transfer the responsibility of the materials being issued to the consuming department through signature-of-receipt on the stores requisition.

EXHIBIT 29: Efficient Storing, Inventory Management & Issuing

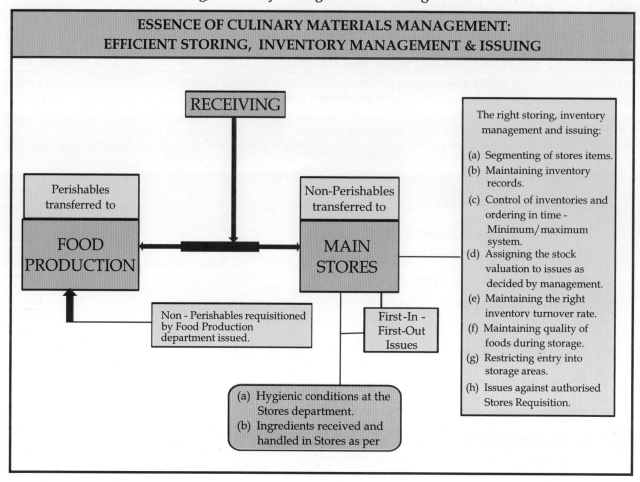

10 ECONOMICS OF FOOD PRODUCTION AND FOOD SERVICE

Essence of the Module

This module explains the essentials of economics of food production, its benchmarks, and the controls in food production processes to achieve cost efficiency. The module details the needs and methods of producing the right quality and the right quantities of menu items. It also deals with the economics of food service.

Module Objectives and Competencies
After going through this module the reader would be competent to:

1. Link planning of right food production to value received by the customer.

2. Understand the concept of planned food production.

3. Understand the planning of food production for a chain operation.

4. Explain the planning of quality and quantity food production and its three control stages.

5. Establish the five standard cost control tools:

   - Standard purchase specifications: their importance and linkages to food production.

   - Standard yields: linkages to food production, saleable weight, production loss, yield test report, cost per portion of raw meat, meat-to-wastage ratio, and yield in absolute terms and percentages.

   - Standard recipes: definition, sub-recipes, chaining of recipes, components, benefits, formats and process of standardization of a recipe.

   - Standard portion sizes: importance and tools to measure.

   - Standard portion costs: arriving at standard portion costs.

6. Explain the importance of volume forecasting for food production.

7. Explain how planned food production pays.

8. Examine the importance and methods of forecasting of quantities of food production:

   (a) Experience of chefs.

   (b) Using the value of trends.

   (c) Using sales history.

   (d) Fixed portion production method.

   (e) Top-up method.

   (f) Weighted average method.

9. Detail the importance of "service guarantees".

10.1 INTRODUCTION TO ECONOMICS OF FOOD PRODUCTION AND FOOD SERVICE

The following are the key objectives of culinary business:

1. to offer great value to customers and to stakeholders. (The concept of value has already been discussed in Module 1: "The Culinary Business"); and

2. to generate revenues and profits.

Profits are the key prerequisites of a business. It is good business if a culinary outlet is able to meet the above two key objectives. Direction-led controlled food production ensures working towards the goals of quality, cost effectiveness, and enhanced possibilities of customer satisfaction.

Culinary business should define standards of quality and quantity of food production. All foods are perishable and deteriorate with age. Overproduction of food encourages spoilage, wastage, pilferage and unauthorized consumption. Menu items prepared especially for the customers are produced using standard recipes, the right and often expensive ingredients like cuts of meats or expensive seafood. In addition to the cost of food materials, time, love and labour is spent in such production. Spoilage, wastage, pilferage and unauthorized consumption besides being an economic loss places burden on the kitchen and the production team.

Underproduction of food is not desirable also. Underproduction may lead to many menu items not being available. "Not-available" menu items cause irritation to a customer who would order these menu items and be refused. The business can lose such a customer. The essence of good food production planning therefore is to produce the right quantities. Right food production has a direct linkage to the satisfaction that a customer experiences.

This module is divided into two parts, as follows:

1. Economics of food production.

2. Economics of food service.

For "Economics of Food Service" see p. 198

10.2 ECONOMICS OF FOOD PRODUCTION: FOOD PRODUCTION PLANNING

Food production requires personal supervision and is directed through personal experience. The quality of food production attracts customers to experience the culinary concept and menu offer repeatedly. The quantities of food production vary due to the variation in the size of the customer footfalls. Experience of production staff, aided by tools and methods such as menu engineering works a great deal towards establishing quantities of food production.

Actual food production has three control stages:

1. The preparation for production, referred to as pre-preparation or "prep".

2. The actual cooking.

3. Holding of prepared food post-production.

In essence, planning of food production is simply getting ready for production. Planning of food production ensures that trained cooks with knowledge of the standard recipe, raw ingredients and products, cooking vessels, equipment, and quality delivery systems are available when required. Planning of food production ensures that panic stages, and sacrifice to safety issues is removed, and the production personnel look forward to the pleasures of the cooking process.

10.3 PLANNING OF FOOD PRODUCTION FOR A CHAIN OPERATION

A culinary brand often has several outlets at different locations. The different outlets have an identical culinary concept, and the same culinary product offer. However, due to location related requirements a few of the menu items change to suit local taste, flavour, culinary strength and availability of ingredients. Each of the food production units of the chain is supported and also controlled by the chain strengths in terms of:

1. menu;
2. menu items;
3. ingredients required for the menu items;
4. standard purchase specifications for the purchase of the ingredients;
5. other purchasing and ordering tools like Purchase Orders and Perishable Order Sheet;
6. standards of on-time ordering;
7. selection of the right suppliers;
8. right receiving of supplies;
9. right storing and right issuing of ingredients;
10. proper pre-preparation of ingredients;
11. proper benchmarking of food production standards:

    (a) Standard yield – better saleable value of the raw product;

    (b) Standard recipe – listing food production techniques; and

12. proper benchmarking of food service standards, for example, service guarantees.

Chain operations of culinary business take support from **centralized purchasing as well as from the mother kitchen.**

The cost of ingredients being different at different locations, food cost of same menu items at different outlets may differ. In addition, the sale price of the menu items is also different at different locations.

Each food production unit of the chain is unique. Personal culinary strengths of the Executive Chef or Master Chef define the overall trend of customer affection, and in essence the quantum of food production. Each unit of the chain must develop specific procedures for production planning that are suited to its own unique needs. However, a typical strategy is to first forecast production requirements and then translate these into production plans. This is true even for stand-alone culinary business.

10.4 CONTROLS DURING FOOD PRODUCTION

Controls during food production involve creating benchmarks and adhering to them strictly. Controls during food production are therefore supportive of financial as well as quality goals. The controls during food production have been enumerated in this module, as follows:

1. The understanding of the topic of planning of quality food production.
2. The understanding of the topic of tools of standard cost control.
3. The understanding of the topic of planning quantities of food production.

Planning of food production has two distinct parts, as follows:

(a) Planning quality of food production.

(b) Planning quantity of food production.

10.5 REQUIREMENTS OF QUALITY FOOD PRODUCTION

The culinary concept, its quality and its target customers define and decide the quality of food production. Expectations of customers align with the concept, and present ideas to the requirements of quality operating standards to operators. It is imperative for culinary business to meet and exceed the expectations of the customers.

10.6 STANDARD COST CONTROL TOOLS

Chefs can benefit from the understanding, development and applications of standard cost control tools. These tools guide the chefs to be true to:

- the established quality benchmarks of the culinary business;
- align the business with its concept values; and
- provide the right connotation of values received by customers.

Culinary business must formulate the standard cost control tools for it to succeed. These tools are listed sequentially and are individually explained in detail below:

1. Standard purchase specifications.
2. Standard yields.
3. Standard recipes.
4. Standard portion sizes.
5. Standard portion costs.

Each of these standard cost tools has a certain relationship of cost and of performance on other standard cost tools. These tools provide means for **consistently** purchasing, producing and serving menu items of the required quality.

Each of the above standard cost tools have been detailed below:

10.6.1 Standard Purchase Specifications

Standard purchase specifications incorporate quality requirements and dictate the minimum quality benchmarks that all food products and raw ingredients must meet at the point of receiving. These specifications are the immediate quality links between the business's requirements and the supplier's abilities. (Standard purchase specifications have been discussed in detail in Module 6: "Efficient Management of Purchasing Activities".)

10.6.2 Standard Yields

Raw ingredients, as purchased, cannot be sold, as a finished menu item. Ingredients lose weight during each of the three stages of production, as explained below:

(a) **Loss of weight during the pre-preparation stage:** Ingredients should be processed in the pre-preparation area of the kitchens using standard methods of pre-preparation before cooking. These pre-preparations may be **skilled** meat or seafood fabrication involving trimming of wastage of skin, fat and bones and portioning and/or vegetable fabrication involving stringing, cleaning, cutting and portioning. Ingredients lose weight due to these pre-preparation processes. Conducting yield tests is another activity of the "pre-prep" stage.

(b) **Loss of weight during the cooking stage:** During cooking, due to shrinkage and loss of inherent natural moisture, all ingredients lose weight.

(c) **Loss of weight during the holding and finishing stage:** Ingredients that have not been portioned during pre-preparation stage can be portioned after cooking. Ingredients lose some weight in this stage also.

Yields of raw ingredients, Butcher Yield Tests and Standard Yields

Understanding the concept of yields is important. Given below is the step-by-step understanding of yields of raw ingredients, and yield tests.

1. An important aim and objective of quality purchasing for culinary business is to obtain the maximum yield from raw ingredients.

2. Yields of raw ingredients indicate their useable weight or saleable weight.

3. Yields depend on quality benchmarks of purchase specifications.

4. Standard purchase specifications are made to suit the concept of the culinary business and can be changed.

5. If therefore, the standard purchase specifications are inaccurately defined, or are ambiguous the supplier would have an opportunity to supply raw ingredients which would produce poor yields.

6. Standard purchase specifications acquire the status of "standard" only when the purchaser experiences the raw ingredients and yields thereof and is sure that the specification is right to suit the business and its concept. If not, the purchaser has an opportunity to amend such purchase specification and make it "standard".

7. If, for example, the business requires large amount of boneless chicken, it would be wise to purchase boneless chicken. The standard purchase specifications would be developed accordingly, and the yields would be near to 100%. However, if full chickens are ordered and fabricated, the yield would be near to 44%. This is because the standard purchase specifications for purchase of full chickens are different than those of boneless chicken.

8. Yield tests are done only on 'A' value products. (These have been defined and explained on **p. 19** in Module 1: "The Culinary Business".)

9. Industry practice in India is to concentrate on raw weight (as purchased) yield tests, and not on cooking losses. The efforts and management time that would be required to do yield tests for cooking losses would not be commensurate with the results.

   The difference between the raw weight of the purchased ingredient and the weight of the same when ready for sale is called **production loss.**

10. Therefore, the industry practice in India is to concentrate on Butcher Yield tests. While the nomenclature for such tests remains as Butcher Yield tests, the nomenclature for the department has changed from butchery to meat fabrication department.

11. Standard yields are arrived at by conducting yield tests. While doing a yield test, it is advisable to use as large a sample as possible. Large samples ensure accurate yields.

12. Once standard yields are set for an ingredient, the future yield testing should produce results in line with the standard yields. At times, particular weather and seasonal conditions ensure proper yields. This is particularly so for seafood.

13. During subsequent yield tests, if a higher yield is achieved than the existing standard yield, then the higher yield becomes the standard yield. All future yields are matched against the new benchmark. If lower yields are received than the standard yield, examination must be done to establish the reasons. The reasons may be:

(a) receiving of ingredients was not done according to set standard purchase specifications; and

(b) personnel handling the pre-preparation processes in the meat fabrication department did not have the right knowledge and skills.

14. Specialist suppliers and manufacturers supply ready-to-cook (RTC) products. These are pre-processed meats, seafood and vegetables, mostly sold in a frozen state to the outlet. These may be sold in portions (for example, specific cuts of meat or seafood) or in bulk units (for example, vegetables cut to size).

15. The ready-to-cook meat products are already trimmed of fat, skin and unwanted bones, etc. The ready-to-cook seafood is deveined and is trimmed of shell and tail, etc. The ready-to-use vegetables are cleaned, peeled, made string-free, cut in the required size and shapes, and portioned.

16. Further processing of these ready-to-cook ingredients is not required. Many of these RTC products are individually quick frozen (IQF). Individually quick frozen prawns are one example. Individually quick frozen products facilitate portioning for the purpose of cooking. Many manufacturers also supply portioned frozen meats and seafood in line with the portion sizes of culinary outlets, in a ready-to-cook format.

17. Yield testing for such ready-to-cook products is not required. The standard purchase specifications for all these RTC products describe the nature of their yields. In most cases the yield corresponds or approaches to 100% saleable weight.

18. The above-mentioned factors indicate that standard purchase specification controls the outcome of yield testing and standard yield. Standard purchase specification is a standard cost tool. Hence, we can say that all standand cost tools are interrelated.

19. To understand the process of yield tests the following example has been taken:

20. The Riverside Grill restaurant purchases whole chickens for the purposes of preparing them for Chicken Shashlik, a boneless preparation. The chickens are purchased with the following standard purchase specifications:

   - Broiler chickens with dressed weight in the weight range of 1 kg to 1.2 kg; inclusive of skin and 4 cm neck.

Extracts from the Butcher Yield Test Report file of Riverside Grill restaurant are reproduced in **Exhibit 30, (p. 179)**.

Cost per portion of raw meat

It is easy to relate the cost per portion of raw meat from the above example. The chicken in the above example was purchased @ Rs. 150 per kg. The following calculations would illustrate how cost per portion of raw meat can be related to the selling price per portion of the menu item.

1. Portion size of raw boneless chicken for Chicken Shashlik was decided as 200 gm. Therefore, each kg of raw boneless chicken yielded 5 portions.
2. Chicken purchased = 114 kg.
3. Cost of 114 kg of chicken = 114 × 150 = Rs. 17,100.
4. The saleable yield received after fabrication = 50 kg.
5. Therefore, 50 kg of saleable chicken costed Rs. 17,100.
6. Portions available in 50 kg of saleable chicken = 50 × 5 = 250 portions.
7. The raw material cost per portion = Rs. 17,100/250 = Rs. 68.40

EXHIBIT 30: Butcher Yield Test Report

𝕽𝕲 Riverside Grill		
Meat Fabrication Department		
Date: 14th October, 2015		**Day: Wednesday**
Yield Test Subject: Whole chicken for boneless		
As received:		
1. Weight range specifications (with skin, with 4 cm neck)	:	1000 gm to 1200 gm
2. Number of chickens	:	100 nos.
3. Total weight received	:	114 kg
Yield tests and calculations:		
1. Average weight of the chickens	:	1 kg 140 gm
2. Saleable yield:		
(a) Boneless chicken legs	:	27.600 kg
(b) Boneless chicken breasts	:	14.300 kg
(c) Chicken fillet	:	4.200 kg
(d) Trimming (for mince)	:	3.900 kg
3. Total saleable yield (a) + (b) + (c) + (d)	:	50 kg
4. Wastage, bones and by-products	:	64 kg
5. Percentage of saleable yield	:	$\dfrac{50 \times 100}{114} = 43.86\%$
6. Percentage of wastage, bones and by-products	:	$\dfrac{64 \times 100}{114} = 56.14\%$

The figure of Rs. 68.40 would be entered in the Standard Recipe for Chicken Shashlik as the cost per portion of raw boneless chicken. From this example, it is clear that standard portion size has a bearing on the standard yield and also on the standard recipe. In a similar fashion the cost per portion of raw weight can be calculated and used in other standard recipes.

The cost per portion of raw boneless chicken for Chicken Shashlik can also be related to the sale price. Estimation can be made of the relationship. In the example the Chicken Shashlik was listed as a menu item at a sale price of Rs. 750. The raw material cost per portion for chicken being Rs. 68.40, the relationship can be established. The other ingredients which form part of the standard recipe for Chicken Shashlik would add to the cost of preparation of the menu item. In addition, the cost of accompaniments like breads, mini portion of saffron rice, vegetables, potato preparations, salad, plate garnishes, and speciality and proprietary sauces would add to the cost of preparation of the menu item.

Meat-to-wastage ratio

Understanding meat-to-wastage ratio is an extension of the understanding of yields. Intelligent interpretation of this ratio helps professional chefs to either effect changes in the standard purchase specifications or add values to them. In the above example the boneless chicken constituted 43.77% of the purchased weight. The bones and other wastage constituted 56.23% of the purchased weight.

The physical constitution of an animal like a goat or a sheep, and its meat-to-wastage ratio depends somewhat on the age of the animal. In a similar manner, table birds like chicken, turkey, farm-bred-quails, etc., all have certain meat-to-wastage ratio in relation to their age. Larger and older animals and table birds may give larger meat-to-wastage ratio. The larger yields may be good in terms of saleable portions that would be available after processing, but may not be acceptable quality wise, as the quality of their meat may be tougher than desired. Therefore, a careful balancing of meat-to-wastage ratio in relation to other considerations is vital.

In the above example the meat-to-wastage ratio would be expressed as:

Boneless chicken: bones and wastage :: 50 : 64

Yield can be expressed as **an absolute figure** as well **as a percentage**. In the above example, the saleable yield carries 50 kg in absolute figures and 43.86 as a percentage. In continuation, the yield of wastage can be expressed as 64 kg in absolute figures and 56.14 as a percentage. In the same manner the meat-to-bone ratio can be calculated by using the figure of bones by weight in the calculations.

10.6.3   Standard Recipes

Understanding and Defining Standard Recipes

The menu is the most important link between the culinary concept, the customer and the food production and food service processes. Quality of food production of each menu item is supported by "Standard Recipes".

The word recipe is a generic term. In terms of cuisine a "standard recipe" is a systematic progression of usage of the right food ingredients and food products, either in raw stage or previously prepared to a designated degree (the process being called pre-preparation). This usage of food products or raw ingredients is done through set values in terms of measurements and commands in terms of exact preparation guidelines, often in a step-by-step methodology, and other information specific to the food service organisation such as usage of equipment and tools, the right temperature, and other nuances of food production.

A **standard** recipe and its format is a consolidation of information, using it makes it easier to duplicate the preparation effectively. A standard recipe is a recipe that has been carefully adapted and tested to ensure that it will produce a consistent menu item every time it is used. Standard recipe format is individual to the needs of a business. Permutations and combinations of the content can be used.

The standard recipe has backward integration with the:

(a)   right purchase systems;

(b)   right values of standard purchase specifications;

(c)   right purchase tools, for example, purchase order or perishables order sheet;

(d)   right supplier;

(e)   right values of receiving, storing and issuing food products and raw ingredients required for production; and

(f)   right pre-preparation techniques, yield testing and raw ingredient portion control which support the cost structures of the recipe.

In the hands of trained and skilled food production personnel, a standard recipe does wonders towards all aspects of food quality and presentation values that a customer expects. The quality of food production is forward integrated with the service guarantees. Service guarantees ensure that the baton of quality taken up by production personnel is correctly delivered to the customer.

EXHIBIT 31: Format of Standard Recipe

RG Riverside Grill

Name of the menu item :	
Preparation tools :	Digital Photograph
No. of portions :	
Sensitivity :	

Ingredients	Wt./Measure	Method
1		1
2		
3		2
4		
5		3
6		
7		4
8		
9		5
10		
11		6
12		

Garnish

(a)

(b)

(c)

(d)

Date of preparation of standard recipe :

Recipe prepared by :

Recipe approved by :

Recipe to be reviewed on :

EXHIBIT 32: Format of Standard Recipe

RG Riverside Grill

Name of the menu item :	
Recipe category :	
Type of cuisine :	
No. of portions :	
Preparation tools :	
Sensitivity :	

Ingredients	Wt./Measure	Ingredient Cost	Nutrient's Analysis			
			Proteins	Carbohydrates	Fats	Calories
1						
2						
3						
4						
5						
6						
7						
8						
9						
10						
Nutrients per portion						
Total cost						
Cost per portion						

Method: Pre-preparation						
1						
2						
3						
Method : Cooking						
1						
2						
3						
4						
Garnish :						

(a)	(b)
(c)	(d)
Date of preparation of standard recipe :	Recipe prepared by :
Recipe approved by :	Recipe to be reviewed on :

Note: Standard recipe format is individual to the needs of a business. Permutations & Combinations of the contents can be used. The nutrients under review can be changed to those required, e.g. (a) Saturated fats, (b) Cholesterol, (c) Vitamin A, (d) Vitamin C, (e) Iron, (e) Calcium, (f) Sodium, (g) Dietary fibre, etc.

EXHIBIT 33: Format of Standard Recipe

RG Riverside Grill

Name of the menu item :

Preparation tools :

No. of portions :

Sensitivity :

Digital Photograph

Ingredients	Wt./Measure	Method
1		1
2		
3		2
4		
5		3
6		
7		4
8		
9		5
10		
11		6
12		

Garnish

(a)

(b)

(c)

(d)

Date of preparation of standard recipe :

Recipe prepared by :

Recipe approved by :

Recipe to be reviewed on :

Therefore, right food production and its planning:

- is inspiring to all personnel;
- ensures quality cuisine and menu items;
- ensures that the meal would meet or exceed the expectations of the customer; and
- ensures that the customer has a great dining experience and would surely revisit the outlet.

The brand and economic values of a culinary business are enhanced through repeat visits of customers.

A standard recipe denotes standardization for an organisation or for use of a housewife. In these days of culinary awareness, the standard recipe format used by housewives is also taking shape of a commercial recipe format.

As such a standard recipe brings in consistency in quality and cost control. A standard recipe is one of the standard cost control tools. Used in conjunction with standard portion and service guarantee it introduces higher degree of perfection and efficiencies, enhancing the perception of value by a customer.

It is not difficult to evolve even a simple recipe into a standard recipe. However, converting **a standard recipe** into **a signature recipe** is brief and involves just the masterly touch of an experienced chef who has the values of perfection, fine culinary nuances and experience.

Sub-recipes

Very often the pre-preparation process of a standard recipe involves preparations which when ready become ingredients for the recipe. These preparations are also made in a systematic way into sequential usage of ingredients, in a similar manner as the main recipe. These recipes are called sub-recipes. Examples of sub-recipe are preparation of sauces, marinades, gravies, *tomato concassé*, butter cream, spice blends, etc. The process of using sub-recipes as ingredients for the main standard recipe is called chaining of recipes. The major portion of daily production schedule of a mother kitchen is preparation of sub-recipes.

Components of a Standard Recipe

The standard recipe format, as well as the information that it should present, is individual to culinary business. The completed standard recipe is privy to a limited number of professionals.

The **minimum** information contained in a standard recipe should include the following four:

1. **Recipe name:** It is the name that adequately describes the recipe and is mostly the way the recipe is known against a menu item. These recipes are also used as training tools. The name of a recipe for the purposes of writing a standard recipe is often tweaked to suit training needs or quick remembrance. However, it is wise to write both names on the recipe format – the name as it appears on a menu item and the abbreviated name.

   In case of writing names for ethnic recipes it is desirable to have its translated English name also. The recipe format should use the same language throughout.

2. **Ingredients:** Ingredients should preferably be listed in order of their actual usage. Very often scratch foods form part of the list of ingredients in contemporary cuisine.

   A recipe is considered "standardized" when it uses "standard" measurements. A rule to follow while writing standard recipes is to use the same measurement system throughout the recipe. Most of the world uses the metric system which is an international decimalised system of measurement.

   Very often professional recipes are evolved from household or ethnic recipes. In such cases, it is always desirable to convert the subjective portion of the measurements into objective measurements through the use of weighing or measuring instruments.

Measurements such as "a pinch", "a leaf", "a piece", and "to taste" etc., are permissible. However, measurements such as tablespoons, teaspoons, cups, etc., are typical tools of measurement used for home-style food production, and should be avoided for standard recipes meant for professional food service organizations. These measurements can be easily converted into specific weights or volume measurements.

3. **Ingredient quantity:** The weight and/or volume of each ingredient is listed against the ingredients. This identifies how much of the ingredient was used for the production of the number of portions listed. This helps in costing of the recipe.

4. **Method:** The method lists directions for preparing the recipe. The method of preparation is often written in a sequential step-by-step and easy to understand method. The method should be written in a manner so that the recipe is easy to duplicate. The method for the sub-recipe is also written in the same manner. The section of method is often split into two distinct components as

   (a) pre-preparation; and

   (b) cooking.

> **Note: Linkages**: Many in culinary business link their standard recipes to the service guarantees for the menu item. This is the forward integration process. Very often, the standard recipes are also linked to the yield tests of the ingredients, especially those of the meats and expensive ingredients. This is the backward integration process. The mention of condiments, proprietary sauces, and pickles, etc., on a standard recipe helps in the process of stores requisition.

However, in addition to the **minimum information** that a standard recipe should provide, as mentioned above, it is a commercial practice to list the following:

5. **Alternative ingredients:** Ingredient that could be substituted for a listed recipe is mentioned. Seasonal availability of ingredients often requires substitute ingredients.

6. **Optional ingredients:** Ingredients that could be added to a recipe to enhance the flavour or acceptability of the preparation are listed. The addition of these ingredients may affect the nutrient analysis and their costing.

7. **Recipe category:** For commercial food service organisations, standard recipes have evolved as training and cost control tools. An effective standard recipe finds a clear path to customer satisfaction and the value for his money.

   Due to this reason, most commercial food service organisations have now made the filing and maintenance of standard recipes a part of the audit trail and regular operation audits.

   If large number of recipes are to be maintained, placing each recipe in a "recipe category" helps data maintenance. The recipe category normally corresponds to the sub-category of the menu, under which the menu item finds itself. For example, a standard recipe for Baked Alaska would be listed under recipe category of desserts in the menu and in the standard recipe filing system.

8. **Cost of ingredients:** A column indicating costs is inserted in the standard recipe format. This lists the cost of ingredients with their unit price and proportionate price of the weight of ingredients used. This exercise supports costing of the recipe, and relating the total cost of production of the recipe to the selling price listed on the menu.

   Purchase price of commodities changes due to market conditions, mostly upwards. Therefore, it is vital to keep upgrading a standard recipe often in the value of the cost of ingredients. Updating of standard recipes is done in commercial food service organisations twice a year. This also allows focussed attention of the chef and the food production team on the recipe and its economic viability.

9. **Portion size:** Portion size is the amount of a single portion in terms of weight and/or volume. Industry standards and the value proposition of a food service organisation decide its portion size.

10. **Recipe yield:** The amount that a standard recipe produces in terms of weight and/or volume or number of portions that are available for service from production of the listed ingredients. The recipe yield informs about the final quantity of the recipe produced.

11. **Photographs:** Photographs of the ready-to-serve preparation are pasted on the standard recipe format. This supports training and service guarantees. The possibility of pasting a digital photograph onto a word file containing the standard recipe, has encouraged chefs to photograph the preparation of a recipe in a step by step process, and paste these photographs on to a standard recipe.

    An essential advantage of using photographs is to identify garnishes and presentation styles. Some recipe formats write the garnishes and presentation styles in addition to the photograph.

12. **Nutrient analysis:** This involves listing nutrients per serving on to a standard recipe. Listing nutrients per serving helps commercial food service organisations such as:

    - hospital catering services;
    - school and college catering services;
    - military catering services; and
    - food processing industry.

    It is imperative for organisations such as above to keep a check on the consumption of nutrients, overriding other considerations. Burgeoning number of restaurants do the same as a service to the customers.

13. **Cooking temperature and time:** Cooking temperature and time are essential nuances of food preparation and of perfecting a recipe. Correct recording of the temperature and its relation to the time that was spent supports correct duplication of recipe. The purpose of preparing standard recipes is to allow for their duplication later, and also by another professional.

14. **Equipment and utensils to be used:** The cooking equipment and utensils to be used in preparing and serving the recipe should be recorded. Quality outcome of certain recipes depends on the equipment and utensils used. For repeat production of the recipe it is important to list these equipment and utensils.

15. **Safety and sensitivities to be careful of:** Specific instructions regarding safety and sensitivities are mentioned in the standard recipe. These instructions draw the attention of the production staff towards the right values of the completion of a recipe.

    Examples of mention of safety issues while preparing a standard recipe involve instructions of usage of equipment or tools or of dealing with hot liquids, etc.

    Examples of sensitivities in a Standard Recipe are in terms of:

    - clear flavour notes. This is typically done in the food processing industry;
    - degree of heat, for example, chilled or piping hot;
    - texture, for example, thickness, thinness, crispiness or golden brown crust;
    - final usage of souring agents like lemon or tamarind;
    - shape, for example, equal size;
    - freshness, for example, freshness of bread;
    - hardness, for example, hard ice cream;
    - crunchiness, for example, crunchy pralines;

- shiny appearance, for example, *velouté* sauce or caramel coating;
- degree of spiciness, for example, end product not to be spicy;
- adequate portions like for thali;
- size, for example, one-bite sized cocktail snacks;
- degree of cooking, for example, avoiding overcooking;
- taste, for example, tanginess of sauce;
- colour, for example, green vegetables; and
- usage of fat, for example, removing top fat.

16. **Tweaking:** Tweaking is the way a recipe can be changed to suit tastes, costs, available ingredients, nutrients per serving, available equipment and utensils or geographical location. Recipes can be tweaked successfully with increase in their health value and without sacrificing taste and flavour. Quantities of certain ingredients can be reduced and certain other ingredients can be replaced. Tweaking normally appears in the form of a note at the end of a recipe.

17. **HACCP guidelines:** Food safety guidelines are either incorporated in a standard recipe format in the steps of production or as a note at the end of the recipe. Many commercial food service organisations write all the HACCP (Hazard Analysis Critical Control Point) information on a separate sheet but in immediate continuation of the Standard Recipe.

18. **Adjusted quantities:** This recipe format is rare, but is followed by canteen / cafeteria organisations for staff members. In such places, recipes can be designed to cater to busy periods and slow period or for a duty period. The number of staff members varies from one shift to another. Quantity of food required to feed them varies accordingly.

    Different ingredient inputs and corresponding recipe yields are noted in this format. For example, a recipe may have ingredient quantities for 50 portions and 100 portions suiting different batch size of consumers. The quantities can be modified with simple arithmetical multiplication or division. For example, a recipe produces 10 portions, and 20 portions are required. Its quantities can be modified by multiplying quantities of each ingredient by 2. Similarly, if the recipe produces 10 portions, and only 10 portions are required, the quantities can be modified by dividing quantities of each ingredient by 2.

    A word of caution: All ingredients of the recipe may not require exact multiplication or division of quantities of ingredients on higher or lower volumes of food production. Certain stronger flavour notes, for example, rosemary; taste notes, for example, tamarind, and certain colours may not require exact multiplication or division of ingredient quantities.

19. **Authorization:** Culinary business ensures that a recipe has been carefully gone through and standardized and that it is the best in terms of value to the customer under the outlet's concept. The recipe should deliver value in terms of quality to the customer, and along with the service guarantees should be a composite tool for the customer's positive dining experience. This is the reason why recipes are authorized by the seniormost chef of the business. Authorized standard recipes have cost control connotations, and only such recipes are considered "final" by the cost control team for the purposes of audit.

20. **Review:** Usually in culinary business review of these recipes is done, at least twice a year. The standard recipe is a benchmark, and the business should examine it along with other benchmarks periodically. In line with this understanding, the date of writing the recipe originally and its date of expected review are written.

> **Note:** Standard recipe format is individual to the needs of a business. Permutations and combinations of contents can be used. A few formats of a Standard Recipe are provided (see pp. 181-183).

Benefits of standard recipes

The main purpose of using standard recipes is to duplicate production of a menu item. Depending upon the format used, standard recipes introduce consistency in terms of quality, flavour, colour, presentation styles, garnish and portion size.

As mentioned earlier, standard recipe is a standard cost tool. Costing of a standard recipe is vital for cost control purposes. In addition, the cost per portion at a given point of time in a year is a financial benchmark. In case of yearly fixed rate contracts for ingredients, consistent recipe cost supports cost control exercise in line with budgeting.

(a) **Food quality consistency:** Success of a culinary outlet depends on the consistency of food quality of its menu items. Customer's perception of value is largely related to consistency of the quality of menu items ordered. Due to the use of standard recipes the production of menu items retains consistency.

(b) **Customer satisfaction:** A customer requires good value. The customer's expectations are required to be met and exceeded on each of his visits. Food quality consistency is an important factor towards customer satisfaction.

(c) **Pre-identification of portions produced:** Standard recipes produce a fixed yield of menu items each time. If a business day's activities require larger number of menu item portions to be readied, the same can be planned easily and vice versa. Intelligently using standard recipes in conjunction with other data such as menu engineering prevents overproduction or underproduction of portions. **Time, care, love, and affection** go in the preparation of food. If the prepared number of portions run out, while the business session is still on, it may be difficult to prepare the same in the right way, while dealing with other orders of the customers.

Pre-identification of portions is very useful, when the menu items are prepared in a mother kitchen and transported to other serving locations.

(d) **Efficient control of food costs:** Standard recipes play a very important role in the overall control system of a culinary operation. With all menu items prepared using standard recipes; food cost control processes get streamlined and can be computerized. Production costs can be calculated easily and accurate information would be available on each cooking occasion standard recipes are used. This is because the ingredients and quantities per portion would be same each time. Standard recipes support menu pricing process and decisions. Standard recipe is therefore an important production tool to deliver quality and for cost control measures.

(e) **Support in employee training:** Training of food production processes to employees is easier with usage of standard recipes. The quality and quantities of the ingredients and steps of production of the recipe are controlled. Estimation of quantities of ingredients for recipe preparation is not required. It is easier to train the employees the nuances of preparing the recipe. With a few rounds of practice, the preparation of the menu item and its presentation styles can be perfected. Training of production of the right quantities is also easier. Standard recipes are therefore a boost to employee's confidence and training systems.

(f) **Ingredient indenting:** Indenting and sourcing of ingredients from the stores or from the market becomes easier because standard recipes provide the right information on the quantity of ingredients that would be used when the recipe is produced. **In addition, this is useful for inventory control purposes.**

The list of ingredients of all the recipes of all the menu items under the command of a unified kitchen and a chef can be used to prepare **master checklists** for the purposes of indenting non-perishables from the stores or perishables from the market.

(g) **Standardized purchasing:** The quantities of ingredients for food production for a specific period can be easily calculated based on the information provided in the standard recipe. This can be easily reformulated into purchase requirements. This is especially so for large industrial catering establishments, wherein the types of menus and their rotation is limited.

(h) **Support in defining effective work practices:** The format for a standard recipe also lists the equipment used for production and often for service also. Hence, properly developed recipes also define effective work practices. Standard recipes combined with service guarantees are indicators to kitchen stewards to be ready with the production and service equipment within easy reach and in sufficient quantities, especially during the peak periods of business.

(i) **Applied nutrition:** In hospital and airline catering it is important to keep the desired and planned nutrition values of each recipe intact. Standard recipes support this need. The standard recipe format for such needs should have calculation of nutrients for each ingredient. If nutrients for each ingredient of a recipe are available, the nutrients per portion can be easily calculated.

> **Note:** Nutrients under review can be changed to those required, e.g. (a) saturated fats, (b) Iron, (c) Vitamin A, (d) Vitamin C, (e) Cholesterol, (f) Calcium, (f) Sodium, (g) Dietary fibre, etc.

The process of standardizing and evolving recipes

The process of standardizing and evolving recipes is **not a magical process**. Any recipe can be made into a standard recipe.

Case A: Preparing standard recipes through systematic addition of values to an existing recipe.

Case B: Preparing standard recipes through the culinary expertise of a chef or a cook. This process involves writing of the standard recipe prepared by the chef in a sequential way.

Case A: The process of **standardization** in the case of an **existing recipe** is as follows:

1. Understanding the recipe in the present format.
2. Identifying the ingredients.
3. Keeping an accurate weighing scale and volume measuring cups handy. If the original recipe was prescribed in terms of spoon measures then standard spoon measures should be available. Weighing, even for liquids is always accurate in relation to measuring.
4. Other standard sized equipment and tools should be used, for example, usage of a standard portion size of caramel custard mould.
5. Keeping all vessels and equipment prescribed in the recipe ready. If vessels and equipment are not specified, reading the recipe and identifying the possible vessels and equipment.
6. Preparing the recipe as the methodology prescribes.
7. Garnishing and presenting the preparation as directed, or using own expertise to do the same.
8. Keeping notes of the steps used in the cooking process, including temperature and duration for which the temperature were used.
9. Inviting knowledgeable persons, gourmets and chefs who had experienced and tasted the preparation earlier, or who can give valuable suggestions to set the recipe right.

   Preparing the recipe again

   Making changes in quality, quantity, flavour, taste, texture, colour, appearance and nutritive values, if required:

   - By changing the quantities of ingredients.
   - By adding additional or optional ingredients.
   - Through the use of additional cooking steps or reducing cooking steps.

- Through the change of temperatures and cooking timings at each temperature stage.

- Through change of cooking vessels and equipment.

- Through innovative changes in the method of cooking, usage of substitute ingredients, flavour and taste notes, finishing touches, appearance and introducing "professional" garnishes.

10. Arriving at the right finished culinary product through permutation and combinations of the above. In case the yield is not as per the desired quantity the quantities of ingredients can be adjusted. The final step involves the writing of the standard recipe on the basis of values explained above. A standard recipe format is individual to the user.

The following steps would help in creating a good standard recipe in addition to the values of the format decided to be adopted:

(a) The ingredients should be listed in the sequence they were used.

(b) The steps of production should be written in detailed and exact language.

(c) Writing the portion control system, e.g., by way of a mini casserole, an *entrée* dish, a custard mould, main ingredient's finished weight, etc., ensures further accuracy.

The essence of a good standard recipe is that anybody using it can duplicate the product. Once the written standard recipe is ready, it should be cooked and tried by **other members** of the production team. Even minor variations in quality or quantity of ingredients, equipment or temperature can make a big positive or negative difference. In a similar manner as above, the recipe should be corrected if required. The standard recipe should yield culinary products of the desired quality and quantity.

Most culinary business solicits support from even their customers to perfect a standard recipe.

Case B: Capturing the **culinary expertise:**

It is easy to prepare standard recipes from the expertise of a chef or a cook. If the chef or a cook is able to deliver the values of a culinary product excellently his performances can be watched and recorded. This is a simpler process of standardizing recipes. This process is adopted in culinary business on a consistent basis.

The chef or cook explains the preparation of the recipe. A rough structure of the recipe in terms of the ingredients required and the step-by-step method of preparation is written down. A fixed quantity of each ingredient, including liquids, is kept ready, preferably by weighing them. The equipment and vessels that the chef requires are kept ready.

The chef uses his culinary skills, and experience values and prepares the recipe, using ingredients in quantities to perfectly present the dish. The chef uses the ingredients in a step-by-step method which is recorded by another chef or cook. The observer chef or cook also records the approximate time taken at each step of the method of preparation and the approximate cooking temperature during the particular step. With the use of an accurate weighing scale, the left over quantities of ingredients are measured. The difference in the quantities is the quantity that was used for the preparation.

The rough structure of the recipe which was prepared earlier is corrected. Ingredients or steps that were missing earlier, or any nuances that the chef explains while cooking the recipe are recorded and the recipe is ready for further experimentation.

The chef prepares the recipe again, with the help of adjusted ingredients. Any gaps in the earlier observation are noted carefully. The recipe is perfected once again through the efforts of the chef (demonstrator) for the values of the recipe in terms of quality, quantity, flavour, taste, texture, colours, and nutritive values.

As mentioned above, the essence of a good standard recipe is its duplication by anybody. A **different team member** prepares the recipe. It is garnished and finished as required.

A panel of team members, chefs or any external gourmets including customers provides expert comments and if required corrections are made. The yields are adjusted if required. The ingredients and step-by-step method of production are recorded in the standard recipe format with values as explained above. The standard recipe format is used as the property of the culinary business.

Costing of recipes

In order to make any selected menu item a complete meal, certain additional preparations are offered. Examples of these preparations are *Amuse bouches*, variety of dinner rolls and breads, salads, optional or additional sauces, salad dressings and potatoes for European meals. For an Indian meal the combination offerings could be Indian breads, curd or raita, dal, kachumber salad, pickled onions and papad, etc.

The cost of each of the accompaniments can be obtained from a pre-costed recipe for that item. Pre-costing is the method of ascertaining the cost of identified quantity of each ingredient required by a standard recipe or sub-recipe.

If the customer has a choice of selecting the accompaniments then the combination of the most popular and expensive accompaniments should be taken as the cost of accompaniments for each of the menu item with which such accompaniments are offered.

Very often suitable accompaniments to the menu item to add to the satiety values and to the total meal experience are provided. These accompaniments could be as simple as condiments, proprietary sauces or pickles, etc. These are presented to the customer as a part of the food service.

Purchase, preparation and offering of all these items as accompaniment add to the cost of the menu item. Combination of costs of the menu item prepared as per its standard recipe and the cost of accompaniments would be the real cost of the menu item. At times however, it is difficult to apportion costs of such value additions to individual menu items.

Costing of recipes helps in relating the cost of the standard recipe to the sale price of the menu item. Proportionate cost of accompaniments, which form part of the menu item offer, are included in the costs.

10.6.4   Standard Portion Sizes

The decision of fixing the quantity of a standard portion in respect to a menu item is vital to the success of the business. Standard portion size is not an arbitrary decision. Fixing a portion size requires the following:

- Examining the culinary concept and customer expectations.
- Standards of portion size of similar preparations in the market competition.
- Examining and costing of necessary accompaniments to the main menu item.

Larger-than-required portion sizes reduce the saleability of other menu items; introduce sharing of the menu item between customers, and a possible customer insistence of carrying left-overs in a "doggy-bag".

One of the vital delivery requisites of a culinary business is to provide the customers the same quantity of all menu items on each service occasion. This fixed quantity is known as **standard portion size**. Customers should not get a smaller or larger portion than the one decided by a culinary business for any menu item. Standard portion also allows for the menu item to be correctly placed on the service dish or plate.

Once customers experience the portion size, it becomes difficult to reduce the size. (Module 4 "Menu Engineering: Culinary Business Analytics" also examines the issue of standard portion in relation to the success of individual menu item as well as the entire menu.)

Portion control tools: Weighing and measuring equipment and tools that help in dishing out the right quantity of portion are known as portion control tools. A few examples are:

- A ladle, e.g., a soup ladle.
- Standard measurement cups, e.g., soup cups.
- Scoopers, e.g., an ice-cream scoop.
- Cake divider.
- Moulds in which a culinary product is prepared, e.g., a caramel custard mould.
- Quarter egg cutter.
- Calibrated litre cups.
- Weighing scales.

All the above are examples of portion control tools. Employees should be trained in the usage of portion control tools.

10.6.5 Standard Portion Costs

The standard recipe should be costed in relation to each of the ingredients it uses in proportion to their quantity usage, and as per the current purchase price. If the menu item is offered combined with other accompaniments, as mentioned above, then the cost of these accompaniments would form part of the calculations. The costs arrived at in this manner should be divided by the number of portions the recipe produces. This would give the standard portion cost for that menu item.

The standard portion cost is therefore defined as the cost of one portion of cooking a menu item through the use of a standard recipe. This figure becomes a benchmark for all future calculations, and is a **standard cost tool.** Standard portion costs of all the menu items must be calculated as these are one of the contributory factors for selling price of the menu items. Standard portion cost is the basis of multiple type of calculations and applications of the menu engineering process.

10.7 PLANNING FOOD PRODUCTION AND FORECASTING QUANTITIES

It is important to plan quantities of a particular menu item to be produced for a day. In a similar manner food production planning should be done for all the needs of the day, of the week, and of the month.

Forecasting quantities of food production and planning of food production are integrated requirements. The process starts with forecasting the volume of sales for a day. Different methodologies are adopted for forecasting the food production quantities in relation to expected volume of sales for the day. In a similar period food production is planned for larger periods, for example, a week. It is imperative for the commercial success of a business to plan production.

The following are the aims and objectives of food production forecasting and planning:

(a) To facilitate the purchasing of food products and raw ingredients required for food production in time. Many food products and raw ingredients require pre-preparation before actual cooking can take place. All purchased meat products need further fabrication to get the right portions or cuts for the specific requirement of the business. In addition, sufficient levels of all the perishables are required to be maintained.

(b) To facilitate the stores requisitioning process.

(c) To reduce losses of **overproduction** due to unauthorized consumption and wastage.

(d) To arrange for personnel who are trained to produce the right quality.

(e) To avoid possibilities of insufficient food production.

(f) To support cost control systems.

(g) To introduce financial accountability.

(h) To analyze the difference between actual and potential portions sales.

(i) To gear up the food production facilities to meet the forecast demands.

The process of food production planning is to set up an initial forecast in advance. This forecast is used for planning and ordering ingredients and other food products. The initial forecast would estimate portions of menu items to be produced. In case there are a number of culinary outlets within the same premises, for example, in a hotel, the production planning of each outlet has to be done individually. While forecasting the footfalls, the following are taken into account:

(i) Earlier portion sale figures.

(ii) Business scenario and financial conditions of the market.

(iii) Weather conditions.

(iv) External market factors like:

- Sporting and/or social events.

- Business and political meets.

- Local, national and international events / disasters.

These factors have possibilities of creating larger or lesser than normal business to the outlet's catchment area. À la carte culinary outlets are particularly subject to the above.

Production planning should be done especially for food promotions. In case of higher than normal business activity in one outlet of a hotel due to a food promotion event, other outlets should re-plan their food production. Depending on the geographical location of the culinary outlet and its brand strengths, the higher number of footfalls due to such food promotions events may result in lesser business in the other outlets.

Closer to the actual date of production, these estimates should be carefully adjusted, and a more accurate forecast should be made. There are a number of aids or management tools that may be employed to assist the forecasting and planning of production. The tools aiding decisions on "right' quantities of food production could be used individually and also in combination with other methods.

The methods of forecasting the **quantities** of food production are:

1. experience of the chefs;

2. examining trends of culinary business in the geographical area;

3. examining sales histories and using menu engineering methodology;

4. using the fixed portion production method;

5. using the top up production method; and

6. using the weighted average method

10.7.1 Experience of Chefs

The experience of a chef and group of chefs is invaluable for determining quantities of food production. "Gut-feeling" and "intuition" add worth to the "experience-value" of a chef. This is supported by data produced through computer systems.

The experience of chefs helps in estimating which of the menu items would move faster, and which need enhanced quantities of production. While à la carte business can be judged statistically on these issues, for buffets and banquets it is "gut feeling" and "intuition" which are aided by pure experience. A combination of cuisines is often offered to customers for banquets. Quantities of food required to be produced for each cuisine would again be the experience value of the chefs for deciding which cuisine or which culinary preparation is likely to be most popular and which should be produced in maximum quantities. The decision would be subjectivity led.

10.7.2   Using the Value of Trends

Trends in culinary business change due to:

- type of customers and their requirements;
- market conditions; and
- culinary skill sets in terms of recently appointed chefs.

Unknown and un-exhibited talents of the performing chefs are exposed through food festivals and food promotion events. Food festivals and food promotion events help set trends and increase footfalls into the business. Culinary trends are also set in motion by fresh culinary activity at the banquets. Clever interpretations of trends help in deciding food production quantities for a day.

Trends for à la carte business come out clearly when earlier data is maintained in the form of sales histories. This is easy these days through the usage of computers.

Trends of consumption help in identifying quantities of products required for expected food production activities for a particular forthcoming period. Using the value of trends for forecasting volumes of food production for a day or for any period is a subjectivity-led method.

Expectations of customers change. So do quality benchmarks. These quality benchmarks in case of food production can be those of the:

- quality of food;
- quality of service; and
- quality of ancillary experience.

Therefore, **quality is not a fixed standard.** It evolves as expectations of the customers and the market change. Expectations of food quality and food service change:

- when a new culinary brand enters the market and also due to its marketing;
- due to enhanced culinary awareness of customers; and also
- due to repositioning of the culinary concept or change in the culinary business plan.

Quality is relative to market perceptions of what is correct and relative to the type of the culinary business and also to the cost of the dining experience.

10.7.3   Using Sales Histories

Sales histories are used to identify popular menu items and consumption patterns. In continuation, sales histories help in identifying portions of menu items required for expected production activities for a particular forthcoming period.

Number of portions consumed by customers on earlier occasions is analyzed in relation to the total number of footfalls during the same period. This helps in identifying portions of menu items required for a particular forthcoming period.

In the following example sales histories are used to predict portions of menu items required. The sales history of the à la carte restaurant Riverside Grill for the month of December 2015 presents the following data:

EXHIBIT 34: Using Sales Histories

RG Riverside Grill

Number of Portions Sold in the Month of December 2015
Menu Item: Chicken Steak. *Four Pepper Jus*

Date	Day	Total customers of the day	Portions sold
1.12.2015	Tuesday	130	15
2.12.2015	Wednesday	142	17
3.12.2015	Thursday	128	18
4.12.2015	Friday	135	22
5.12.2015	Saturday	155	22
6.12.2015	Sunday	162	26
7.12.2015	Monday	125	12
8.12.2015	Tuesday	140	14
9.12.2015	Wednesday	137	19
10.12.2015	Thursday	128	19
11.12.2015	Friday	132	21
12.12.2015	Saturday	160	22
13.12.2015	Sunday	165	27
14.12.2015	Monday	130	14
15.12.2015	Tuesday	134	13
16.12.2015	Wednesday	131	18
17.12.2015	Thursday	134	19
18.12.2015	Friday	136	22
19.12.2015	Saturday	155	24
20.12.2015	Sunday	158	23
21.12.2015	Monday	122	12
22.12.2015	Tuesday	135	14
23.12.2015	Wednesday	133	17
24.12.2015	Thursday	142	18
25.12.2015	Friday	162	23
26.12.2015	Saturday	175	25
27.12.2015	Sunday	180	28
28.12.2015	Monday	126	14
29.12.2015	Tuesday	130	16
30.12.2015	Wednesday	135	18
31.12.2015	Thursday	138	19
Total		4395	591
No. of Days		31	31
Average		141.77	19.06

The above data indicates that in the month of December 2015, the average number of customers per day were 142. The average sales of number of portions of Chicken Steak *with four pepper jus* were 19. This gives one guideline of portions of the menu item to be produced subsequently.

On Sunday 27.12.2015, the restaurant received 180 customers and 28 portions of the Chicken Steak were sold. This relates to 15.6% of customers ordering the menu item. Once the total number of customers expected for the forthcoming Sunday, i.e., 3 January 2016 is estimated, the percentage can be used to estimate the number of portions of the Chicken Steak that should be kept ready.

The case study further assumes that the number of expected customers would be 200 due to the higher tourist group movements for Sunday 3 January 2016. Further assuming that the same percentage of customers would order the Chicken Steak, the guideline for production planning would be to keep 200 × 15.6% = 31 portions ready. This method creates possibilities of using trends of portion consumption in relation to the number of customers, using days of the week or weekends as guiding point.

The process is repeated to estimate production requirements for all other menu items, and for all days in the period of forecast. Menu engineering worksheets especially the Menu Item Analysis helps in understanding of the consumption pattern of à la carte menu items. Production quantity levels of the immediate future can be determined accordingly. This method of using sales histories for forecasting of food production for a particular day is subjectivity-led.

10.7.4 Fixed Portion Production Method

This method is predominantly used in outlets which are family or chef owned and run. The critical success factor of these restaurants is the superlative quality of food produced, and a product which is impossible to duplicate and be available elsewhere. A customer does not feel cheated or offended if the prepared number of portions run out on one of his visits. In fact, the customer is prepared to arrive early on his next dining occasion at the same restaurant or reserve certain number of portions beforehand.

The limitation in food production quantities happens due to:

- limited quantities of raw materials available;
- requirement of specialist ingredients; or
- labour and efforts required by the chefs at such outlets.

The chefs produce only a specific number of portions of each of the menu items which they are sure of selling. In addition, the portions to be produced on a day are the same as on any other day. This is an objectivity-led method of forecasting volumes of food production.

The chefs produce each menu item with lot of love, care and in a "straight-from-the-heart manner, and also as per their experience with a successful recipe. Once these portions are exhausted, the chefs do not want to produce additional portions in hurry for unexpected demands. Very often, customer orders for other menu items are pending to be executed.

The author was a witness to such practices in a number of restaurants located in European countries, especially in non-principal towns.

10.7.5 Top-up Production Method

This system of food planning and production works in a manner akin to the top up method used in financial matters. Petty cash expenditures of a cashier are reimbursed in a similar manner – only that much fresh funds are given to the cashier as he has vouchers for.

A certain fixed number of portions are planned for production for a day or for a period. This figure is arrived at by checking sales history data. The portions of each menu item sold are listed chronologically on a spreadsheet.

On the day of the production, the previous day's figures of consumption or sales are checked. The production is done only for the number of portions sold to bring the stock level up to the fixed number of portions. This system is especially followed in a factory style of food production operation like in the food processing industry and in mother kitchens. The top-up method of forecasting volumes of food production is objectivity-led.

10.7.6 Weighted Average Method

With the weighted average method it is possible to calculate quantities in terms of à la carte portions likely to be ordered by customers for a day. Food production planning can take direction from the statistical data presented by the method.

Weighted average method is a part of **mathematical finance**. The applications of mathematical finance and those of the weighted average method are used for needs of diverse industries. For culinary business this forecasting method depends on analysing past à la carte portion consumptions at **identical time intervals** and taking into account the total number of customers who placed orders for the menu item during the subject meal period or day. Weighted average method is a progression of data points, **measured at successive times spaced at uniform time intervals.**

The weighted average method essentially analyzes data from a chronological sequence. It provides weights for data from the sales history. It treats the most recent sale figures as the one with the most bearing on the requirements of forecasting. The assumption is that the most recent sales figure would be the true picture of the expected sale of immediate future, if measured at identical time intervals. The most recent sale figure gets the "heaviest" weight. In continuation the method assigns lesser weight to figures from the sales history in a reducing manner from recent to older chronological occurrences.

In essence the weighted average method heavily depends on **trends of consumption of the immediate past to forecast quantities required in the immediate future.**

Case study: Forecasting quantities of food production using weighted average method:

Data was extracted from the sales history of the à la carte restaurant Riverside Grill. A study was done on 1 January 2016. Figures of portions of the menu item Chicken Steak *with four pepper jus* sold on each of the previous five Tuesdays were taken. That ensured that the study was done of sales at identical time intervals. The sales figures of each of the previous Tuesdays were considered data points. The requirement on 1 January, 2016 was to project the number of portions that were **likely to be sold** on Tuesday 5 January, 2016, which was placed at an identical time interval in the immediate future. Weights were assigned as explained above.

Date	Day	Portions Sold	Weights Assigned
29.12.2015	Tuesday	16	5
22.12.2015	Tuesday	14	4
15.12.2015	Tuesday	13	3
8.12.2015	Tuesday	14	2
1.12.2015	Tuesday	15	1

The study having been conducted on 1 January, 2016, the following steps were taken to project the number of portions that were likely to be sold on Tuesday, 5, January, 2016.

1. The number of portions of Chicken Steak sold on each Tuesday in the case study to be multiplied by its respective weight and the values totalled:

   $16 \times 5 + 14 \times 4 + 13 \times 3 + 14 \times 2 + 15 \times 1 = 80 + 56 + 39 + 28 + 15 = 218$

2. The total of the weighted figures (218) to be divided by the sum of its weights:

   $$\frac{218}{5+4+3+2+1} = 218/15 = 15$$

The weighted average method projected on 1 January 2016 itself that approximately 15 portions of Chicken Steak were **likely to be consumed** on Tuesday, 5 January, 2016. The reader would be enlightened to know that Riverside Grill restaurant actually sold 16 portions of Chicken Steak on Tuesday, 5 January, 2016.

The weighted average method for forecasting volumes of food production is limited to à la carte business and is subjectivity-led as it is based on assumptions. Larger sample size always provides more accurate results in comparison to results provided by limited data points. The method works well when chronological data of several months is required to be analyzed in the above manner. Weights are provided accordingly. Computers help to do the necessary task faster.

> **Note 1:** In actual practice, culinary business uses more than one of the methods of forecasting volumes of food production in conjunction with each other.
>
> **Note 2:** The author has successfully used the above mentioned methods of forecasting volumes of food production, often in conjunction with other methods **earlier on also** in his career as a professional chef.

10.8 ECONOMICS OF FOOD SERVICE

10.8.1 Service Guarantees and their Importance in Culinary Business (Exhibit 35, p. 201)

In terms of a culinary product offer the customer demands consistency in:

- quality of the food preparation;
- quality of the service; and
- quality of attention post-service and consumption.

Consistency in the above relates to positive dining experience and good value of money spent by him.

There are many known factors during **service** as well as **post-service** of food. Standard operating procedures of the business prescribe handling the service and post-service aspects of food service. It is **service guarantees,** in addition, which provide an opportunity of declaring information related to **food preparation and presentation**, including food styling, which would relate to values of consistency if these are delivered perfectly.

Cuisine and culinary performances are subjective in nature. The effort of an efficient culinary business should always be to create as many parameters of objective delivery, as are possible. Service guarantees identify and define these **objective** parameters.

Declared service guarantees are therefore symbols and reflections of a culinary business's efficiency and its zeal to provide continuous and consistent value to a customer for his meal. Service guarantees reflect the technological superiority and technological inclination of the organisation.

Standard recipes are privy to the chefs and to limited number of operators. This is done to prevent information of the nature of intellectual and professional property rights leaking to competition.

Service guarantees are designed to inform the food production and food service staff of important and sufficient parameters of food production and service. Service guarantees are therefore tools with which production and service staff are aligned and duty bound to deliver.

Service guarantees therefore help in effective training especially of service personnel. The mark of good food delivery benchmarks are service personnel's ability to be able to explain the menu items in terms of their preparation, portion size, and related information in answer to customer queries at the time of ordering food or in an effort to up sell food.

Service guarantees are zero-defect, zero-variable and zero-tolerance benchmarks. Various values of service guarantees are contained in a tabular word file format in a binder. Each menu item of an outlet's menu is represented by a page in the binder. Even non-menu items are represented through pages in the binder. Soft copies of service guarantees can be maintained in the computer. The following information is provided by the service guarantees format in respect of each menu item:

1. Name of the culinary outlet.

2. Menu category in terms of soups, salads, main course or desserts, etc.

3. Name of the menu item.

4. Description of the menu item for service personnel. The description is short, crisp and explains the preparation and finishing style of the menu item including its garnish and also the accompaniments. A contemporary option is to guide the service personnel about suitable wines and spirits to be paired with the menu item.

5. Selling price of the dish.

6. Its method of cooking.

7. Pick-up time/service time. This ensures fast and efficient delivery and that the service personnel are ready to pick up an ordered item in time. It relates well to the promise a service personnel can give to a customer. The knowledge of pick up time is also useful in spacing more than one order for the same customer or same table. The knowledge is also useful for picking up ready-to-serve menu items from different sections of the kitchen for the same table. This reduces possibilities of late deliveries for lady customers causing embarrassment for other gentlemen customers on the same table whose orders are ready.

   Pick-up time is often sectionalised as per the sections of the menu, for example soups and salads take 10 minutes, the main course 30 minutes and desserts 10 minutes, etc.

8. Major ingredients used in the preparation.

9. Portion size.

10. Required serviceware.

11. Pick-up point.

12. Garnishes.

13. Accompaniments.

14. Service style and whether it is a hot or a cold service.

The service guarantee format is accompanied by a photograph of the menu item. This is digitally pasted on the format and print-outs taken. The photograph provides standardized appearance of the menu item as it would appear when it is ready for pick-up.

Culinary services in a hotel present a different possibility than a stand-alone culinary outlet. In hotels, multiple food service outlets are available. Often same menu items are available in different outlets. It is possible in such cases that service guarantees for the same menu item are different for different outlets. An example is service guarantees in respect of a 24-hour restaurant and a 24-hour room service. Service guarantees may change as per operational needs in many parameters, for example:

- Selling price.
- Pick-up/service time.
- Serviceware.

The presentation style may also change, which would also mean that the photograph would present the difference clearly.

Many hotels provide for separate kitchens for in-room dining service. In such cases the pick-up points mentioned in the service guarantees for in-room dining would be different from the pick-up points of the same menu items served in another outlet.

Culinary business displays service guarantees in printed and framed format, often with large font sizes, on the walls, near the food pick-up counters.

The purpose of the display is:

- providing avenues for refresh training inputs;
- providing instant reference for the benefit of food production and service staff;
- creating feeling of pride regarding quality of food production and delivery among staff members; and
- Providing instant help and guidance in case of a dispute between the service and production personnel. Service guarantees remove ambiguity.

Customers often like to walk through the kitchen and observe chefs while their ordered food is prepared for service. Earlier on it was not possible for customers to walk into a kitchen.

However, contemporary kitchen infrastructure is inviting and chefs take a lot of pride in the quality of sanitation standards of their kitchens, and also in their methodical culinary performances.

The practice now is to allow customers to the kitchen. Displayed service guarantees present a very impressive, heart-warming and systematic professional touch to the customers during their visits to the kitchen. The guarantees reflect the attitude of the service personnel, their pride, knowledge, ability and willingness to work as a team. The guarantees also exhibit the initiative of the service staff to provide quality cuisine to the customer with faultless service standards. The display also ensures that service personnel remain "on-their-toes", which, in turn, ensures great values of the dining experience to the customers.

Kitchen stewards are responsible for providing pick-up dishes at the pick-up points in time. Service guarantees ensure that they are knowledgeable about the requirements.

Service guarantees are not standard cost control tools, and are not part of the financial audit trail. However they are indispensable for culinary business for its operational and financial success. The understanding of service guarantees can be successfully applied to any area of hospitality operation.

The final presentation style of the menu item should be captured in a colour photograph. This photograph should be inserted in the service guarantee format of the menu item or should be linked to it. Service guarantee of each menu item is a formidable benchmark towards customer satisfaction, cost-effectiveness and accountability.

When similar culinary outlets and menu types with similar culinary offerings exist in the same marketplace, it is service guarantees, accompanied by quality of food production, ambience of the restaurant, the quality of the service personnel and their delivery which would create the enhanced footfalls of the customers into the business.

EXHIBIT 35: Specimen of Service Guarantees

RG Riverside Grill	
Serial Number	DESSERT – 10
Name of the Dish	BANANA SPLIT
Description of the Dish	An All American favourite ice cream based dessert. Full meal by itself. Fresh split Bananas with trio of Ice Creams: Vanilla, Chocolate, and Strawberry topped with whipped Cream, Chocolate sauce, and lightly roasted California almond wafers. Garnished with destoned cherry, orange segments, and served with many speciality accompaniments.
Area of Operation	"RIVERSIDE GRILL" Restaurant.
Selling Price	Rs. 375.00
Method of Cooking	Pantry speciality involving usage of bought-out ice creams, bananas, cream and nuts. Chocolate sauce is prepared with a mixture of cocoa powder, sugar and water. Almond wafers are lightly roasted in the oven.
Ingredients	One large scoops each of Vanilla, Strawberry, and Chocolate ice creams. + Ingredients of the accompaniments.
Pick-up Dish	*"RG" monogrammed cold half plate.*
Pick-up Point	Main kitchen pantry.
Pick-up Time/ Service Time	Seven minutes after ordering.
Portion Size	One large scoop of each of Vanilla ice cream, Strawberry ice cream, and Chocolate ice cream and accompaniments in listed quantities.
Garnish	20 gm of chocolate sauce, 15 gm lightly roasted almond wafers sprinkled, one ice cream wafer, one de-stoned red cherry without any blemish, three segments of canned mandarin orange, almond *tuile*, sweetened cream spiral (20 gm)
Accompaniments	Extra chocolate sauce (30 gm) + two Brownie wafers (25 gm) + two no. *biscotti* wafer (20 gm) + small sauceboat of sweetened whipped cream (30 gm), two Strawberry marshmallows (5 gm), two Black-currant jujubes (5 gm)
Service Style	Pre-plated / pre-portioned, Coffee Shop style of service.
Hot/Cold Food Service	Cold service.

10.9   END OF MODULE NOTES

10.9.1   Cost-effectiveness in Food Pre-preparation Processes

Ingredients require pre-preparation before actual cooking. Pre-preparations may be for meat or seafood and include trimming away of wastage of skin/shell, fat and bones and their portioning. Pre-preparations for vegetables involve stringing, cleaning, cutting and portioning, etc. The understanding, **key areas** and **success factors** which would work towards cost-effectiveness of pre-preparation processes are listed below. The food production department must:

1. conduct yield tests on 'A' value raw ingredients using as large as-is-possible sample size. Match successive yield tests against standard yields. Identify the reasons of differences, if any between different yield tests. Select the best results as the future standard yield;

2. amend standard purchase specifications to suit the culinary concept/menu items for better yields;

3. use **or avoid using** scratch foods, ready-to-cook foods and individually quick-frozen products depending upon the culinary concept and volumes of business and profitability; and

4. ensure systematic preparation of sub-recipes with a similar and cost-effective manner as for standard recipes. Daily food production schedules include preparation of large number of sub-recipes.

10.9.2   Cost-effectiveness in Food Production Processes

The understanding, **key areas** and **success factors** in relation to food production processes to be cost-effective are listed below. The food production management must:

1. enforce and implement the standard cost control tools;

2. use authorized standard recipes to ensure consistency in quality of food production. The consistency in quality supports value creation to the customer and inherently the cost-effectiveness of operations;

3. review and cost out the standard recipes periodically;

4. ensure availability of tools to measure standard portion sizes. Larger-than-required portion sizes reduce the saleability of other menu items;

5. forecast the volume of sales;

6. control the quantities of food production required for the day/chronological period. During higher than normal business activity due to food promotion in an outlet, replan the production of other outlets; and

7. ensure a tight-fisted approach to authorization of ingredient requisitioning from stores as well as purchasing of perishables and highly perishables.

> **Note:** Standard recipes have backward integration with the right pre-preparation techniques, yield testing and raw ingredient portion control, supporting the cost structure of the recipe. The standard recipes and food production techniques have a forward integration with service guarantees for each menu item and with food service techniques.

10.9.3 Cost-effectiveness in Food Service Functions

Operational cost-effectiveness of a culinary business requires not only reduction in costs but enhanced capacity utilization. The **key areas** and **success factors** in relation to food service functions are listed below. The food service managers must:

1. keep a continuous check on the outlet's capacity utilization;

2. utilize capacities of the trained personnel;

3. take positive steps to improve footfalls into the business. Enhanced footfalls relate to cost-effectiveness;

4. introduce mandatory 'zoning' during periods of leaner business;

5. introduce additional revenue generating opportunities, for example, sale of by-products which may bring in larger revenues; and

6. ensure that 'zero-variable' **service guarantees** are strictly followed. The compliance would ensure food delivery consistency.

> **Note:** Quality and consistency of cuisine, food service and intangible services like attending customers during dining and afterwards relate to positive dining experience and good value of money spent by the customer. When similar offerings exist in the same marketplace, it is the **service guarantees** and their strict compliance, which would enhance customer footfalls.

10.9.4 A Satisfied Customer

The supply markets for culinary business are becoming dearer. The additional cost burden cannot be borne by customers constantly. Culinary business should create inherent efficiency in operations, especially in the food production and food service deliveries, and also be cost-effective. The understanding of the finer nuances in relation to the customer and the **success factors** for a great dining experience are listed below:

1. The customer is becoming increasingly knowledgeable and selective on the matter of cuisine.

2. Quality of dining experience is relative to:

    (a) a customer's and market's perception of what is correct,

    (b) to the culinary concept, and

    (c) to the costs to the customer.

3. A truly valuable dining experience for customers is when they depart from the culinary outlet with a feeling of having received full value for money spent, or better still, more than their own expectations.

4. Quality dining experiences are the results of a combination of quality cuisine, quality food service, quality of intangible services, quality up-selling, and consistencies of delivery of product and service.

5. Great dining experiences ensure repeat visits which, in turn, ensure enhanced brand and economic values for the culinary business.

EXHIBIT 36: Economics of Food Production and Food Service

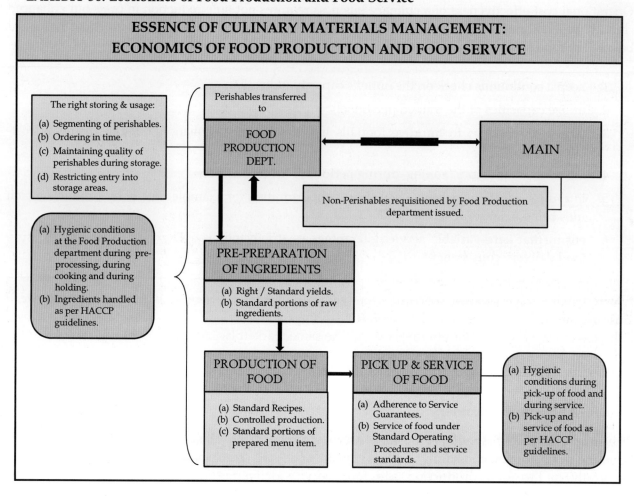

11

CONTROLS

Essence of the Module

Profits are the key prerequisites of doing business. To ensure higher revenues and higher profitability, personnel in management of culinary business must ensure in-built and preventive control measures and the right documentation to ensure accountability of its staff. This module establishes the importance of controls towards the success of the food & beverages outlet.

Module Objectives and Competencies
After going through this module the reader would be competent to:
1. Understand the importance of perishability of food materials in relation to their control.
2. Identify the goals of controls for culinary business.
3. Explain functional and operational areas.
4. Delineate the importance of effective controls.
5. Identify the eleven control points and explain the control actions at each control point.
6. Detail the control documents that are required at each functional or operational area.
7. Identify the roles of the food & beverages controller.

11.1 INTRODUCTION TO CONTROLS

An essential typicality of culinary business is the range of materials it uses. The most important materials purchased are food products and food ingredients. All foods perish with time, while some foods are easy and quick to consume even in their as-received state. These factors, as well as convenience of their availability in immediate environments, induce employees to commit thefts and other malpractices in the operations of a culinary business. Besides purposeful negligence by the purchasing and receiving departments, malpractices also include pilferage and unauthorized consumption of food products, ingredients as well as menu items ready to be served to the customer. Often it is difficult to prove malpractices having taken place minutes after their occurrence.

If higher-than-possibly-required quantities of food products and ingredients are purchased spoilage would result. Spoilage of food leads to wastage. Poor handling including poor food production techniques and/or poor storage conditions also lead to spoilage and wastage of food materials. Food products and ingredients are prone to varying degrees of spoilage and thereby wastage during the process of:

1. receiving;
2. storing;

3. issuing;

4. pre-preparation;

5. storage — temporary or long term — before food production;

6. food production;

7. holding (intervening period between food production and food service); and

8. food service.

Food products and ingredients get progressively expensive per unit of purchase from one business year to another. It is not right to place the entire burden of rising purchase costs on to the customer. Effective controls are the answer to resist and restrict increase in menu item selling prices.

11.2 GOALS OF CONTROL

The above are the important reasons why controls are imperative to the survival as well as success of a culinary business. The management must ensure that robust and comprehensive control measures are developed to eliminate or reduce possible losses. The control processes should ideally be of the **preventive** genre instead of the **corrective** genre. There are four goals of **effective** controls in culinary business. The mechanisms of the four goals overlap each other in a running business. The four goals are:

1. Quality control.

2. Quantity control.

3. Budgetary control.

4. Financial control.

11.2.1 Quality Control

Quality control enhances the efficiency of operations. Quality control also ensures higher quality of dining experience for the customer. Quality control requires introduction of systems which would ensure adherence to laid down standards and policies. Quality control can be used as an important tool of the culinary business in relation to the generic as well as local competition. Examples of quality control are **adherence** to:

1. standard purchase specifications;

2. standard recipes;

3. standard portion sizes; and

4. service guarantees.

11.2.2 Quantity Control

It is an important function of any business to purchase the right quantities of raw materials, to control their receipts, storing, production and sales. Food products and raw ingredients are the predominant materials for culinary business. These are perishable and can be used only till these are safe for human consumption. Statutory laws define and decide the period of usage of any particular food product or raw ingredient.

Quantity checks are mandatory in the following functional and operational areas:

- At receiving area to check and receive the quantities of perishables, non-perishables, highly perishables and other requirements.

- At stores department to store the quantities of all supplies in their right places and under the right storage conditions. The stores department checks the quantities of supplies independently through a process called "blind-receiving".

- At stores department to calculate the quantities of non-perishables to be ordered.

- At the time of issue from stores to check the quantities of issues against the quantities authorized by the user department through the Stores Requisition.

- At the meat fabrication area to check the quantities of yielded non-vegetarian raw ingredients and to ensure the efficiency of the meat fabrication/yield testing process. Quantity checks are also mandatory at the meat fabrication area to ensure that the quantity of wastage is acceptable as compared to the results of earlier yield tests.

- At the pre-preparation area to check the quantities of produce of sub-recipes and to check that the quantities of wastage and spoilage are within limits.

- At the food preparation areas and around food pick-up counters to check the quantities of wastage, spoilage and unauthorized consumption of ready-to-cook raw ingredients as well as ready-to-serve menu items. Wastage and spoilage should be in limits and there should be no unauthorized consumption.

- At food preparation area to calculate the quantities of perishables and highly perishables to be ordered.

Quantity control is aided by inventory control. Inventory control deals with taking regular inventories of actual stocks in stores and within the food production area and matching these with records. In case of any variance in the physical stock position of any stock keeping unit and the corresponding records, immediate investigation, rectification and future course correction is mandatory. Inventory control includes encouraging high inventory turnover and low inventory in stores. Inventory control also means ordering the requirements in time, and only those quantities of each stock keeping unit that are required. Inventory controls allows the culinary business to effectively organize **funds for other operational needs.** Examples of inventory controls are:

- Action taken on inventory records.
- Control of purchase requisitions.
- Control of stores requisitions.

11.2.3 Budgetary Control

Budgets for the business year that follows are decided in advance of the start of the year. Budgetary controls ensure that the operators maintain revenue and expenses within budgets. Examples of budgetary control are:

- Daily sales reports.
- Provision of comparatives of operational expenses in relation to the same period of the previous year.

11.2.4 Financial Control

Many activities are part of financial control, as follows:

- Control of the income and expenditure.
- Provision of accurate financial records.
- Safeguarding the materials.

- Establishment of preventive systems to avoid malpractices, pilferage and unauthorized consumption.

- Establishment of right processes to stop or reduce wastage due to spoilage.

- Ensuring that local and national laws related to food and beverages are adequately followed and that the business does not suffer from want of information and/or action regarding statute-linked requirements.

Examples of financial control are the availability of:

- Purchase orders, Open Purchase orders and Fixed Rate contracts.
- Daily Receiving Report and invoices.
- Records of standard yields.
- Daily sales reports.
- Records of warranties received while receiving food supplies, wherever applicable.

Financial control is integrated with audits and yearly financial statements. Accurate financial records should be available for immediate reference as well as for future.

11.3   FUNCTIONAL AND OPERATIONAL AREAS

The following are the functional areas of a culinary business:

(a)   Purchasing and supplier management.

(b)   Receiving.

(c)   Storing and inventory control.

(d)   Issuing.

(e)   Food & beverages controls.

The following are the operational areas of a culinary business:

(a)   Pre-preparation of food.

(b)   Food production (including food production planning).

(c)   Food service.

(d)   Kitchen stewarding.

Functional areas support the operations of culinary business. The functional areas are related to materials management. Each functional area has forward and backward linkages and integration with other functional areas. The functional areas have forward integration with the operational areas, thus constituting a complete cycle of materials management. Functional areas must be kept integrated for value addition as well as cost-effectiveness.

11.4   REQUIREMENT FOR CONTROLS

This module started with the understanding of the range of food materials that a culinary business uses. The perishability of the materials is an intimidating factor if not handled properly.

The range of food materials introduces susceptibility of the business to **financial losses** through spoilage, wastage, theft, and malpractices. Malpractices include pilferage and unauthorized consumption of as-purchased foods as well as prepared menu items which are ready for service.

Purchasing higher-than-required quantities and poor handling of food materials including poor food preparation techniques add to the vulnerability of the business. These are the typical possibilities which need to be prevented or controlled to cut short losses.

Financial losses are attributed to poor management and lack of supervision. Employees take advantage of the gaps in controls and supervision and resort to malpractices. Instead of remedial action post-losses, it is important to set up specific benchmarks, controls and a report-back system. The objective of food cost control is **not limited to report-back**. Actions are mandatory to correct cause of any loss or possible loss immediately.

11.5 CONTROLS IN CULINARY BUSINESS

To control means to obtain the maximum value **of all unavoidable costs at the least expenditure point.** Operators must enforce higher accountability amongst personnel to fulfil the execution of the four goals of effective controls detailed earlier in this module. Operators must regularly use statistical data for analyses of their business. Controlling activities of functional and operational areas to achieve maximum value of all unavoidable costs is the responsibility of each and every member of the team, and not of the controller alone.

Controls of one functional area often overlap that of another. Effective controls require rotating personnel within the functional areas. Rotation of personnel of the functional areas is achievable in culinary business as all functional areas report to the finance department. Rotation of personnel ensures increased reliability and flexibility. Rotation also ensures that the personnel do not form a dishonest partnership with suppliers.

11.6 AIMS AND OBJECTIVES OF EFFECTIVE CONTROLS

The control system should be cost-effective and balanced against its benefits. The controls department must ensure that reports, analyses and other information reach the operators when they need it so that a meaningful response can follow. The aims and objectives of effective controls are ensuring the:

(i) directions to operators in terms of budgets, revenues and cost parameters;

(ii) cost-effectiveness of operations;

(iii) higher profitability of the culinary business;

(iv) required compliance to statutory laws;

(v) required compliance to laid-down standards and policies of the business;

(vi) safeguarding of assets;

(vii) authorization for a deviation and its record on file with a note on the reason/reasons;

(viii) personnel of functional and operational areas are cognizant of their controls-related duties;

(ix) highlighting of weakness in the system and recommending corrections through a committee approach and involvement of field experts;

(x) culinary business responds positively to disruptions in the market and business environments;

(xi) culinary business evolves with each passing business year – by introducing positive changes in standards and/or policies;

(xii) records are in order for the purposes of various audits;

(xiii) financial reports to the stakeholders – published or otherwise — are transparent and accurate; and

(xiv) management did everything possible to cut short losses.

The success of a culinary business depends on many factors. The "right" commercial launch is preceded by several control actions which are taken in a sequential order leading up to the day of the launch. All such control actions are grouped under Control Point One.

The menu is the most important tool and **the link** between the culinary concept, customer, food production and food service processes. The success or failure of food and beverages operation is directly linked to the menu. Control actions in relation to the menu are grouped under Control Point Two.

Once the business is launched, many control actions are mandatory at each **control** point of the materials chain – within the functional areas as well as within the operational areas. There are 4 control points in **functional areas**, and five control points in **operational areas**. The eleven control points and their aims and objectives are listed below.

11.7 CONTROL POINTS (Exhibit 38, p. 217)

EXHIBIT 37: Control Points: Aims and Objectives

Control Points	Aims and Objectives
1.	This control point deals with control actions prior to the launch of the business.
2.	This control point deals with control actions in relation to the menu.
Control Actions in Functional Areas	
3.	This control point deals with control actions during purchasing and supplier management.
4.	This control point deals with control actions during receiving.
5.	This control point deals with control actions during stores management.
6.	This control point deals with control actions during issuing.
Control Actions in Operational Areas	
7.	This control point deals with control actions during pre-preparation of food.
8.	This control point deals with control actions during preparation of food.
9.	This control point deals with control actions during food service.
10.	This control point deals with control actions during kitchen stewarding.
11.	This control point deals with control actions by the Food & Beverages Controller.

11.7.1 Control Point One: Before Launch / During Repositioning of a Culinary Business

The start of culinary business or its repositioning is an important function in relation to the future impact on effective control of the business. The **control actions** before launch or during repositioning are:

(i) Positioning/repositioning of the operational benchmarks.

(ii) Ensuring a price, quality and service relationship within the culinary concept and the menu offer for the benefit of the customer.

11.7.2 Control Point Two: The Menu

It is imperative to sell **all** the menu items, indicating that each menu item is popular. It is equally important to sell each menu item profitably. Popularity and profitability of each menu item establishes the success of a menu. Menu engineering reports give instant indication to each menu item's popularity and profitability. The reports must reach the operators daily and well in time before the process of food production **planning starts**. Operators must regularly study the menu engineering reports and take corrective actions. The **control actions** in relation to the menu are:

(i)   If required, planning to prepare higher or lower quantities of menu items. (quantity control).

(ii) If required, changing the composition and/or presentation of menu/menu items. (quality control).

(iii) If required, changing the price points of the menu items (financial control).

Control actions in functional areas:

11.7.3   Control Point Three: Purchases and Supplier Management

A standard purchase specification for purchase of each food product and ingredient has to be laid down as per the requirements. Standard purchase specifications which match the values of the business concept ensure maximum yields. The following are the **control actions** while initiating purchases:

(i)   Avoiding over-specification of the quality benchmarks. The standard purchase specifications must be in line with the culinary concept (quality control).

(ii)   Purchasing the right quantities of food products and ingredients (quantity control).

(iii) Ensuring preventive and remedial actions against malpractices in the purchasing system (financial control).

(iv)   Reducing subjective purchasing through fixed rate contracts (financial control).

(v)   Avoiding emergency purchases (financial control).

(vi)   Purchasing requirements at the right price – lowest total cost of each stock keeping unit to be purchased against standard purchase specifications (financial control).

(vii) Modifying menu/menu items to eliminate/reduce purchase of food products and ingredients of a seller's market (financial control).

(viii) Eliminating arbitrary decisions and implementing a committee approach towards higher objectivity of the operations of the purchase department (financial control).

(ix)   Ensuring selection of the right supplier (financial control).

(x)   Ensuring ambiguity-free processes in dealing with the supplier (financial control).

Control related documentation at the purchase department:

- Standard purchase specifications.
- Purchase orders.
- Open purchase orders.
- Fixed rate contracts. The records must include documents of price negotiations.

11.7.4   Control Point Four: While Receiving Supplies

The ownership and responsibility of the supplies in all respects is transferred from the supplier to the purchaser, immediately on signing the supplier's delivery invoice. The following are the control actions during the receiving of supplies:

(i)   Quality to be received (quality control):

- Receiving the supplies in conformation to quality standards as prescribed by standard purchase specifications agreed to between the supplier and the purchaser.

(ii) Quantities to be received (quantity control):

- Receiving supplies in strict conformation to orders placed.
- Checking the quantities of perishables/highly perishables against the Perishables Order Sheet/Butchery Order Sheet.
- Checking the quantities of non-perishables against the Purchase Order.
- Checking non-food supplies for the culinary business against the Purchase Order.

(iii) Personnel to check (quality control):

- Ensuring availability of knowledgeable and trained personnel from the user department to check quality of ordered supplies. It is mandatory for the user department to support receiving activities.

(iv) Control of malpractices (financial control):

- Controlling of malpractices through setting up of guidelines.

(v) Transferring the accepted supplies to their right storages immediately (financial control).

(vi) Ensuring availability and usage of correctly calibrated weighing scales and measuring equipment for quantity checks (financial control).

(vii) Ensuring availability and usage of equipment to check quality, e.g., lactometer (quality control).

Control related documentation at the receiving department:

- Standard purchase specifications.
- Daily receiving report and invoices.
- Short-supply note.

11.7.5 Control Point Five: During Stores Management

Conducting regular inventories of stored items is vital for the following reasons:

(a) To match the actual inventory with the inventory in records.

(b) To analyze consumption patterns of successive business periods.

(c) To transfer the value of the closing inventory of each financial year into the financial statements of the year and list the same as assets.

The following are the **control actions** at stores:

(i) Avoiding stock-outs. However, maintaining of low inventories to:

- ensure optimum product quality (quality control);
- reduce spoilage (financial control);
- reduce operational expenses. Low inventories allow funds to be used for other operational expenses (financial control); and
- eliminate employee theft (financial control) .

(ii) Achieving control and reduction in inventories to lowest possible levels through:

- improved forecasting;
- closer monitoring; and
- improved delivery performances of suppliers.

    (All these are financial controls.)

(iii) Maintaining high inventory turnover rate. Low inventory turnover rate must be prevented at all costs. Low inventory turnover rate indicates that stocks were over-ordered. Over-ordered food items run the risk of:

- losing freshness (related to quality control);
- spoilage (financial control);
- losing on yields (quantity control); and
- usage under pressure to avoid crossing "best-before" dates (quality control).

(iv) Checking regularly for expired items and immediately segregating them from non-expired stock (quality control).

Control related documentation at the stores department:

- Purchase requisitions and its supporting documents.
- Inventory records: Physical inventory or perpetual inventory or computerized inventory.
- Records of stores requisitions.

11.7.6 Control Point Six: During the Process of Issuing

Daily requirements of the consuming department have to be communicated to the stores department in advance through an authorized Stores Requisition. The following are the **control actions** during issuing:

(i) Issuing **just what** is requisitioned-for. Mistakes in issuing, by oversight or by design, reduce the operational profitability (quantity control).

(ii) Transferring the responsibility of the materials being issued to the consuming department through signature-of-receipt on the stores requisition (financial control).

(iii) Restricting entry of personnel into stores (financial control).

(iv) Establishing issue timings for each user department (financial control).

(v) Checking the items for expiry date before issuing to user department (quality control).

Control related documentation at the stores department, for purposes of issuing is as follows:

- Records of stores requisitions.

Control actions in operational areas:

11.7.7 Control Point Seven: During Pre-preparation of Food

The **control actions** during the pre-preparation of food are:

(i) During meat fabrication, yield testing and packing (quantity control):

- Conducting yield tests on all non-vegetarian ingredients and 'A' value raw ingredients. While conducting yield tests it is important to use as large a sample size as is possible. The largest yield is taken as the Standard Yield for future.
- Matching results of successive yield tests against the Standard Yield.
- Identifying the reasons of variances, if any, between Standard Yield and results of successive yield tests. If the successive testing yields higher usable values, the same has to be taken as the future Standard Yield.
- After portioning, packing fabricated ingredients for a la carte portion size or in bulk for banquet/buffet cooking.

- Using contemporary packing techniques like vacuum packing.
- Placing weight, portion and date tags on each packing or using the bar-coding system for the same.
- Using/issuing the packed portions chronologically – strictly on the first-in-first-out basis.

(ii) During production of sub-recipes (quality and financial controls) :

- Ensuring systematic preparation of sub-recipes with a similar and cost-effective manner as is done for standard recipes. Daily food production schedules include preparation of large number of sub-recipes.

Control related documentation at the pre-preparation stage:

- Chronological records of yields conducted on 'A' value products.
- Chronological records of fabrication of meats, poultry, and seafood.
- Chronological records of inventory – identifying the quantities of portioned and packed raw ingredients placed in deep freezers at the right temperatures. These inventory records correspond to matching dates, colour or barcodes on the packed portions.
- Chronological records of preparation of costly sub-recipes.

11.7.8 Control Point Eight: During Food Production

Traditionally, food production was of a subjective nature. Chefs were skilled but remained tuned to food production only. However, contemporary chefs are not only skilled, but educated, and trained to add the extra human touch in dealing with customers and to deal with the task of increasing profitability of the culinary business. **Contemporary food production is led by high degree of objectivity.** Higher objectivity supports control of food costs and operational expenses. Earlier, chefs liked to maintain kitchens as their "domain". Today's chef works through a committee approach. On their own, or through co-workers and controllers, chefs must take the following control actions:

(i) Enforcing the usage and implementation of the standard cost control tools (financial control).

(ii) Using authorized standard recipes to ensure consistency in quality of food production. Standard recipes have backward integration with the right pre-preparation techniques, yield testing and raw ingredient quantity control, supporting the cost structure of the recipe. The standard recipes and food production techniques have a forward integration with service guarantees for each menu item and with food service techniques (quality control).

(iii) Reviewing and costing the standard recipes regularly and whenever market prices change. Established culinary business reviews and cost standard recipes twice a year (financial control).

(iv) Ensuring availability of tools to measure standard portion sizes (financial control).

(v) Forecasting the volume of sales (financial control).

(vi) Controlling the quantities of food production required for the day/chronological period ahead through a planned approach and synergizing with the menu engineering reports and expected sales. During higher than normal business activity due to food promotion/food festival in an outlet, re-planning the production of other outlets (quantity control).

(vii) Ensuring a tight-fisted approach to authorization of stores requisitions as well as purchasing of perishables and highly perishables (quantity and financial controls).

(viii) Eliminating or conscientiously reducing unproductive costs: spoilage, wastage, pilferage, and unauthorized consumption. This is achieved through planned food production, use of standard recipes and control (quantity control).

(ix) Being in regular touch with the market for new, improved or cheaper products which may be applicable to the operations (financial control).

(x) Being in touch with the purchase department and individual suppliers for information on market prices to ensure price competitiveness (financial control).

(xi) Being in touch with the stores department to reduce possibilities of non-moving or slow-moving food products and ingredients in stores and utilizing these creatively (quantity control).

(xii) Using or **avoiding** using scratch foods, ready-to-cook foods, outsourced ready-to-serve food items and IQF (individually quick-frozen) products. Deciding in relation to the culinary concept and volumes of business and profitability (financial control).

The chefs control food pre-preparation as well as food production. The control related documents maintained at the food production department are as follows:

- Food production related standard purchase specifications.
- Standard recipes.
- Standard portions of all menu items.
- Service guarantees of all menu items.
- Chronological records of menu engineering reports and action taken.
- Standard portion costs of all menu items.
- Comparatives of operational expenses in relation to same period of the previous year.
- Daily sales report of each outlet in case of multiple culinary outlets.
- Reports of gross and net revenues related to approved budgets of the department.
- Daily and monthly food cost reports.
- Approved budgets of revenues, profits and expenditures.
- Fixed rate contracts.
- Other rate lists.
- Records of specific benchmarks.

11.7.9 Control Point Nine: During Food Service

The **control actions** during food service are:

(i) Adhering to declared service guarantees (quality control).

(ii) Ensuring enhanced capacity utilization of the restaurant area (financial control).

(iii) Ensuring there are no leakages in revenues arising out of manipulation of customer checks (financial control).

Examples of revenue leakages in relation to customer checks are:

- Not raising checks for orders.
- Not settling checks though payment has been received.
- Voiding of checks without justification.
- Rotation of checks.

11.7.10 Control Point Ten: Within Kitchen Stewarding Department

The **control actions** by the Kitchen Steward and kitchen stewarding personnel are:

(i) By introducing accountability in the issue of tools, kitchenette equipment and service gear. Using the power of inventories and demanding action to reduce losses due to irresponsible handling, theft and breakages (financial control).

(ii) Reducing wastage of cleaning material, if any (quantity control).

(iii) Taking positive steps, for example, through structured employee training, daily briefing, and by creating general awareness to control energy costs. All wasteful expenditure must be stopped. Planned food production supports the right usage of energy (financial control).

11.7.11 Control Point Eleven: Controls by the Food & Beverages Controller/Food & Beverages Controls Department

The Food & Beverages Controls department controls the **right** purchase, storage, issue and consumption activities of the food production and food service departments. It also controls the materials management related activities of all functional departments. The controls department regularly analyzes each of the operational expenses in relation to the same business period of the previous year. The analyses are shared with the operators. The operators are expected to immediately execute corrective measures for control of any operational expense. (The reader may like to revisit **operational expenses on pp. 42, 219**).

The following is the documentation maintained at the food & beverages controls department:

- Standard purchase specifications.
- Fixed rate contracts of operational departments.
- Other rate lists.
- Purchase requisitions.
- Purchase orders.
- Open purchase orders.
- Daily receiving reports and invoices.
- Chronological records of short-supply notes.
- Perishables order sheets.
- Butchery order sheets.
- Record of standard yields.
- Regularly costed standard recipes – for food production as well as for the beverages.
- Records of decided standard portions of all food and beverages menu items.
- Chronological records of menu engineering reports.
- Standard portion costs of all menu items.
- Daily and monthly food cost and bar cost reports.
- Daily sales reports of each outlet in case of multiple culinary outlets.
- Approved budgets of revenues, profits and expenditures of each revenue area.
- Reports of gross and net revenues related to approved budgets of each culinary outlet and comparatives of the same in relation to same period of the previous year.
- Comparatives of operational expenses in relation to same period of the previous year.
- Inventory records.

Note: Culinary business working with property management systems or SAP system, etc., maintains the documents in digital version.

EXHIBIT 38: Controls in a Culinary Business

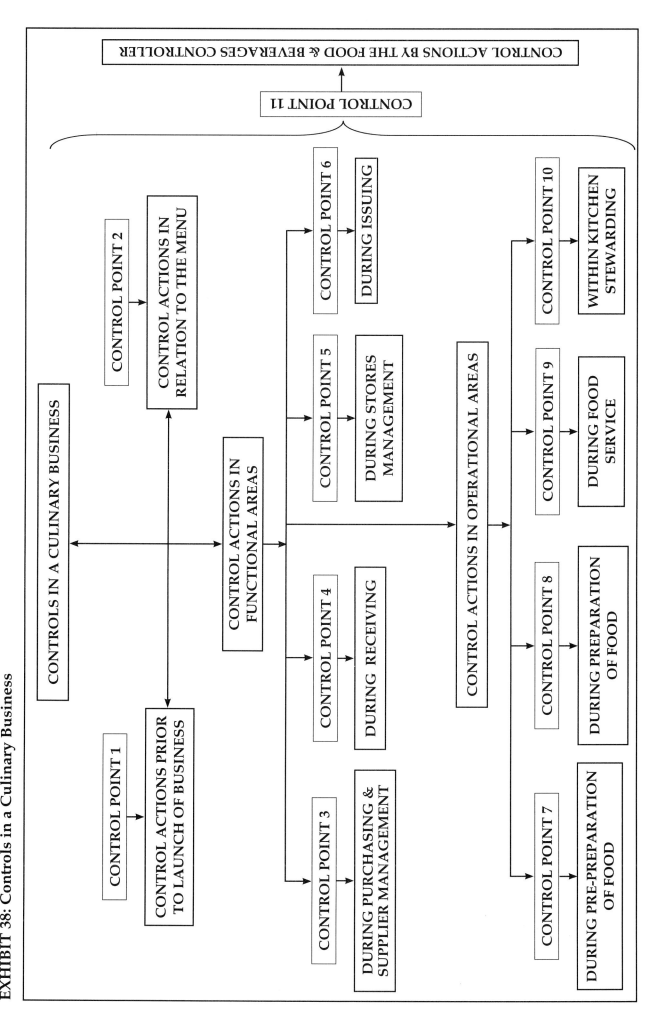

11.8 ROLES OF THE FOOD & BEVERAGES CONTROLLER

Chefs and operators are skilled and technical personnel. The chefs and operators of a culinary business conscientiously get involved in quality food production and food and beverages service in a manner befitting their training, skills and earlier exposure to the hospitality industry. The operators also get involved in ongoing customer-centric requirements including efforts to increase footfalls into the business as well as enhancing quality-led business.

Right documentation ensures accountability from personnel of functional and operational areas. Documentation is **mandatory:**

(a) to enable established norms of the business;

(b) for audit purposes;

(c) to be answerable to stakeholders of the business; and

(d) to respond to statutory compliances.

Ensuring higher profitability and attendance to laid-down processes requires attention to regular actions within the functional and operational areas.

Operators often miss out on concentrated efforts to control costs, to be in line with budgets and the required control-related documentation. Their attention has to be redirected to such specific as well as dynamic needs of the business.

The Food & Beverages Controller ensures that all functional area personnel and operators **fall in line.** The business goals of the culinary business are achieved through individual as well as collective efforts. The most important role of the Food & Beverages Controller is therefore to guard the business interests and regulate laid-down guidelines of performances. The controller is responsible for all the goals of effective controls. These goals are related to quality, quantity, budgetary and financial controls.

The controller is duty bound for action in the following diverse activities:

1. Handling of reports.
2. Inventory control.
3. Prevention of malpractices.
4. Revenue control.
5. Supply contracts and negotiation process.
6. Purchase process.
7. Receiving of supplies.
8. Statutory requirements.
9. Outdoor requirements.
10. Maintenance and upgradation of documents.

11.8.1 Handling of Reports

(a) **Issue of reports:** The controller issues the following reports:

- Daily Food Cost report.
- Daily Bar Cost report.
- Daily Menu Engineering reports.
- Daily Sales Report for F&B outlets.

- Daily Cover Report for F&B outlets.

- Variance analyses. (These are described below under Note 3.)

> **Note 1:** Most operations combine the daily sales report and daily cover report for F&B outlets. The report clearly identifies the average cover sale which is alternatively known as average check.
>
> **Note 2:** Menu Engineering: The controller must issue the menu engineering reports of the previous day in respect of each outlet **in time**. Provision of the reports in time allows operators to study and analyze these reports in relation to the sales reports of each outlet, and in relation to general business environment, especially if the outlets are within a hotel. The operators are expected to take immediate corrective actions and plan the food production accordingly.

To enable the menu engineering process the controller is responsible for updating the portion cost and menu selling price of each menu item in the Point of Sale (PoS) system or property management system.

> **Note 3:** Operational expenses are always related to net revenues. At the end of each month, the controller issues report of comparatives of operational expenses in relation to same period of the previous year in respect of each user department. The controller prepares monthly variance analyses of the budgets, sales, and operational expenses. The analyses are sent to the concerned operators. Subsequently, a meeting of all the operators, the controller and management personnel takes place. During this meeting the operators are responsible to present the possibilities of reducing the operational expenses of their department. The sales reports, budgets, net and gross revenues are also discussed in this meeting to identify actions to be taken.

(b) **Action on reports:** The controller acts on:

- The Daily Receiving Report in respect of individual suppliers together with related invoices. These are sent to the controller after the signatures of the head of the user department. The invoices are checked and processed for payments. To authorize payments is the responsibility of the controller.

- Any other verbal or written report indicating requirements of specific controls at a specific area and/or on any specific day. Requirements of specific controls can arise due to any negative performance as indicated by any of the variance analyses or report of suspected or actual malpractice.

11.8.2 Inventory Control

The values of the year-end inventories are added as assets of the business in the financial statements of the year, and the value is carried forward to the next business year. For a business whose capital is owned by public, the calculation of the value of the quarterly inventories is as important as the calculation of the value of the yearly inventory. It is the duty of the controller to ensure that all inventories are conducted correctly. The types of inventory controls are explained below:

(a) **Stores inventory:** In association with the stores personnel, the controller is jointly responsible for taking monthly inventories of the stores, and ensuring the **right** turnover of each and every stock keeping unit into profitable food production. The quarterly, half-yearly and yearly inventories are conducted by several officers, including deputed officers from the operations. The inventories are reconciled with the records.

The Euro-American format of storing perishables and highly perishables has been explained on **pp. 45, 152**. If the business is operating under the Euro-American format the monthly stores inventory includes conducting inventories of non-perishables, perishables and highly perishables.

The controller must advise the food production and food service departments of any stock remaining in stores for unusually longer than earlier or not moving out at all into usage.

(b) **Inventory of perishables and highly perishables:** As per hospitality business norms in India, the chef controls the perishables and highly perishables. The chef or his representative takes daily inventories and places orders for fresh purchases as per business needs. These inventories are linked more to the experience values of the chef and customarily not done with measuring equipment. (The reader can revisit the same under the topic of Ordering of Perishables on p. 93).

The controller is responsible to take monthly, quarterly and yearly inventories of perishables under the control of the chef. Under the Euro-American system the inventories of perishables and highly perishables are taken in the same manner as inventories of non-perishables.

(c) **Liquor store inventory:** Liquor store inventory has been taken up under statutory requirements.

(d) **Inventory of the bar/bars and service bar:** Quantities of different alcoholic beverages are measured at the close of business hours on each day. The inventories have to be reconciled with the:

- Closing stock of the previous business day.
- Bar Order Tickets of the day.
- Bills presented to the customer.

In case of any discrepancy the controller takes the desired action.

(e) **Inventory of food & beverages outlets:** Food and beverages outlets use food items like condiments, oil and vinegar cruet sets, proprietary sauces and mouth fresheners. The controller takes monthly inventories of such items and takes suitable action if food or beverages shortages occur.

(f) **Kitchen stewarding stores inventory:** Kitchen Steward is responsible for:

- Installed kitchen equipment.
- Issue of freshly purchased kitchen and kitchenette equipment to the food production department and to its chefs.
- Issue of required tools and service gear as well as crockery, cutlery and glassware to food and beverages service handlers.

In that capacity he is also responsible for the custody and inventory of such items. He is required to keep track of breakages and prepare a periodic (usually, weekly) breakage report to management with his analysis, assessment and reasons for the breakages.

He is required to carry out a quarterly physical inventory of crockery, cutlery and glassware jointly with a representative from the controller's department. The physical inventory must match with the inventory records maintained by him. Differences, if any, are required to be explained by him after analysing and assessing such differences.

11.8.3 Prevention of Malpractices

The controller is responsible to prevent malpractices. The details are presented below:

(a) Malpractices in the purchasing system: (The reader may like to revisit **pp. 114-117** and onwards for the types of malpractices common to the purchasing system. The methods to reduce the cost of purchase have been detailed on **p. 117** and onwards.)

(b) Malpractices at the time of receiving. (The reader may like to revisit the topic of Cost Controls in the Receiving Functions on **p. 144** for details of malpractices and how the business can safeguard its interests.)

(c) Malpractices in the form of pilferage and unauthorized consumption: Prevention of such malpractices is achieved through various means like:

(i) Synergies of the menu engineering reports with food production process.

(ii) Restricting duty meals to be consumed only at the designated cafeteria.

(iii) Reconciliation of Kitchen Order Tickets (KOTs) and Bar Order Tickets (BOTs) with customer's bills.

(iv) Surprise spot checks at the outlets.

11.8.4 Revenue Control

All hotel operations run an inherent risk of revenue leakages at the outlets. Typical examples of such leakages are:

(a) Order is not processed in the system but served to the guest. This could either result in unauthorized consumption or payment not going to hotel's account but to the pockets of F&B personnel.

(b) Payment is collected against a check but not settled in the system for unduly long period.

(c) Order is served but check voided without justification or valid reason.

The F&B Controller is responsible for checking and ensuring that such revenue leakages are avoided or at least minimized. Some of the typical actions to control such leakages are as follows:

- Conduct spot checks at outlets to ensure that order is opened for all guests seated at the outlet.

- Conduct spot checks at the kitchen pick-up counter to ensure that all orders ready for pick-up are supported by system generated KOTs (Kitchen Order Tickets).

- Investigate all cases of delays in settlement of checks in the system.

- Ensure that all void checks are justified and authorized by designated personnel.

11.8.5 Supply Contracts and Negotiation Process

The role of the controller is vital to the success of the yearly contract and negotiation process.

(a) A month before the renewal of yearly contracts for supply of all the materials required by the business, the controller issues the existing standard purchase specifications to the user departments. If during the course of the business period the operator has felt the need for any of these specifications to change, the controller is intimated, along with reasons for change. The changes are incorporated in the standard purchase specifications for the next purchase period.

(b) The standard purchase specifications are the same for all the prospective suppliers. Based on the standard purchase specifications the prospective suppliers quote their best rates. The comparatives of these quotes are prepared by the controller. These comparatives are updated during and immediately after each round of negotiation.

(c) In the case of competitive bidding process, the role of the controller remains the same.

(d) The process of negotiations with the prospective supplier is done through a committee approach. The committee for negotiations for supply of culinary materials is formed by:

- The head of finance of the business or his representative.

- The chef or his representative.

- The F&B Manager or his representative.

- The Purchase Manager or his representative.

If and when required during this process, the controller steps in with any market information or data from existing records.

(e) When the supply contracts are finalized and awarded, the controller or the purchase manager circulates the contract documents to the concerned departments. The contract documents include the final and agreed-to standard purchase specifications.

11.8.6 Purchase Process

The controller regulates the purchase process, often as a follow-up.

(a) The stores management forwards purchase requisitions to the purchase department for action. At a later date, the controller examines the ordering in relation to the dynamic changes in the consumption pattern of different stock keeping units.

(b) The chef is responsible for preparation of the Perishables Order Sheet and the Butchery Order Sheet in time. These documents list the purchase of perishables and highly perishables. Copies of the two order sheets are sent to the controller. Alternately, the two order sheets are forwarded by the receiving department along with the DRR and supplier invoices. The controller identifies purchasing of higher quantities of perishables and highly perishables in relation to the normal pattern of their purchases. He is duty bound to reconcile the higher quantities through discussions with the chef.

(c) If the business follows the Euro-American format of storing, the stores management prepares purchase requisition for non-perishables, perishables and highly perishables. This is forwarded to the purchase department for action. In addition to the non-perishables the right quantities of perishables and highly perishables must be ordered. This is achieved through active consultations between the controller, the stores personnel and the chef.

11.8.7 Receiving of Supplies

(a) The controller is not responsible to check the quantities and quality of supplies received. However, the controller has the right to conduct surprise on-the-spot checks, and is duty-bound to act in case of suspected or actual malpractices.

(b) On receipt, the supplies are immediately transferred to their respective storage areas. Normally, it is the duty of the stores management to store the supplies in a manner to ensure right storage conditions and optimum quality of the supplies till such time as these are requisitioned by the user department. In case of spoilage due to any reason the controller steps in to arrest further spoilage.

(c) The controller checks the availability and usage of correctly calibrated weighing scales and measuring equipment.

11.8.8 Statutory Requirements

The controller is:

(a) Involved in the process of liquor licence applications and purchase of liquor in time as per local laws.

(b) Responsible for the maintenance of liquor stores, and reconciliation of stocks-in-hand with stocks on records.

(c) Responsible for daily reconciliation of bar stocks.

(d) Responsible for filing of warranties received from suppliers for food products and ingredients. Warranties safeguard the interests of the purchaser.

11.8.9 Outdoor Requirements

(a) The controller is member of the committee for regular market surveys. At the end of each of the market survey the controller or the Purchase Manager or their representatives prepare a report and complete the checklist. The report and the checklist are forwarded to the operators, senior management and concerned departments for action.

(b) In case of any short supply, the controller ensures that open market purchases are made within a reasonable period to avoid disruption in the process of food production.

> **Note 1:** The action on open-market purchasing in case of short supply differs from one business to another. However, hospitality business allows such purchases without involvement of the controller. In such cases, the norm is for a team consisting of an employee of purchase department and a representative of the chef to do such open-market purchasing.
>
> **Note 2:** Rule of thumb requires the controller to control all out-of-the-ordinary cash outflows.

11.8.10 Maintenance and Upgradation of Documents

The documents to be maintained by the controller have been detailed earlier in this module. These documents support efficiency of operations and availability of data whenever required in future.

(a) The Controller maintains and updates chronological records of yield tests conducted by the meat fabrication department on 'A' value products – especially the non-vegetarian raw ingredients.

(b) Under the Euro-American system, the packed and ready-to-store portions of non-vegetarian raw ingredients are the responsibility of the finance department. Issues of these ingredients are handled in the same manner as done for issues of non-perishables. The controller is responsible for:

- Regular inventories of such fabricated ingredients.
- Questioning poor yields, if any against standard yields obtained earlier. Records are maintained for the same.

If higher yields are obtained the fresh yields are taken as the benchmark Standard Yield for future.

(c) Each menu item of the food & beverages department must have a standard recipe to ensure its right production. The controller maintains records of standard recipes used by the food production as well as bar service operations.

(d) Food & Beverages controller is responsible for costing standard recipes initially and whenever prices of any of the constituent ingredient changes. If standard recipes are tweaked due to repositioning efforts of the business, these are costed again.

(e) The service staff place food orders on the kitchen through a KOT. and beverages orders on the bar/service bar through a BOT. The controller reconciles these order tickets with the customer's bills. The controller maintains these documents. This task is now easy with property management systems and computerization.

(f) The controller is not responsible to decide or maintain the standard portions of the menu items. However, he maintains records of standard portion costs of all menu items.

11.9 END OF MODULE NOTES

To control means to be in command – in command of revenues, of expenses, and of the business. To control means not to be caught by surprise by disruptive forces in the business environments.

12

KITCHEN STEWARDING

Essence of the Module

This module examines the role of the Kitchen Steward and the stewarding department towards the success of the food & beverages outlet. Food production as well as food service must progress in a perfectionist manner. It is the role of the Kitchen Steward and his team to assist the food production and food service personnel. Food should be produced and served within the framework of the culinary concept, service guarantees, hygiene and HACCP control, statutory laws and the decided economic standards of the business.

Module Objectives and Competencies
After going through this module the reader would be competent to:
1.   Understand the diverse roles of the kitchen stewarding department.
2.   Identify the control functions that the Kitchen Steward plays.

12.1 THE ROLE OF KITCHEN STEWARDING

In addition to its quality and unique service guarantees food served in any culinary outlet must be prepared hygienically and must be safe to eat. Chefs and other operators must be sensitive to their sacred duty of safeguarding the health of their customers. Customers trust the culinary outlet for the same. Contamination of food can be effectively prevented by knowledgeable and conscientious food production, food service and kitchen stewarding personnel.

Menu items ready for service can get contaminated and unfit for human consumption due to contaminated raw ingredients and/or unhygienic food handling. This includes non-compliance of personal hygiene mandates by food handling personnel.

Food can also get contaminated due to **non-food sources** during pre-preparation, preparation and holding processes. The contamination could be due to poor equipment hygiene or unhygienic conditions in the food production area. The kitchen steward and the kitchen stewarding personnel play a crucial role in preventing such contamination through compliance of their duties and responsibilities.

The kitchen steward is responsible to the F&B manager as well as the chef. The kitchen steward through personnel under his command is considered to be the conscience keeper of an efficiently run culinary business. All production areas and equipment, as well as all service gears that come into contact with the hands of the food handlers and/or the customer's mouth must be cleaned as per established hygiene and HACCP principles. Hygiene regulations would increasingly get stricter in the years to come; and many would take the form of statutory laws, mandating food handling personnel to incessantly evolve in their knowledge and skills.

In addition to matters of hygiene, the kitchen steward and his team have numerous other responsibilities. The kitchen steward uses checklists to ensure adherence to standard operating procedures as well as sequential operations of a period – a day, a week, a month and the year.

The duties and responsibilities of a kitchen steward and the kitchen stewarding personnel are listed below:

12.1.1 Cleaning of Food Production Areas

The responsibility is to ensure in-depth cleaning of all areas. It should be feasible to regularly clean the otherwise difficult-to-access areas, for example, under the equipment. Fixed equipment should be dismantled for thorough cleaning. High standards of hygiene and sanitation are mandatory in all food production and ancillary areas like:

(a) Pre-preparation.

(b) Meat fabrication.

(c) Speciality/satellite kitchens.

(d) Staff cafeteria.

12.1.2 Fire Safety

Fire safety in food and beverages production and service areas is a joint responsibility of the Chef, the F&B Manager, and the Kitchen Steward. All food & beverages personnel must be trained in the use of fire safety equipment and must be knowledgeable about:

(a) Safety procedures.

(b) Working of fire-safety alarms.

(c) Usage of firefighting equipment and extinguishers.

(d) Emergency evacuation procedures.

Fire in the kitchen often spreads through the dispersion of flammable oil in ducts and vents. An important duty of kitchen stewarding is to regularly clean, degrease and air-dry the exhaust systems – ducts, hoods and filters. Modern exhaust systems are integrated with firefighting and self-cleaning mechanisms. For purposes of firefighting fire extinguishers and sand-filled fire buckets are normally kept in food production areas.

12.1.3 Safety in the Kitchen

Accidents must be prevented in food production areas. 'On-contract' workers and all food and beverages personnel must be trained for safe work practices and safety in kitchen through structured sessions. In addition, food production and kitchen stewarding personnel must be trained for safe usage of kitchen equipment and tools as well as for their safe and hygienic cleaning process. The important safety requirements are as follows:

(a) Written safe handling practices for all equipment should be displayed next to the equipment. Food handling and cleaning personnel should be trained accordingly.

(b) The gas bank, the gas connections, the gas valves and the pressure regulators must be checked regularly for leakage, and action taken accordingly.

(c) Floors must be maintained in good condition. Floors, water traps, floor drains, drain covers and external grease traps must always be kept clean and dry to prevent accidents. The passages in-and-around the food production area must be kept free of obstacles.

(d) When not in use and during cleaning the power supply to equipment must be turned off.

(e) Charcoal must be safely stored and safely used. Flying charcoal dust must not get into food.

(f) Solid fuel used for buffet chafing dishes is a dangerous material if it comes in contact with food. In addition to harmful chemicals, solid fuel emits toxic fumes. It should be used carefully. Evolving food service solutions use electrical energy/ induction heating systems to keep food hot in chafing dishes.

(g) Cleaning supplies – scouring powders, detergents and sanitizers must be stored separately and used with extreme care. On no account should the cleaning supplies mix up with food. Cleaning/ sanitizing solutions should be used carefully and leftovers, if any, should be disposed safely.

(h) Equipment and tools used for cleaning should be cleaned, disinfected or sanitized, dried and stored in properly designated areas.

12.1.4 Equipment and Tool Positioning

Rightly equipped and well-functioning kitchen is a chef's delight. The kitchen steward must ensure that equipment is placed in a manner which is safety, hygiene and facility oriented.

(a) Food production, kitchenette and food service equipment must be available when required. All such equipment must be washed, rinsed, sanitized and placed in their designated places. Extra service equipment must be carefully stored in kitchen stewarding stores.

(b) Equipment such as cold stores, deep freezers, ice cream freezer, milk cooler, sandwich station, pick-up counters, display cases, range-top stations, ovens, combi-ovens and hand sinks should be cleaned and sanitized at least once in each shift. These often have many difficult-to-access components. All these equipment should be dried to ensure safe working conditions.

12.1.5 Equipment Maintenance

(a) All equipment must be maintained to deliver optimum performance. All equipment should ideally have a maintenance schedule. Preventive maintenance is the best option for mechanical or difficult-to-replace or indispensable equipment. The kitchen steward acts as a liaison with the engineering and maintenance department for regular as well as preventive maintenance. Yearly maintenance of certain equipment is often outsourced to professionally competent agencies, for example, those representing the manufacturer.

(b) Special service gear, for example, silverware should be maintained as per standards.

12.1.6 Waste Management

Kitchen steward must ensure segregation of garbage and its proper storage under the right storage conditions till the time it is removed from the property. The garbage room should be sanitized after each use.

12.1.7 Purchasing and Receiving

The kitchen steward must:

(a) ensure that cleaning products and sanitizers of the right quality and diversity are purchased and used for different requirements;

(b) be involved in market research for labour and time saving equipment, cleaning products and methods;

(c) be involved in the process of receiving materials for the stewarding department; and

(d) prepare the list for annual capital expenditure for food production and food service equipment. Popularly called the CAPEX plan, it includes planning for purchase of kitchen equipment.

12.1.8 Miscellaneous Duties and Responsibilities

The kitchen steward must:

(a) take positive steps to control energy costs – electricity, power, gas, charcoal, etc. All wasteful expenditure should be controlled. Planned food production helps right usage of energy. (The reader may like to revisit the topic of control of costs of water and energy resources in Module 3: "Costs: Core of Culinary Economics".)

(b) ensure that pest control activities take place as scheduled. Installed pest control systems include effective air-curtains, and ultraviolet lights to control flying insects.

(c) ensure supply of utilities when required. These utilities are cooking gas, compressed steam, and electrical power.

(d) ensure right functioning of support systems like:

- lighting;
- exhaust;
- refrigeration; and
- heat, ventilation and air conditioning (HVAC) systems. The HVAC system should guarantee fresh air flowing into the kitchen and prevent flow of fumes into the guest areas.

(e) ensure right functioning of systems like telephones, POS terminals, and public address systems in food production areas and on food pick-up counters.

(f) plan duty rosters carefully to ensure that knowledgeable, well-trained and sufficient number of stewarding personnel are available at peak times of the day. Duty rosters should be made to ensure a smooth round-the-clock operation.

(g) plan a chronological cleaning schedule of all kitchen areas and equipment. A cleaning schedule works like a **stretch goal.** A detailed cleaning schedule is supported by a checklist which helps to identify if any equipment or kitchen area has not been attended to in time.

(h) ensure adequate hand disinfection facilities and availability of disposable gloves.

(i) ensure that the requirements of buffet set-ups, for example, chafing dishes are washed, rinsed, sanitized and handed over to the food service personnel, in time.

(j) ensure return of the following after an outdoor event:

- all kitchen and kitchenette equipment;
- service gear.

Detailed returnable gate passes are made before any food material or equipment or service gear is taken away from the property. Every item must be brought back to the property and accounted for; and

(k) must ensure all safety precautions are taken for outdoor events to safeguard the personnel and guests.

Note: The duties and responsibilities of a kitchen steward for outdoor events are extensive, but fall within the points (j) and (k). It is not the scope of this book to provide details.

12.1.9 Inventories

The Kitchen Steward is responsible for issue of equipment, tools and service gear, crockery, cutlery and glassware to food and beverages handlers. In that capacity he is also responsible for the custody and inventory of such items. He is required to keep track of breakages and prepare a periodic (usually weekly) breakage report to management with his analysis, assessment and reasons for the breakages.

In addition, every quarter he is required to carry out a physical inventory of crockery, cutlery and glassware jointly with a representative from the Controller's department. The physical inventory must match with the inventory records maintained by him. Differences, if any, are required to be explained by him after analysing and assessing such differences. In this capacity the Kitchen Steward can also seek explanations from the food production and food service personnel for the reasons for the breakages or inventory differences and caution them if these are more than the accepted norms.

12.1.10 Audits

The kitchen steward and kitchen stewarding personnel participate in audits conducted for various requirements. These audits are:

- Hygiene audit.
- Operations audit.
- Safety audit.
- Water safety audit.

12.2 ATTIRE AND TRAINING OF KITCHEN STEWARDING PERSONNEL

Many kitchen stewarding personnel have duties in guest areas, for example, while setting up the buffet stations. The uniforms of kitchen stewarding personnel must reflect well-cared for as well as hygienic appearance. **Pride in job performance** must be visible in the attire and actions of kitchen stewarding personnel. Regular and specific training as well as daily briefing is mandatory to achieve this requirement.

12.3 END OF MODULE NOTES

The kitchen stewarding career is as rewarding as any of the other careers in the operations of a culinary business. Large number of hospitality professionals, including the author started their careers from the kitchen stewarding department.

The job of a Kitchen Steward is commitment to safe and efficient food and beverages operations. He must be knowledgeable about his responsibilities and execute these in a chronological sequence. He should use teamwork and committee approach towards execution of each day's work schedules. The Kitchen Stewards' position requires strong interpersonal skills and problem solving abilities.

13

OBJECTIVITY AND SUBJECTIVITY IN CULINARY BUSINESS

Essence of the Module

This module deals with key points and ideas to encourage higher objectivity in the operations of culinary business.

Product designing is largely led by objectivity in most types of business and manufacturing industries. Traditionally, culinary business has been a "touch and feel", creativity-led and subjective business in nature. Contemporary forms of culinary business – either as stand-alone entities or within a hotel are considered "revenue, profit and cost centres". Profits are the key prerequisites of culinary business. The enabler for higher profitability is enhanced objectivity in operations.

Module Objectives and Competencies
After going through this module the reader would be competent to: 1. The need for chefs and operators to develop potential.   2. To understand the borderline between creativity and objectivity-led processes.   3. To identify objective processes and products in the earlier modules.   4. To identify subjective processes in the earlier modules.   5. To facilitate quick reference of objective processes, objective products and subjective processes to the text of the modules.   6. To list the aids to achieve higher objectivity in operations.

13.1 INTRODUCTION TO OBJECTIVITY AND SUBJECTIVITY IN CULINARY BUSINESS

The author wishes to reiterate the importance of the very first paragraph of this book. The success of any culinary venture definitely depends on the knowledge and skills of its chefs and operators. Chefs and operators must remain in a mode of self-actualization and continuously develop their own potential.

As it has been scientifically proven, the left hemisphere of the brain is goal-oriented and is always eager to reach conclusions. The left hemisphere is also responsible for logical-language based analytical and rational capacities and conclusions. The right hemisphere of the brain is responsible for creativity and dreaming of options. The activities of the right hemisphere of the brain are more of inspirational nature. The chefs and operators of the culinary business must exercise and continuously train both the hemispheres of the brain for success.

Before proceeding any further in this module, it is important to understand what is *objectivity* and *subjectivity* in culinary business. Quite simply, objectivity is the tangible data and information side of culinary business—the aspects one can measure. They are the facts that keep one focused on the goals of the business, tracking benchmarks, budgeting, auditing, materials management, quality control, sales revenue, gross profit margin, etc. Essentially, anything that can be backed up with solid data is objective. Appropriate tools must be set up to ensure objectivity norms are met.

On the other hand, *subjectivity* refers to those emotional aspects of the business when one relies on intuition or gut, or individual taste. *Subjectivity* often has a basis in reality, reflects the current perspective, and cannot be verified using **facts and figures only**. Some important aspects include: customer value evaluations, menu engineering, evaluation of suppliers performance, cooking processes, etc.

The culinary business must encourage creative processes. The business must support a work ecosystem wherein goal-oriented operating systems, the existing knowledge and skills of the chefs and operators converge with the creative impulse, evolving technologies, modern techniques and processes and strive for new, creative and perfectionist cuisine. Usage of technology, digitalization and property management systems would introduce higher objectivity in the culinary business.

13.1.1 Balance in Objectivity and Subjectivity

It is the key to running a successful culinary business. It any one aspect is weak, it would spell the eventual demise of the business. A business with overly objective approach will meet all the targets, yet, being weak in the subjective area, will soon confront abandoning customers, vendors and high turnover in staff. The business will eventually fail to meet its objectives because its staff would become callous and insensitive, lacking qualities needed for greater performance. The awareness of the complementary role subjectivity and objectivity play in the business is crucial to success.

The author wishes to take the reader throughout the contents of the modules presented earlier to identify objective processes and products and subjective processes. None of the modules presents any subjective product. The author has advised the reader on the methodology to progressively convert the culinary product into an objective product through the use of recipe control and service guarantees. When high expectations from the customers and the market interface with the culinary concept, service guarantees, tangibles and intangibles of the culinary business, objectivity prevails.

13.2 OBJECTIVE PROCESSES

(a) **Process of delineating the culinary concept and business plan:** The process of arriving at a well-positioned business plan involves subjective processes. However, once a business plan is made, it reflects objective benchmarks which are ready for execution. The culinary concept and business plan can evolve towards higher revenues, or towards higher value proposition or towards higher quality infrastructure, in turn, enhancing customer satisfaction.

(b) **Process of price point decision:** Price points for the sale of menu items can be decided in a subjective manner. However, objectivity-led decisions on price points are the ideal solutions. Objectivity-led fixing of price points for the sale of menu items is a process which requires detailed examination of the

- culinary concept;
- uniqueness of the culinary product/concept;
- existing performance of the menu item;
- total cost of selling of the menu item; and
- competition from a similar culinary offer/menu item in the same geographical market.

(c) **Process of setting benchmarks:** Setting up of benchmarks is an important exercise. Once benchmarks are fixed, actual of future performances can be measured against these. Variances observed during this exercise can be analyzed, and reasons established. Subsequent corrective action ensures efficient operations. All benchmarks are objectivity-led.

(d) **Processes of budgeting:** Budgeting is an important exercise of setting standards of financial and operational performance for a start-up as well as for a running culinary business.

(e) **Processes of auditing:** Audits are vital support functions for the operations of culinary business. Auditing is an objectivity-led process. All listed benchmarks and their performance parameters are listed and formulated into checklists. Auditors work against ready-to-use checklists and keep evolving these in line with the evolving business. Auditing functions have been greatly facilitated by computerization and property management systems.

(f) **Generic materials management processes:** The important **aspects** of the materials management processes are 'materials', 'time', and 'space'. The operation of the materials management system aims to overcome the problems of 'supply', 'distance' and 'time', in order to obtain product for the minimum cost under the constraints of established standards of production and service.

The entire materials management process, except a few elements of supplier management as well as food-production management, is highly objective in its design and delivery.

(g) **Specific purchase department's processes:** The following are the processes and responsibilities of an efficient purchase department:

(a) Materials purchasing.

(b) Quality improvement.

(c) Cost management.

(d) Suppliers management.

(e) Inventory management.

(f) Office & records management.

All processes mentioned above except "supplier management" are objectivity-led functions.

(h) **Specific supply-receiving processes:** The incoming supplies should be checked for their quality against standard purchase specifications and quantities against what has been ordered in the Perishable/Butchery Order Sheet/Purchase Order/Open Purchase Order. The professional experience and competence of the personnel of the consuming department is invaluable in checking supplies. The process is objective in nature, due to strict laid-down benchmarks.

(i) **Specific stores and inventory management processes:** The following stores management processes are objectivity-led:

(a) Physical inventory system.

(b) Perpetual inventory system.

(c) Minimum/maximum inventory and ordering system.

(d) System of maintaining bin cards.

It is imperative for culinary business to:

(a) maintain a high inventory turnover as per hospitality industry standards; and

(b) reduce inventories to lowest possible levels in line with "supplier efficiency" and the consumption patterns of each of the stored items.

The inventory control processes implemented by quality-led culinary business are objectivity-led processes as these function within the framework of established benchmarks. Management of stocks through use of bar-coding systems, computerization, and property management systems works towards enhanced objectivity.

(j) **Process of instituting service guarantees for menu items:** Quality-led culinary business examines and experiments with a number of service designs for each menu item before the launch of the menu. This examination/experimentation involves presentation styles, and other value components of the service guarantee format.

Creativity is highly desirable and in normal course of actions till the point of finalization of each of the menu item. However, once finalized, the service guarantees take over and chefs are restricted from subjective impulses of creativity till the menu item is re-examined. Re-examination of each menu item is an important and regular exercise and is facilitated by the menu engineering processes. The service guarantees are therefore objectivity-led. Subjective and creative changes are not acceptable till the time of re-examination of the entire menu as well as individual menu items.

The above detailed objective processes are presented below to enable the reader with quick references to text within the book.

S. No.	Processes	Re-visit Module No.	Module Name
1.	Delineating the culinary concept and business plan	1	The Culinary Business
2.	Deciding the price points of menu items	1	The Culinary Business
3.	Setting up of benchmarks	1	The Culinary Business
4.	Setting up processes of budgeting	1	The Culinary Business
5.	Processes of auditing	1	The Culinary Business
6.	Generic materials management processes	5	Culinary Materials Management: The Concept
7.	The specific purchase department's processes: (a) Materials purchasing. (b) Quality improvement. (c) Cost management. (d) Inventory management. (e) Office & records management.	6	Efficient Management of Purchasing Activities
8.	Specific supply-receiving processes	8	Right Receiving
9.	Specific stores and inventory management processes	9	Efficient Storing, Inventory Management and Right Issuing
10.	Instituting service guarantees for menu items	10	Economics of Food Production and Food Service

13.3 OBJECTIVITY-LED DOCUMENTS

Objectivity-led documents are explained below.

1. **Budgets:** Chefs and operators must have benchmarks of revenues, profits and expenditures to work against. An approved budget is an objective document.

2. **Purchase Requisition:** Purchase Requisition lists items to be purchased to replenish depleting stocks. This is forwarded by the stores management to the purchase department. The property management system or computerization of the minimum/maximum inventory and ordering

system facilitates churning out specific and unambiguous details of the quantities of each of the stores items to be purchased.

3. **Perishables Order Sheet and Butchery Order Sheet:** As per Indian hospitality industry norms chefs control the management of perishables as well as highly perishable (butchery) items. The ordering of the perishables and highly perishables is done with the help of the Perishables Order Sheet and the Butchery Order Sheet. In small sized business the two order sheets are combined.

Once ordered, the Perishables Order Sheet as well as the Butchery Order Sheet and the contents within are objective in nature. Copies of the two order sheets are provided to the receiving department to enable receipt of these items strictly against quantities ordered.

4. **Purchase Order and Open Purchase Order:** Either of these is prepared by transferring details of items and their quantities to be purchased from the Purchase Requisition. Either of these is prepared in the name of specific suppliers. These are also controlled by property management systems or computerization.

5. **Daily Receiving Report:** The receiving personnel prepare the Daily Receiving Report (DRR). Information from the supplier's delivery invoice and the receiving department's notes is collected and made into the DRR. Separate daily receiving reports are made for different consuming departments. The DRR is authorized by the chef or by the head of the consuming department. The authorization confirms that the "right" products have been received.

6. **Short-supply note:** In case the ordered supplies have not been received or they have been supplied in quantities short of the required, the receiving department writes the shortfall on a document called the "Short Supply Note". This is sent to the head of the respective consuming department.

7. **Documents of stores management:** The documents of stores management are all objectivity-led documents. These are all specific and do not have any ambiguity on the stock keeping units in stores, those to be ordered or those to be issued. The following are documents of stores management:

   (a) The physical inventory format.

   (b) The bin card format.

   (c) The perpetual inventory format.

   (d) The minimum/maximum inventory and ordering system format.

   (e) The stores requisition – requisition by consuming department, records kept in stores.

8. **Standard cost control tools:** These are benchmark-linked documents. There is no ambiguity or subjectivity in compilation of these documents. These are:

   (a) Standard Purchase Specifications: All standard purchase specifications are zero-defect, zero-variable and zero-tolerance in nature. There is no ambiguity about the quality between the purchaser and the supplier.

   (b) Standard yields.

   (c) Standard recipes.

   (d) Standard portion sizes.

   (e) Standard portion costs.

The above detailed objectivity-led processes are presented below to enable the reader with quick references to text within the book.

S. No.	Document	Re-visit Module No.	Module Name
1.	Budgets	1	The Culinary Business
2.	Purchase Requisition.	6	Efficient Management of Purchasing Activities
3.	Perishables Order Sheet and Butchery Order Sheet.		
4.	Purchase Order and Open Purchase Order.		
5.	Daily Receiving Report.	8	Right Receiving
6.	Short-Supply Note.		
7.	Documents of stores management: (a) Physical inventory format. (b) Bin card format. (c) Perpetual inventory format. (d) Minimum/maximum inventory and ordering format. (e) Stores requisition.	9	Efficient Storing, Inventory Management and Right Issuing
8.	Standard cost control tools: (a) Standard purchase specifications. (b) Standard yields. (c) Standard recipes. (d) Standard portion sizes. (e) Standard portion costs.	6 10	Efficient Management of Purchasing Activities (b), (c), (d), and (e) Economics of Food Production and Food Service

13.4 SUBJECTIVE PROCESSES

1. **The process of evaluating value:** The customer establishes the values of his dining experience each time. The customer compares the value in relation to his dining experience for a similar culinary offer elsewhere. During subsequent visits he compares the value received in relation to his earlier visit. The quality of food is not the only criteria for a customer to patronize or re-patronize a culinary offer in the market. A customer assesses a culinary product line for diverse values. The values depend on the:

    (a) quality of the culinary product;

    (b) quality of the tangible and intangible services; and

    (c) quality of the ambience and other features.

    Value assessment is therefore a subjective process.

2. **The processes of menu engineering:** While most components of the menu engineering exercise are objectivity-led, menu engineering does have its own subjectivity components. The subjective components are as follows:

    (a) Menu engineering does not respond to items ready for sales, or those that are partially cooked, but not sold. Fast and efficient delivery of ordered menu items against individual service guarantees is facilitated by semi-preparation of a pre-planned number of portions of all à la carte menu items.

(b) The calculations of menu item cost price are limited to the costs mentioned in the Standard Recipe Card. The inputs are sometimes inaccurate and approximate.

(c) Menu engineering process does not accurately point to portions of food items lost due to spoilage or unauthorized consumption.

3. **The processes of purchase cycles:** The only subjective part of the purchase cycles for perishables, highly perishables and non-perishables is the part relating to "supplier efficiency".

4. **The process of determination of quantity of perishables:** The process involves subjective evaluation of quantities to order and precedes the actual ordering.

   The chefs normally maintain safety stocks of all perishables and highly perishables. The safety level for each ingredient allows for delays of supplies due to market conditions or/and delivery performance of the supplier. The safety level also allows for unusual and higher-than-estimated consumption, for example, requirement of unannounced banquets.

5. **The process of evaluation of supplier's performance:** The supplier is evaluated at the end of each purchase period for his tangible and intangible performance such as:

   (a) Quality performance.

   (b) Price performance.

   (c) Delivery performance.

   (d) Relationship performance.

   The supplier's quality, price and delivery performance can be measured in objective terms. However, relationship performance is typically an intangible performance parameter and is subjective in nature.

6. **The process of development of suppliers:** Once selected the supplier must be developed via structured inputs. The supplier must be in total understanding of the purchasing organisation's business, and its vision and mission. The process of development of suppliers ensures that they take pride in supplying to the purchaser. The process of development of suppliers is subjectivity-led, and depends on the supplier's educational background.

7. **The process of cooking:** The actual cooking processes are subjective in nature. By combining various raw ingredients, in specific measures and preparing them through specific step-by-step methods, chefs create **well-defined and specific** culinary preparations.

Note: The author wishes to reiterate that for quality conscious culinary business the ready-for-service culinary product assumes an objective nature due to exact cooking processes and requirements to adherence to service guarantees of each of the menu item.

---

8. **The process of forecasting food production volumes:** There is no fool-proof method to forecast the volume of food to be prepared either for à la carte or for banquet business. (The reader may like to revisit the methods of volume forecasting for food production explained in Module 10: "Economics of Food production and Food Service".)

   In this module, the author has attempted to bridge the gap between subjective quantities of food production and objective quantities of food production. All the methods that have been explained have elements of subjectivity. **However, the author has successfully used these methods in his career as a professional chef.**

   The above detailed subjectivity-led **processes** are presented below to enable the reader with quick references to text in this book.

S. No.	Processes	Re-visit Module No.	Module Name
1.	The process of evaluating value	1	The Culinary Business
2.	The processes of menu engineering	4	Menu Engineering: Culinary Business Analytics
3.	The processes of purchase cycles	6	Efficient Management of Purchasing Activities
4.	The process of determination of quantities of perishables	6	Efficient Management of Purchasing Activities
5.	The process of evaluation of supplier's performance	7	Selecting the Right Supplier
6.	The process of development of suppliers	8	Right Receiving
7.	The process of cooking	10	Economics of Food Production and Food Service
8.	The process of forecasting food production volumes	10	Economics of Food Production and Food Service

13.5 AIDS TO HIGHER OBJECTIVITY

(a) Evolving benchmarks.

(b) Service guarantees.

(c) Checklists.

(d) Templates.

(e) Formats.

(f) Formulas.

(g) Colour photographs of steps of recipe production.

(h) Colour photograph inserts to aid standard purchase specifications.

(i) Technical and performance specification to aid the standard purchase specifications of non-food items.

(j) Scaled drawings to aid the standard purchase specifications of non-food items.

(k) Quality warranties of as-supplied ingredient or food product.

(l) Guarantees of supplies.

(m) Colour-coding applications.

(n) Time and date tagging.

(o) Bar-coding system.

(p) Audit trail.

(q) Control points.

13.6 END OF MODULE NOTES

A running culinary business must maintain a balance between objectivity and subjectivity. It must deliver tangible and intangible values to its customers at every moment of truth.

Scalability of the business is dependent on creating a robust template of the business. The process of creating a template must include the subjective and objective processes as well as objective documents which spelt success for the existing business. The template is often fine tuned and tweaked to suit the new circumstances.

Contemporary management systems depend on banks, institutional investors and venture capitalists to scale up their business. In such cases, it is important to maintain an objectivity-led ecosystem in the existing business. This eco-system would drive accountability at the work place. Measureable indicators of the success of the business and existing data support bidding for funds for further investments and scaling up.

EXHIBIT 39: Objectivity in Quality of Food Production

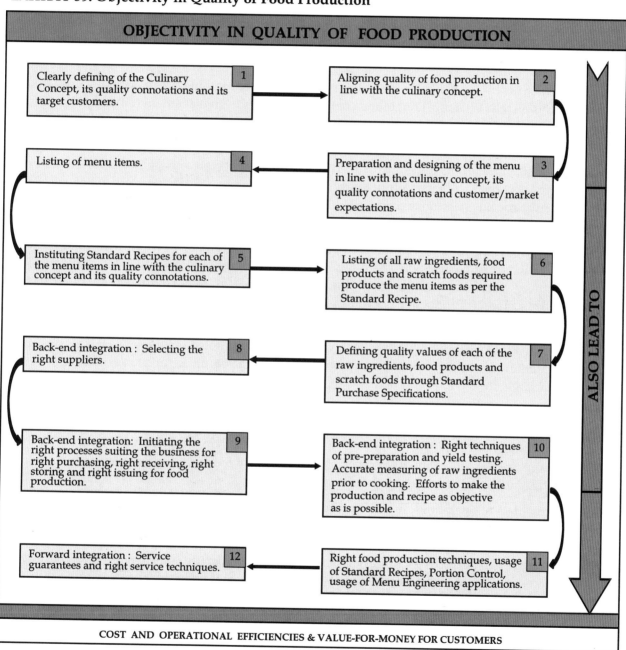

FINAL COMMENTS ON "CULINARY ECONOMICS"

Operators of culinary business must maximize value to its customers in relation to the culinary concept, through the establishment of benchmarks at each stage of materials management. Operators must strive to introduce and maintain higher levels of objectivity in operations.

Earlier chefs were highly skilled in the culinary arts, but were semi-literate or illiterate. The situation has changed completely. Chefs are literate and come from hospitality management/culinary management institutes. Most chefs have international exposure. Culinary business employing skill-trained and knowledgeable chefs can exercise higher levels of objectivity in the operations.

As is eminently clear from the contents of this module, higher objectivity in operations is linked and directly proportional to higher profitability and to the success of the business. Chefs as well as operators of culinary business must strive for higher levels of objectivity to secure higher revenues, lowest administrative costs and higher profits. Creativity must be supported by objective processes.

Subjective purchasing should be eliminated or reduced through fixed rate contracts. Items required for food production must be available when required. Stock-outs should be eliminated and emergency purchases reduced. Menus and menu items should be modified to eliminate or reduce purchasing of items of a seller's market. Production standards must ensure authorized consumption only. Wastage must be eliminated or reduced wherever possible.

Subjective processes should progressively yield to objectivity-led processes. Higher objectivity requires elimination of arbitrary decisions and introduction of a committee approach. Food production and other operations should have measureable indicators. **What gets measured gets focused, improved and managed.**

To exemplify how subjective processes can yield to objectivity-led processes, the author has provided a flow diagram below illustrating how 12 steps can lead to objectivity in quality of food production. It is also clear from the flow diagram how objectivity in quality of food production also leads to cost and operational efficiencies and value-for-money for customers.

Cost effectiveness of operations, higher profitability of the culinary business, and economics of food production is the theme of this book. The first module started with that theme. As a final tribute to the contents of **all** the modules of this book the author presents a comprehensive process chart entitled **"Cycle of Strength: Cost-effective Culinary Operations"** is given on **p. 240**. The process chart details the critical success factors of the processes for cost-effectiveness of culinary business.

Culinary Economics

The market for culinary business is burgeoning in geometric progression each year.

Thousands of forms of culinary business close down within the very first year of operation. Most of these have good concepts, involve large capital, and are started with the right intentions. The failure of the business happens mostly due to operational inefficiencies and cost-overruns.

The author is sanguine in his belief that failure of some of the world's best culinary business and inherently their chefs, if it has happened, is due to their poor knowledge and application of **culinary economics**.

This book would prove invaluable for Students, Trainers, Faculty Members, F&B Managers, Chefs, Venture Capitalists, Consultants, Auditors, and Controllers in Food & Beverages, and Hotel Industry.

EXHIBIT 40: Cycle of Strength: Cost-Effective Culinary Operations

CYCLE OF STRENGTH COST-EFFECTIVE CULINARY OPERATIONS

A SATISFIED CUSTOMER

1 DELINEATING THE CULINARY CON-CEPT FOR COST-EFFECTIVENESS

2 UNDERSTANDING THE COSTS OF CULINARY BUSINESS

3 COST-EFFECTIVENESS THROUGH MENU ENGINEERING

4 UNDERSTANDING BASICS OF CULINARY MATERIALS MANAGEMENT

5 COST-EFFECTIVENESS IN PURCHASING FUNCTIONS

6 COST-EFFECTIVENESS IN SUPPLIER SELECTION

7 COST-EFFECTIVENESS IN RECEIVING FUNCTIONS

8 COST-EFFECTIVENESS IN STORES & INVENTORY MANAGEMENT

9 COST-EFFECTIVENESS IN ISSUING FUNCTIONS

10 COST-EFFECTIVENESS IN FOOD SERVICE FUNCTIONS

11 COST-EFFECTIVENESS IN FOOD PRODUCTION PROCESSES

12 COST-EFFECTIVENESS IN FOOD SERVICE FUNCTIONS

13

CULINARY ECONOMICS

- PROFITS ARE THE KEY PRE-REQUISITES OF CULINARY BUSINESSES.

- CULINARY OUTLETS-WITHIN HOTELS OR AS STAND-ALONE OUTLETS - ARE ALWAYS COST, REVENUE AND PROFIT CENTRES.

INDEX

Index

Index

Index